Tales of a Huggable Vicar
STUMBLING TOWARDS INTEGRITY

– HUGH MADDOX –

An environmentally friendly book printed and bound in England by
www.printondemand-worldwide.com

Mixed Sources
Product group from well-managed
forests, and other controlled sources
www.fsc.org Cert no. TT-COC-002641
© 1996 Forest Stewardship Council

PEFC Certified
This product is
from sustainably
managed forests
and controlled
sources
www.pefc.org
PEFC/16-33-415

This book is made entirely of chain-of-custody materials

i

www.fast-print.net/store.php

Tales of a Huggable Vicar – Stumbling Towards Integrity
Copyright © Hugh Maddox 2011

ISBN 978-178035-215-2

First published 2011 by
FASTPRINT PUBLISHING
Peterborough, England.

Tales of a Huggable Vicar
STUMBLING TOWARDS INTEGRITY

"You always were a good hugger!"
– a surprised military man when I had comforted both his wife and him.

Dedication

This book is dedicated to my oldest friend, Roger Musker, and to his lovely and talented wife, Alison. They insisted I write it, and demolished all my excuses for delaying.

Also to all my family, whom I love, and who have given me so much love and support. Profound thanks to Kay Grynyer who offered to type this book, using a computer instead of my fountain pen dipped in ink, - Ann Miller for her comments and all the friends who have encouraged me and offered advice.

Introduction

I hope that you enjoy this story of my life. Possibly you will occasionally chuckle and may be intrigued by my memories of wartime and the following years – how different were assumptions about life in those days.

Perhaps, along with me, as my attitudes slowly change, you may also observe some of my new insights into life and the nature of God; and you may feel encouraged by my failures.

I dare to hope that the tragedies I have experienced, both in the lives of others, and in my own, may have shaken some of the dogmatic certainties and commitments of youth. I hope that my theology of life is now both deeper and wider.

Hugh

Chapters

Chapter I

FORBEARS - inspiring and daunting - India -
Edinburgh - Medicine

I have some colourful and worthy ancestors; it was a
daunting task trying to live up to them.

The Vicar's daughter, Mary Anstey, had an affair with
George Pitt, first Lord Rivers. She was known as the Belle
of Trumpington, the village just outside Cambridge. Her
father was a well fed eighteenth century incumbent, living
in an elegant Vicarage. Mary's portrait shows her to have a
lovely face and an alluring figure, with just a hint that she
knew of those charms which had captivated the noble Lord.

She gave birth to his son and gave the boy the name
George Nesbitt Thompson, in memory of her fiancé who
had died, and also of her mother, born Mary Thompson, of
Trumptington Court.. He went to India and ended up as
the personal assistant and close friend of Warren Hastings,
the Governor-General; he was the common ancestor of
both my father and mother who were second cousins. The
Thompsons were a godly, hard-riding aristocratic lot; in the

middle of the nineteenth century, many of them were on the Viceroy's Legislative Council in India, where they had served for generations.

Hugh Inglis was another forbear of the eighteenth century; he was from Kingsmills, near Inverness, and he married Catherine, daughter of the Maclean of Duart Castle, that most romantic sight on the Island of Mull; I am very proud of my Highland ancestry. Hugh used his ship to bring arms from France for Bonnie Prince Charlie. I suppose that today we would call Hugh Inglis a gun-runner for terrorists. Their son, Alexander Inglis, went to South Carolina, and I have seen his will giving his dozen slaves their freedom; he had taught them Gaelic and I like to think that he treated them well. He was exiled from the United States for supporting King George. Later, Alexander was killed in a duel, but his children remained in Scotland.

My maternal grandmother was Eva Inglis, daughter of John Inglis from Inverness. He was in line to be the Lieutenant Governor of the United Provinces in India, with a knighthood and life style of royalty; but he resigned from the I.C.S. because of the more harsh, arrogant imperialistic attitude of the new Governor-General after the Indian Mutiny. (War of Independence?)

My grandmother's sister was Dr Elsie Inglis who founded and led the Scottish Women's Hospital, staffed entirely by women. She took them to Serbia, our allies in the First World War. You might say she was Scotland's Florence Nightingale, sometimes operating for thirty six hours on end, and organising hospitals in horrendous conditions. They were captured by the Germans; she was ordered by an officer to sign a document; he said "Sign, or I will make you!" She closed her eyes, folded her arms, this tiny middle aged Scotswoman, and said "Make me!" She awaited a blow, but when she opened her eyes the officer had gone. She wrote to my mother, her beloved niece, "It was a great day when I discovered that I did not know what fear was."

Elsie died in 1917 of cancer and exhaustion; there was a state funeral for her in St Giles Cathedral in Edinburgh, with silent crowds lining the streets as her little coffin was carried past on a gun carriage. She had been inspired by God, and had total trust in Him.

My father's mother was Grace Monteath, the daughter of Alexander Monteath who served in India until he inherited the small estates of Duchaly and Broich in Perthshire. My father's father was Ernest Maddox. As children we were told of his great absent-mindedness; he boarded a steamer in Bournemouth to go to their cottage in Swanage for the weekend, only to find himself on a ship bound for America. Fortunately it stopped at Cherbourg and he was able to return to England before too long.

This grandfather was also a world famous eye surgeon. Whenever I go to a new optician and the light of a red bar is used to test for stigmatism, the optician casually says, "Oh, by the way, this is called the Maddox Rod , invented in the 1920s." When I say "I know, he was my grandfather", the optician nearly falls over with surprise and respect.

Ernest Maddox and Grace Monteath met and married in Edinburgh where the first four of their thirteen children were born. They were devout Plymouth Brethren, drawn by the simplicity of life and belief of those Biblical Christians, in contrast to the lax lifestyle and formal worship of the established churches.

My mother's father, John Shaw McLaren, was also an Edinburgh surgeon; his father was a leading citizen of

Edinburgh, and his mother a Muir, another family serving in India. A Shaw ancestor of the eighteenth century was the first Scots Lord Mayor of London, Sir James Shaw – for years we had his beautiful Georgian silver tea set.

My grandfather gave up his established practice and teaching post in Edinburgh to found a hospital in India, where he trained some of India's first women doctors and where my mother was born. They returned to Edinburgh where, as a young woman, my grandmother had run a club for wild young men.

Sadly, of my four grandparents, my mother's mother was the only one I knew, and she died when I was seven, but I believe they all had a great sense of life lived in obedience to God. I am told that the McLaren grandparents combined this with a very practical outlook on life, with much fun, music, and an elegant way of living. Those were the days!

My father was wise, quietly distinguished; he was a truly integrated person, both sensitive and strong. He was courteous, a gentleman. On his death somebody wrote "Eddie had that lovely gentle wit, modesty and charm – he just suffused goodness in every circle and at every range. He was lovely to look at, with the sweetest smile, lovely, especially at the age of 80". My aunt Eva was devoted to him and gave him an ashtray which she had found; on it was written, "It is hard to be humble when you are as great as I am." "True", he replied with a smile, "but I manage". Once, with mock satisfaction, he was pointing out to the family and guests how noble he had been to have laid the breakfast table for everyone. With impish satisfaction one of the guests pointed out that he had forgotten the egg spoons. "Spoons will be served hot in the morning" was his quick reply.

My mother was another wonderful person. She and my father had an exceptionally strong and loving marriage; their friends would tell us children how lucky we were, as their marriage was one in a million. If they ever had a row, which I doubt, we never heard it; this gave us great security, but an almost impossible example to follow! When she was nearly ninety she was travelling back from Dorset to London by train. She fell into conversation with an elderly gentleman sitting opposite her. At Clapham Junction he said,

"Would your son mind if I asked you to marry me?"

She was tickled by the idea, but politely declined.

At 107 my mother was probably the oldest living Cambridge graduate, having been born, in India in 1904. She was perfectly fulfilled and happy running the home, looking after her husband and children. She would often say it was the most important job in life, that if you brought children into the world, it was no hardship to sacrifice yourself for them – it was just natural to put their needs first. She was a very loving and much loved lady, adored and respected by all – a good listener with a sweet smile for children. A passionate Scot, she also had a strong personality and it was a blessing and a great privilege to be able to look after her in her great old age. Because of her independent spirit, it had been hard to do so before! She had only started putting a little hot water in her cold morning bath when she was eighty.

The stories about my ancestors which I heard when I was growing up had a profound influence on me. My loving parents were far too wise to say that I should be like these distinguished forbears, but I suppose that I just breathed in the influence of these family members when I was at a very impressionable age.

We had a decoration given to Aunt Elsie by the King of Serbia. It was a reminder that I was born into a tradition of heroic service to help the wounded, and also that she had moved in the highest circles. How was I, little Hughie, to follow in these tremendous footsteps, when in my youth and early manhood I thought that I had neither the compassion, the qualities of leadership, or the self discipline needed?

Perhaps the stories of my ancestors, the positions they held and the friends they had, led me to want to move in more grand circles myself? I think this paradox of compassion and upper class living led me in later life to want to be both a slum priest and one of the landed gentry! I allowed myself to live under an unnecessary tension and a pressure to succeed and impress.

Chapter II

WARTIME CHILDHOOD - Gloucestershire -
London - the air raids

I am told that I was in a hurry to come into the world. At the time, my parents and my three year old brother, Colin, were living in the White House, not in Washington, but Putney, a happy, roomy house with a big garden. They were away for the weekend, and had to come hurrying back to London for my birth which was earlier than expected, Friday 9th July, 1937; later I was often reminded that "Friday's child is loving and giving". As with Colin and Alison, I was born by caesarean operation – so was Julius Caesar and also Macduff, who fulfilled the three witches prophecy that Macbeth would not be killed "by any man of woman born." Macduff was "from his mother's womb untimely ripped". Apparently I was looked after by Nurse Burr, my father's beloved nurse, and a nursery maid as well. What different times!

Of course I have no memories of those early days but I am told that I wanted to be like Colin, my older brother, in every way. We each had a jar of tadpoles; Colin's died, and later I was found pouring my jar into the grass in the garden. My mother said "Oh, but Hughie, yours are still alive." "No they're not, they're dead. They're very, very dead!" Early signs of hero worship and of the tendency to give more significance to feelings than to facts?!

My own first memories are of our time at Hardwicke Court in Gloucestershire, where we had gone to escape the Blitz. The house had been requisitioned as a nursing home; Aunt Eva was there as the assistant to Dr. Crichton-Miller. It is a large, elegant Regency country house, built of Cotswold stone, standing at the end of a long drive through the park. Outside was a cobbled courtyard and stables, where we played. The other side of the farmyard were sheds; we discovered, beneath the cobwebs of years, an old carriage, good for cowboys and Indians, or grand people going to a ball. I also remember playing amongst the R.A.F. lorries which were lined up in the park in front of the fine house.

Hardwicke was the home of Olive Lloyd-Baker whose ancestors had owned the estate for generations. Later, my Aunt Eva married Bill Murray-Browne, Olive's cousin and heir to the estate, so Hardwicke was to play an important part in my life over the years.

The Chandlers were a lovely old couple who lived in a cottage behind the stables; I think he had been a groom for many years, and they both spoke with a soft Gloucestershire burr. When Alison was born Chandler knew it was a girl because he had seen three magpies in the field that morning – "one for sorrow, two for joy, three for a girl and four for a boy." You could avoid the sorrow, of course, by saying "good morning magpie, good morning magpie, good morning magpie, where's your wife, where's your wife, where's your wife?" It had to be said before he flew off.

I loved the Chandlers and I believe they loved me. I was about five at the time. I remember with horror how I came out of their cottage one day to see a dead horse being winched onto a lorry. There is something profoundly disturbing about seeing such a large dead animal being dragged along. No wonder that I have never forgotten it.

When Alison arrived we were her devoted brothers for ever. I remember visiting my mother in hospital and giving her my green lorry, my most prized possession.

About this time my mother had a very vivid dream – she was walking down a road with her Aunt Elsie who kept saying "don't go to the left Amy, don't go to the left." When she looked back, on the left of the road, there was a vast hole.

By now, 1942, the first wave of German bombing had stopped. My father was working in London and we were to join him. The White House had been requisitioned so he looked for a house to rent, if possible, on the sunny side of the street. He couldn't find one, although there was a "To Let" sign for such a house, which he didn't see. So we moved into 57 Chartfield Avenue, opposite. I went to my first school there. All I can remember is watching the nativity play and my great distress at seeing Joseph and Mary being so rudely turned away at the door, over and over again. My first religious experience.

I was aged about six and Colin nine, and I remember going off with him, sandwiches prepared for us by our mother in our pockets, and "exploring", going alongside a railway track and the banks of a canal.

The raids started again with the terrifying wail of the air raid siren, the thud of bombs, - quiet, then finally the enormous relief of the steady note of the "All Clear"; although the siren might sound again, later in the night. In the morning Colin and I had great fun picking up the pieces of shrapnel. One night, in the middle of a raid, there was an almighty crash. The ceilings came down and the doors and windows were blown in. When my mother looked out in the morning, instead of the house on the sunny side of the street, there was a bomb crater, the enormous hole, which she had seen months earlier in her dream.

My Uncle Moray came next morning and escorted Alison and me to Stonehouse in Gloucestershire. By this time Aunt Eva had married Bill Murray-Browne. He was a doctor in this large village about six miles from Hardwicke. Uncle Bill and Aunt Eva couldn't have been kinder, but I remember feeling rather lost and bewildered as I sat at their dining room table. As a little boy it seemed to me to be very large. The portraits of Uncle Bill's ancestors looked down on us. Grannie was living with them at this stage, and I remember sleeping in a little bed in her room. She was very sweet to me and I became devoted to her.

I made a trainer plane from wicker chairs and cushions on the big lawn in front of the house; she sat in the front seat and I was in the back, instructing her. When she described the contraption as a "trailer" I fell out of the plane and rolled on the grass, collapsing with laughter. I gasped out, "it is a trainer, not a trailer; Oh Grannie". "I understand now" Grannie replied "but Mr Churchill must be very short of manpower if he is calling up old grandmothers of 78 to train as his pilots." "It doesn't matter how old you are", I said scornfully, "Only the instructor matters, and I am instructing you." And so, with terrific revving noises we flew high in the sky. All this is described at greater length in a letter which she wrote to my mother. Grannie was a sport.

Back to the war years – after a time it was considered safe and wise for me to join the rest of the family in Woldingham, although I seem to remember the terrifying sound of the flying bombs overhead, on their way to London; but, mercifully, none of them cut out and exploded anywhere near us. For some months we lived with the Nordens, with its big, rambling garden. I remember being told not to walk over a rickety little wooden bridge that crossed a small gully, but I couldn't resist the temptation, walked, broke it and fell. I was all right, but poor Uncle Hubert was not pleased! Even so, he let me sit in his beautiful big Austin and exciting open Sunbeam Talbot (what a wonderful name!) and pretend I was driving.

Towards the end of the war my father bought Edghill for £2,000. It lived up to its name, and had a garden and wood, with a magnificent view over the valley. The drawing room had a french window each side of the fireplace, as well as windows both ends of the room. It was a light, lovely room with many happy memories, Father romping on the floor with us, Colin and I sharing an armchair crouched over the wireless to listen to Just William, (we did not have television till my early teens) or sitting round the fire on a Sunday afternoon all reading our books; we were also allowed to read at the dining table.

Edgehill had been requisitioned during the War and was used by Canadian troops; they had burnt some of the staircase to keep warm and painted much of the glass in the windows, instead of using curtains for blackout. The whole garden was on a slope and shortly after we moved in, two men, one called Osborne and the other, a powerful giant with the name of Smallbones, dug out a series of terraces; one for football and cricket, one we called the Castle, and the third was for a tiny swimming pool, about twelve feet by six, later lengthened. We children had enormous fun, even when the water was green by August. Although many of our neighbours were much richer than we were, few, if any, had swimming pools in those early days, so they would come round to us. The three Shaw boys used to bring round a school friend, Furse Swann.

Osborne became our gardener, cycling in from Caterham twice a week. We did not call him Mr. Osborne, although Colin called him Tom. Colin was always more truly democratic than his younger brother; he always had a more direct human approach to people. I am afraid that I absorbed the belief that the hierarchical structure of society was natural and good. I took in all the guidance about the upper class ways of saying and doing things as if they were part of the moral guidance about kindness, honesty etc, which I received at the same time. So I thought it was wrong to hurt somebody's feelings, and it was also wrong to use certain words, instead of drawing-room or lavatory or to hold my knife a different way. Sadly, in a child's eyes, this implied there was something WRONG with people who were different from us, and so "below" us! It was all right for servants to speak in a different way, but not friends. It is appalling, isn't it? But all too common, I fear. Of course, my parents did not say this, or even think it, but as a child I put two and two together, and made five. Sadly, it is the start of the process of "us" and "them", the educated and the uneducated, white and black, British and foreigners, the dehumanising process that lies behind all racial contempt and made it acceptable, in Nazi eyes, to gas Jews, and for

Southern whites to lynch black slaves, feeling that Jews and slaves were not fully human.

Back to Edgehill – while they were digging out the swimming pool, Osborne and Smallbones wore their khaki battledress tops, as so many men did in those days; awe-inspiring for a small boy. I remember the joy and relief at the ending of the war; we had bananas for the first time, and ice cream in a cone. I had nearly finished mine, with just two inches left of cream-filled cone. I asked Colin "What do I do with this?" "I'll show you," he said, and ate it!

Chapter III

WOLDINGHAM - happy years - Edinburgh - Arran - Dartmoor - France - Lady Docker

During all of my childhood I hated Hitler as a monster, and all Germans with him – after all, hadn't they nearly killed us? This hatred was enforced during my teens by the black and white war films, where all the German soldiers seemed to be bullies speaking in a hated language. Of course, I have met many wonderful German men and women since, especially at Christian gatherings. Later on, like many others, I was much influenced by Dietrich Bonhoeffer, a devout, learned, disciplined prophet and pastor whose *Letters and Papers from Prison* inspired many who were seeking for "religionless Christianity". Bonhoeffer was hanged by Hitler in 1945.

Edghill was to be our home for about the next fifteen years, during my childhood, teens and early twenties. Woldingham was a very good place to live, with lots of similar families in easy cycling distance. To start with I went to Croftdown, the local dame school where I was rather frightened of the lady teachers; and then, at about nine, I joined Colin at St. Michael's Limpsfield, a boarding school for the daughters of missionaries and a prep school for boys.

There must have been some enjoyable times with the other boys, but I was afraid of the headmaster, Mr. Williams, and hated one of the Masters, a big, sallow faced, critical, sarcastic man. Even when I was playing cricket and made a mistake, I always had an explanation ready in my mind – the sad need to justify myself set in early. When lying in bed I would imagine that I was leading a medieval cavalry charge and, armed with a lance, would be chasing this Master, fleeing in front of me – what satisfying revenge! I like to think that such bullying prep school masters no longer exist.

It was probably the next year, round about 1947, that we had our first Arran holiday. We went to Edinburgh by train, all the carefully packed trunk and cases having been sent on ahead, Passengers Luggage in Advance. When we arrived at the Waverley Station I was disappointed not to see everybody wearing the kilt; I certainly was. We were to stay for a night or two with my uncle, Moray McLaren, and his wife, Lennox Milne. He was a great character and one of my heroes. He was of striking appearance, short, with a high forehead, large eyes, and the downturned McLaren mouth, which could break into a wicked grin when he told a racy story. He could do an imitation of any accent necessary, whether Glasgow, Cockney, French or whatever the story needed. Years later, I remember walking with him near Lloyd Square in London; it was a misty night and we could see a nun, in full black and white habit, standing in the doorway of the convent and beckoning to one of the servant girls, locked in a fond embrace with her lover, on the other side of the street. As we passed, Moray raised his hat, and in his fruity voice, with a hint of humorous reproof, quietly said, "Sister, God is love!" I was very tickled. His voice was known throughout Scotland, as he was an established broadcaster and writer, - a real Edinburgh character. At that age I had never met anybody like him; he wore a bow tie, used a silver snuff box and red handkerchief. He had reacted against the Church of Scotland of his youth, and had become a very committed Catholic, talking so naturally of Our Lady and the saints, as if they were personal friends, the world of the spirit being very evident, and heaven more real than earth. He had led a colourful life as a young man, and some of his problems stayed with him for much of his life. He was enormously grateful for his wife, Lennox Milne, Scotland's leading actress, for the support she gave him, saying that she was as good as she was beautiful. She had that long Scottish face and large eyes. I was very fond of her, and had enormous respect for them both.

So after Edinburgh, we went to Ardrossan Harbour, via Glasgow. In those early days we sailed to Arran in the Glen Sannox, one of the superb 1930's Clyde steamers, long, low, with plenty of wood and brass, and a speed of seventeen knots; she had no bow thrusters, and so in Brodick Bay she turned in a wide circle, with the Castle and the mountains of Goatfell and the Sleeping Warrior in the background – a wonderful sight. Later, when we brought the car, Father had to drive it on and off the steamer over two wooden planks, sometimes at quite an angle, if the tides were high or low. On the return journey the car occasionally had to share the deck with cattle. When the steamer left the pier, at the end of people's holidays, the sorrowful travellers would throw pennies onto the pier as the boat slowly pulled away, and we children delightedly scrambled after them.

Later, this was thought unsafe, and so loo rolls were thrown instead; it was an amusing sight, seeing the rolls unfurl and the paper flutter in the wind – but it was not so rewarding for the children. Still later, a larger ferry was built, the Caledonian Isles; it was much higher, the pier had to be rebuilt, and the public were kept at a safe distance, so, alas, no pennies, no loo rolls – ah me!

On our first crossing the waves were large, there were no stabilisers, the boat tossed and yawed and poor little Alison was seasick. We stayed at the Gwyder Lodge Hotel, right on the seafront, with its magnificent view over the bay to the mountains. We hired bikes for the fortnight and cycled everywhere, so we could roam around the hills and glens and bathe in the burns. We hired good old wooden boats from elderly Mr. Henderson and his powerful son, Johnnie – when speaking to each other they used the Gaelic, the ancient lovely poetic language of the Highlands. We rowed across the Bay to the pier, to the beach of the Duke's bathing place, or up the Rosa burn.

I was a passionate little Scot, as both my father and mother had Scots blood, and my mother was brought up in Edinburgh. I frequently read H.E. Marshall's "Scotland's Story", a large book, written on thick paper and with wonderful pictures. I loved all the legends and the heroic stories of William Wallace and also Robert the Bruce, from whom we are descended. Of course, in much of her history, Scotland's enemy was England, which has always produced some confusion in my inner being, as I am half English, brought up in England and speak like an Englishman; but the emotional pull of Scotland is immensely strong. The very word on the page affects me deeply, as does the map of Scotland, with its romantic outline of all the Western Isles; or when I hear the tones of a Scot's voice, and above all, the sound of the pipes, which often brings me to tears, whether the massed bands of pipes and drums or the sound of a lone piper on the seashore. It is uncanny, but it must be deep in the blood, absorbed with my mother's milk and strengthened by all her stories. An obstinate Scot's patriotism can be irritating to others! Even so, I still thrill to the words of Walter Scott's poem:

> *"O Caledonia, stern and wild,*
> *Meet nurse for a poetic child;*
> *Land of the brown heath and shaggy wood,*
> *Land of the mountain and the flood,*
> *What mortal hand can e'er untie the filial band*
> *That knits me to thy rugged strand?"*

And Robert Louis Stevenson's:

> *The yellow rose of all the world is not for me*
> *All I want is the little white rose of Scotland*
> *That smells sharp and sweet*
> *And breaks the heart.*

Back to Surrey and to St. Michael's Limpsfield. When I was nearly twelve we were told, at short notice, that the boys prep school was to close; so I went to a prep school in Purley. I was far from happy there, and was terrified of the Headmaster. One night, when I came home I was physically sick with anxiety. When my father returned from London and heard my story, he rang up the Headmaster and told him that I would not be going to his school any more. The Headmaster said, "You can't do that, because I won't refund next term's fees", to which my father replied, "I would gladly pay for Hugh NOT to go to your school". What a father! No wonder that I felt safe with him and trusted him. It was the same with my mother; whenever life was difficult at school, I would say to myself, "Oh, I wish Mummy were here!" It became a sort of mantra, and I even used it in my mind when the sergeants in the Army were shouting at me; I'm glad I did not say it aloud! I suppose it is rather like the grown men who go on using a bedtime prayer which they used as children.

My mother usually said our prayers at night, but occasionally my father would, and I was impressed by the way he knelt down at my bedside, and said quite grown up prayers; it was a picture of the strong man being humble before God. We had lots of the small books about Jesus, his stories and his healing miracles. I came to love Him very much. I also had a calf bound Bible, with the very realistic paintings by William Hole. I was reluctant to turn the pages and see the pictures of Jesus being flogged and crucified; it was so, so sad. While I was still young, we once went down to Bournemouth for Easter, and travelled in the car on Good Friday; somehow I was not comfortable with this, feeling that we should have been with Him. I think I sang, under my breath, "There is a green hill......"

Once, after a day in Edinburgh, I was locked in sadness, and found it difficult to tell anybody what it was about. Finally, I was able to say that I was thinking of an old tinker woman trying to sell white heather in Princes Street. As we walked past her and bought nothing, in my innocent ignorance, I thought of her climbing the Pentland Hills in search of white heather among the purple – and then nobody wanted it! I felt so sad for her.

We went to Church in Woldingham most Sundays, and in my teens still felt that Sunday should be a quiet family day. Occasionally the Rector called – I remember thinking him rather old and ineffectual – I suppose I wanted him to talk about God, instead of making social chit chat. He was a wise old bird, however, and when I was about sixteen he asked me to help him at the altar; in other words, he got me robed and the other side of the rail.

Thinking of the different schools – I wonder why I was so frightened of the teachers? I suppose that it was partly because I was a sensitive little boy, and partly the kindness at home was so different from the angry discipline at school. We never had any punishments at home. I will give you an example. The road from the station to our village came beside the bottom of our wood. Nearby was an electric storehouse or telephone exchange, and we would climb to the top, where there was a concrete parapet round the roof. One day we threw some conifers at passing cars and then ducked behind the parapet, very pleased with ourselves; but one of our neighbours saw and recognised us as he was driving past, and told my parents. My father explained to us that this was dangerous and could have caused an accident. I think we immediately realised how wrong it was, said sorry, and that was that. There was no need for an artificial punishment – the sense of shame at having possibly caused an accident was quite enough.

When I was about nine, Colin started weekly boarding at St. Michael's; I always looked forward to his coming home on Sundays; but some little thing would upset me soon after his arrival. I wouldn't talk about it, became moody, hated myself and probably spoilt the day for everybody. I did not have trouble with this sort of thing for many years, but then it became a problem once again. Alison and I remained very close at this stage; she nobly took part in the little plays I produced; I also used to love dressing up to look like a soldier in medieval times; we even had real cavalry sabres, which we clashed together in what could have been fatal fight.

When I left the horrid prep school I went for a year to the Purley School of Commerce and Languages – a priceless time. I sat in a class of rather dim witted teenage girls who were trying to get into typing school. I was taught by Mr. Thetford, a kindly man, looking rather like a portly George Formby; he used to play tennis with me, to give me some exercise, but even so I did put on plenty of puppy fat and was known in the family as "the rotund little gentleman". I walked up the road from our house in the morning, and was driven to Purley by a kindly neighbour, who worked in London, going in his wonderful pre-war Bentley, his pretty daughter at his side. In Purley I had my lunch every day in a café, egg and bacon, beans or chips, a twelve year old, sitting there happily reading the Beano. What a hard life! Mr. Thetford coached me well, and I got good marks in my Common Entrance to follow Colin to Gresham's. The next year, (while at the school), I sat for another exam and was awarded a scholarship; much jubilation.

Round about this time Colin and I stayed with Monsieur et Madame Derouet in Boulogne. My father was on the Council of the Law Society, the governing body of solicitors throughout the country; in mock humility he always pretended that they had made a mistake, that they had really wanted another solicitor named Maddox. Anyhow, he and my mother met this French lawyer and his wife on their official visit to London. Our whole family stayed with them in their typically French town house, with its shutters, in Boulogne. I was surprised and ashamed to learn of the terrible destruction to the harbour and part of the town which had been caused by British bombs. They explained that the raids were to destroy the German defences there. I also remember being very bored while the grown ups talked during the many courses of dejeuner, a meal which lasted about two hours.

Later, Colin and I were asked to stay with the Derouets on our own, to improve our French. We stayed one night with a doctor friend of theirs, because they had a son, Pierre, of our age. During the night I needed to pee several times and had forgotten where the lavatory was, so I learnt the trick of peeing in the basin, which has been useful on many occasions since. I also rapidly developed severe stomach pain. The doctor immediately diagnosed acute appendicitis, and told M. Derouet that I should have an operation straight away. Being a lawyer, he refused permission because he did not have my father's consent, and my father couldn't be contacted. After some hours, and heated French argument, the doctor insisted, and the last thing I knew was my lying on the operating table, with white masked doctors crouching over me. I awoke in a room of my own, and as soon as I moved I felt a stabbing pain from the wound; when I cried out, a French nun, with no English, came to me. It was a strange experience for a twelve year old. It must also have been desperately worrying for poor Colin, who, at the age of only fifteen, felt responsible for me, until my mother joined us the next day. I think I stayed in this Catholic Hospital for nearly a fortnight. When we sailed back to Folkestone, my father was there, with an ambulance waiting, expecting to see me coming out on a stretcher. Instead, I emerged on the shoulders of a burly French sailor, waving the air gun which the doctor had given me. What a mercy that we had been staying with him during that terrible night. I believe that my appendix can still be seen in a silver and glass casket in Boulogne Cathedral.

We also had another remarkable French holiday. One of my father's clients was Norah, Lady Docker, the wife of Sir Bernard, the Chairman of Daimlers and BSA. He seemed to me to be a kindly dignified old buffer, whereas she was a very colourful character, often in the Daily Express because of her extravagance and occasional outrageous behaviour. But she was also very kind, inviting all five of us to join them on their yacht Shemara for a week's holiday in the South of France. When my father hesitated she tactfully said, "Oh, and Shemara's service starts at Heathrow," so she paid for our flight as well. It think it was the first time any of us had flown; it was about 1950; and it was exciting and alarming, especially when the old plane bumped during turbulence. When we arrived at Nice we were driven to the quayside in two open Daimlers. Wow! Shemara was beautiful, shaped like a small traditional liner, with a crew of thirty and a first class cook; the food was delicious – even the toast was special. We swam in the warm Mediterranean Sea, either diving in from a ladder on the side of the ship, or from a speedboat steered by Norah's son, Lance Callingham. It was a fantastic experience, but we also looked forward to the freedom of Arran where we could come and go as we liked and roam freely over the hills and swim in the burns.

One evening we were all having dinner in an outside restaurant in Monte Carlo (as you do!). I was sitting near the Captain of Shemara, a fine man, kindly, but with great authority, and looking very distinguished in his white uniform, the sort of man I instinctively respected. I saw him look at the dance floor and say to his neighbour, "I hate to see a white woman dancing with a black man. Where's her self respect?". As a hero-worshipping thirteen year old I assumed his attitude must be good. It took me some years to realise that he was tragically and dangerously wrong.

Chapter IV

TEENAGE YEARS - Greshams - liberal education - sport - acting - Chapel

When I was just thirteen, I followed Colin to Gresham's. It had been founded in the sixteenth century by Sir John Gresham as a grammar school for the boys of Holt in Norfolk. I believe that some leases of property in London fell in round about 1900, and the school was re-founded as a public school. It remained a non-fee paying school for local boys but now had four boarding houses as well. Because it was founded just a bit later than many of the Victorian minor public schools, Gresham's had a more liberal approach to education, with very little beating, only a minimal system of fagging and an emphasis on art, music and woodwork as well as the traditional subjects and sports; it was a very good size, with only 4 houses and about two hundred and fifty boys. We boasted that W.H. Auden and Benjamin Britten had been at Gresham's. It was a fairly privileged all-male education. I was very lucky – but there were also some attitudes to un-learn.

In the first year I shared a bedroom in the Headmaster's private part of the house with two others; one was Roger Musker, who became a very good life long friend

We were allowed to have our bicycles at school, and it gave us a sense of freedom to be able to cycle out to the heath and play games. Of course, sport was important to most of us; we played every afternoon, rugger in the Michaelmas term, hockey in the Lent term, and cricket, tennis and swimming in the summer. I hugely enjoyed acting in the house plays, once as the French cavalry officer in the 'Bridge of Estaban'. We went to see the other house plays. I was very moved by 'Journey's End' – my first insight into the hell of the trenches in the First World War, or the Last War as we heard it called when children. The School had an open air theatre in the woods and I had small parts in the annual production of Shakespeare.

I also remember the moment when a master came into our classroom and said, "The King has died." We stood in shocked silence. I suppose we had not realised how ill he had been. During the War I often had a bedtime fantasy, either that I was lying flat in a shallow trench with shells flying just over my head; or else I was lying in a line of wounded soldiers and the King and Queen came by to comfort us, and the Queen stopped and talked to me. Like everybody I knew, I was a passionately loyal subject. I also remember Churchill speaking on the wireless that evening, and saying in his unmistakeable voice, "Once again, I can say, 'God Save the Queen'!" He had been a young man under Victoria.

We had the C.C.F. – the Corps, which was compulsory; I quite enjoyed it, the drill, the exercises and the annual week's summer camp; I think I became a Sergeant, which all stood me in good stead when I came to do National Service.

When I was just sixteen I made my first speech in the Debating Society, held in the Big School. I was extremely nervous, but I made myself step forward; later I was one of the first speakers, proposing the abolition of capital punishment. I was asked to be the Secretary, took the minutes and read them out much too fast. I enjoyed life in the sixth form, doing history and English, in a class of about a dozen, including John Tusa, well-known TV and radio presenter and now a life peer. Another member of that small VIth form class was Alan Carr, a kindly boy, old for his years; as a Jew he played the part of Shylock in the Merchant of Venice; I can still hear him saying, with a strong Jewish accent, "If you prick me, do I not bleed, if you tickle me, do I not laugh?" – our common humanity. Holt Taylor was our English master; he had a superbly affected, arty manner and was a brilliant teacher, inspiring us with the liberal ideals of the authors we studied, Shelley, John Stuart Mill, Keats and others.

They all seemed to represent the original ethos of Gresham's, which had become thin on the arts, and the Headmaster was beating boys left, right and centre – fortunately not me! The School prefects went to the Governors and got him sacked – what excitement! I knew them fairly well, as I was in the same class, although I was younger. I was disappointed that I had not been made a house prefect, as it was so important to me to be a leader; but my turn came in my last term, when my exams were over. I did work quite hard – in those days – and went to Corpus Cambridge to sit for the interviews and entrance exam. Colin was already there, following Uncle Moray who, I believe, had been sent down for his wild lifestyle; I think that when he became famous they offered him an honorary fellowship, but he enjoyed turning it down.

Every morning at school we would walk across the playing fields to the Chapel for a short service – a hymn, a reading, and a prayer. Our evening prayers were taken by the Headmaster in the House; it was all part of the natural rhythm of life, the spiritual face of the community, independent of the individual belief or disbelief of the boys. In the sixties, many public schools abandoned corporate public worship and have regretted it since. We were also given two minutes silence in the dormitories to kneel at our beds for our own prayers before lights out; that also reminds me that we had twenty minutes on our beds after lunch every day – an excellent habit which I have practiced all my life!

Our Chaplain was a straightforward Protestant sort of a chap, but not inspiring. He was rather critical of one of the Mirfield Fathers who visited the school, but I was intrigued with this first meeting with a robed monk who talked about the spiritual discipline of his order. It was both deeper and more personal than anything I had heard before.

Very different was another visitor, who had left Howson's the year before. He was at Cambridge, and had been converted by Billy Graham, the American evangelist who had made an enormous impact in the 1950s. I think he was well off, and he did not have much of a spiritual background; but he did have neatly creased thin pale grey flannel trousers; what things we remember! Anyhow, with great awe, he introduced me to the very personal Evangelical tradition, the sinfulness of mankind, the price paid by Christ to the holy God, the full authority of the Bible, especially the words of St. Paul. To avoid eternal death it was necessary to accept our total unworthiness and accept what only Christ could have done for us, giving our lives whole heartedly to Him; in this view there was no other way – no amount of loving kindness to others, no amount of traditional church going would save us. Most nominal Christians, all agnostics and atheists, Jews, Muslims, Hindus or Buddhists (not that I knew much about them) would be in trouble. For an Evangelical, to accept the substitutionery doctrine of the atonement was the only way.

There was something impressive about his sincerity, about the thrill of his discovery of a new way, through his conversion, about the reverence with which he opened his calf bound Bible, which he always had with him. I was at an impressionable age, open to new ideas, and fascinated by this sort of secret society which alone had the key of life. I had always loved God and Jesus, His Son, and in my prayers I now offered myself to Him again.

However, I was never taken in by Billy Graham and his followers; they seemed to ignore the natural love for God held by those brought up in the Church. It seemed to me that they would not acknowledge my own father and mother as fully Christian; this thought confirmed my confidence in questioning the Evangelical approach; at its best it can lead to a genuine, merry commitment to people, but at its worst it can be dogmatic, exclusive and lacking in natural, humorous humanity. You can find my present thoughts about religion in a lecture I have just given to a packed audience in the backroom of a Pub in Wareham. This is in the Appendix.

I took Confirmation very seriously and remember kneeling in front of the Bishop of Norwich, sitting on his throne; he was the old style of Bishop, aristocratic and impressive. I took Holy Communion with great reverence. We often had famous preachers in the School Chapel, but I thought that many of them just waffled for much too long. I thought that I could do better by just telling everybody to love God and be kind to each other. Oh, the arrogance of youth. It makes me smile, though, to think how the good Lord can use the dodgy side of our characters to fulfil his purposes. When I told one of my friends I was thinking of being a vicar, he said that of course I would be a Bishop – ah me.

My last term at Gresham's, the Lent term, was a pleasant and easy one. I had secured my place at Cambridge, I was now a house prefect, I could read and study what interested me, mostly books of a liberal and idealistic nature, and I played hockey.

Chapter V

MY TEENS IN WOLDINGHAM - separate from most
people's world

In retrospect, life in my teens in Woldingham seems very peaceful, in contrast to all that we hear about young people today. The word "teenager" did not exist in those days; instead, adults talked about "boys and girls in their teens". Boys wore the same sort of clothes as their fathers, even if rather untidily. There may have been rebellion – the healthy pulling away from parents, but it was not institutionalised rebellion; that came in the '60's with money being made from the teenage market; there will always be the teenage mood swings, with the onslaught of hormonal change, guilts and yearnings, teenage crushes for your own or the other sex, half boy, half man. Physically I developed at the normal pace, and at an early stage became quite civilised and courteous, enjoying the company of adults, and absorbing all the attitudes of my family without question – rebellion came much later. Delayed adolescence is more difficult and prolonged.

In Woldingham, Colin and I would cycle up to the 9-hole golf course, which was often fairly empty. Mother had a small legacy, and used it to build a tennis court in the garden; we played a lot and had friends around to join us; we were very lucky. I have very happy memories of Christmas – Osborne brought in a full sized Christmas tree for the hall, which was lit with real candles; our presents were always a complete surprise and I loved buying things for each member of the family, and we all wrote affectionate messages on the labels. On Boxing Day my parents often gave a morning drinks party. I enjoyed those adult parties, and learned from my parents the art of introducing people to each other; people still thank me for the ruthless(?!) way I move people around at our parties – often this leads to life long friendships.

"Where did you two meet each other?".

"At one of Hugh's parties".

"Good heavens, so did we"!.

Introductions were more necessary in the 1950's than today; in those days it was not quite the thing to talk to somebody unless you had been introduced.

As children we had been to dancing classes with our friends in Woldingham. At Gresham's, the Headmaster's wife Nancy, heroically tried to teach us adolescent boys ballroom dancing; I think we preferred the vigour of Scottish country dancing. When we were in our teens, in Woldingham, in the early 1950's, we went to a whole lot of parties, either in each other's homes, or in the Golf Club, where there would usually be a live band, including a wonderfully wailing saxophone. Square dancing came in at this time, and a return of the Charleston. It was very different in Arran, where the Highland dancing was wild, and we flung each other around in good Glasgow fashion.

One other memory of Arran was a terrifying climb in the mountains. Colin and I were crossing the A'Chir ridge; the path was easy to follow, with the marks of climbing boots on the rocks: at one stage the path was only six inches wide, with smooth bare rock above us to the right, and a sheer drop of five hundred feet to the left; no ropes of course. As we were coming down Cir Mhor we lost our way in the mist; all around us were huge rock faces, almost vertical. At one stage we had to drop some ten feet down smooth rock; we could not have climbed back, and we had little idea of what lay ahead – it might have been totally impassable – for us, anyway.

Immediately after my visit to Cambridge, for the Corpus entrance interviews and exams, we went to our first Hunt Ball, which was held at Hardwicke Court; it was a most colourful occasion, with the women in dazzling ball gowns, and many of the men in hunting pink tailcoats or military uniform. On our return to Edgehill the telephone was ringing as we came in the front door – it was the Headmaster, an alarming surprise, but he rang to tell me that I had been awarded an Exhibition at Corpus, a minor scholarship; what a moment! It was a good thing that I had failed my driving test the first time, or I would have been even more satisfied with myself.

In the meantime, I went to stay with a Gresham's friend, Henry Coke (pronounced Cook); he had an easy-going approach to life, a ready charm and quick wit. They lived at Weasenham Hall, in Norfolk; it was a large red brick country house. The family had very little money, and virtually lived in the dining room; Henry's ancient, aristocratic father, wearing an old pullover and collarless shirt, sat in a vast chair near a roaring fire – at least there was no shortage of wood. I was taken along an endless corridor to my bedroom, a large grand room with a high ceiling and bitterly, bitterly cold; the fumes and smell of the little paraffin stove only made it worse. We went to a dance next evening and on the way back we gave a lift to one of the Gurney girls, dropping her at Walsingham Abbey – years later I was to go there for Jean's wedding with Patrick Mayhew; he was to become Secretary of State for Northern Ireland.

Mercifully I was not wholly involved in society. Peter Rosling arranged for me to meet Mrs Petrie who lived in a small flat in a very poor street of Bermondsey, which was far from being the fashionable place it is today. I called on her regularly until she died. She was an affectionate, sparky little Cockney, and it was a privilege to have known her; altogether a new and very necessary experience for me.

The summer I had to myself. I went and stayed with various relations, going on my own, as a young adult. At the Mount I heard of Aunt Eva's work with the P.N.E.U. school in the house, and her involvement with other schools and court work. I went with Uncle Bill on his rounds as a country doctor and remember my shocked surprise as we passed some cottages and he said, quite naturally, in his booming voice, "Of course, in those places, there is lots of incest." It all sounded rather matter of fact, just part of country life – brothers and sisters sharing a bed and the human sexual urge stronger than that of the animals on the farm. I stayed with Olive Lloyd-Baker – we caller her cousin Olive, although we were not blood relations – at Hardwicke Court. I went with her when she sat on the bench of the Magistrate's Court and joined her on her visits to the many tenants of her farms and cottages. She had been a racing driver and had a splendid Aston Martin; every time we stopped at a cottage I leapt out and opened the car door for her, waited in the car, and leapt out again when she reappeared. One time she parked near a hedge and it was possible, but difficult, for me to get out; when she returned I received a cold look. At every cottage after that I leapt out!

Olive was a truly aristocratic landowner of the old sort; she hunted, was highly intelligent and at one stage, was the Chairman of Gloucestershire County Council, saying "hounds always work best when led by a bitch". In the dining room, amongst the family portraits, was one of Granville Sharpe; he started William Wilberforce on his mission to free the slaves. I saw a paper Olive had written in the '50s about the future of the Church in the country. It included many of the thoughts put forward by modern thinkers years later, such as lay leadership, shared parishes, multi and ecumenical use of Church buildings etc. One final memory of Olive – on the mantelpiece of her library she had a beautiful comb which had belonged to one of the medieval popes; she used it to comb her lovely spaniels.

I also stayed with Uncle Moray and Lennox in Edinburgh. He showed me the grand elegance of the Georgian New Town, where the respectable and well-to-do lived, and the ramshackle Old Town where the respectable enjoyed themselves at night! These were the two faces of his beloved native city – the two sides that are there in all of us. Moray also knew many colourful rogues in the city through his terrible drinking bouts, to which he still succumbed occasionally. Lennox was a tower of strength for him, loving him and admiring him loyally.

Chapter VI

NATIONAL SERVICE - grim and glamorous

It was 1955, I was eighteen and called up to serve my Queen and country, for Britain still had interests around the world, and conflict was in the air. I started my service at Catterick in North Yorkshire, the camp for basic training for tank regiments – I had a vain hope of a cavalry commission. We received the shock of military discipline the moment we got out of the train and were ordered into the waiting trucks by the transport sergeant – no "please" or "thank you" for many months! We were given our uniforms and had most of our hair cut off, to limit our individuality; unlike today, it was only convicts who had shaved heads; we noticed the contrast between ourselves and the young officers who were fashionably long-haired.

We slept, about twenty of us, in a hut of corrugated iron, with only a coal stove in the middle for heat. Our Corporal was a caricature of the bullying N.C.O., shaven bullet head, peaked cap over his eyes, and a vile little moustache. He delighted in waking us up at five o'clock on a winter's morning by running his stick along the ridges of the corrugated iron, shouting "get up, get up, get your feet on the floor, you 'orrible lot" – a sudden shock and violent awakening, in traditional sadistic Army fashion. We were, of course, a mixed lot, with tough youngsters from the back streets of Liverpool, teddy boys from London's East End – the barber had fun cutting their hair off – as well as the P.O.'s, potential officers. Before going to bed I would read my Bible and kneel for my prayers, as well as slipping out early on a Sunday morning for Holy Communion in the chapel, with only half a dozen others there. It was a wonderful brief interval of calm and sanity. My fellow sufferers in my platoon merrily called me "f....ing 'oly Moses", but in an affectionate and not unkind way; they helped me when I was behind with my kit and protested to the P.T.I. when he made me stand holding my rifle at arm's length for too long, because of some minor failure on my part. I was more amused than shocked by the language, and when somebody could not find an item of kit, we knew just what he meant when he said, "Some f......er' as f......ed me f......er". The same word was used as a pronoun, a verb and a noun. I would join in with the crude songs we all sang, the mildest being a well known old favourite:

> *"I don't want to join the Army,*
> *I don't want to go to War;*
> *I'd rather hang around*
> *Piccadilly Underground,*
> *Living on the earnings of a*
> *High born lady..................."*

The memory of those early mornings still makes me shudder. The dash and barging, to get to the basins and their gift of cold water, the latrine, where you squatted and all could see you – no doors. Having hurriedly dressed we were fallen in and marched at the double to the cookhouse; when we fell out you could be crushed under foot in the stampede to get to the food, vile though it was – porridge thick with sugar, and tinned tomatoes, which I have hated ever since. We spent a lot of time square bashing – not too bad for me because of the Corps at school. Once I was marched off to the guardroom at the double, as the inspecting Corporal found my head dirty. In the guardroom they were comparatively gentle, with the Sergeant saying "What would your mother say about this?" "That it is my dry skin, Sergeant" – but there was dirt there as well. In the evening our foul-mouthed Corporal taught us how to avoid V.D; and with a revolting lear recommended a local whore. At eighteen probably most of us were sexually inexperienced; anyhow, we believed they put bromide in our tea to dampen our desire.

We spent hour upon hour, often late into the night, cleaning our kit. The brass work was pitted and needed an enormous amount of polishing to make it smooth and shiny. Our boots were made of rough leather; with a lighted candle we would warm the back of a spoon and slowly burn off the protruding bumps in the leather – it was rumoured that you could be put on a charge for destroying Her Majesty's property. Personally, I don't think that she was bothered. This was followed by further hours of spit and polish. How I longed for our passing out parade and our first 72-hour leave, with the thought of sitting round the fire at home, and nobody shouting at me. I was given a lift with another P.O., Hankey, who had Pitt-Rivers connections and so was a very distant cousin. He had an open MG and drove at breakneck speed down the A1 at night, taking incredible risks in overtaking.

On returning from leave I found life a little easier, as we were now in a separate squad of potential officers; in other words, we were quickly creamed off, because of A levels, the Corps, or just because of public school? Most of the others had been promised commissions in cavalry regiments and had been at well known schools. They always called me Monty, partly because of my name Monteath, and partly because my large beret made me look like the great Field Marshall.

As P.O.'s we were taken on exercises designed to improve our qualities of leadership. I was given a group of three or four and told to defend a certain hollow on the moor, while at some unspecified time, the officers would attack. Showing great initiative, I moved my men a few hundred yards, so we could ambush the enemy. A brilliant strategy? The officers did not think so! They wandered around looking for us in the dark. We were immediately sent on a five mile run, with rifles and full kit, as a punishment for disobedience. I was not popular.

In mid-December we went to W.O.S.B., the War Office Selection Board, with the hope of being recommended for a commission. We were given the usual tasks – leading a group of four candidates as we tried to get an oil drum over a stream using a plank which was too short to reach the other side; somehow we managed. I hadn't a clue, so asked my men for ideas, and putting on an air of authority, told them to put their scheme into practice. We each had to give a two minute talk on a subject of our choice. I spoke on the Highland clan system; I think my debating experience gave me confidence. We were watched every minute of the day, and at the end I was told I had passed, thank God. On reflection, today, I can see that I would have been deeply mortified had I failed; I would have felt a sense of shame that I had not been thought good enough to be a leader, and this would have stayed with me, not only during the rest of my National Service, but during my years at Cambridge.

I went, almost straight away, to the next Hunt Ball in Gloucestershire, at Haresfield Court; I still had the shaven head of an ordinary soldier, but I could proudly say that I had just passed my W.O.S.B.

And so to Mons – the Officer Training School. It has only just occurred to me that while we were there we never thought of the horrors of Mons in the Great War. I was behind the other cadets training to go into different regiments of the Royal Artillery; their basic training at Oswestry had given them some experience of working with 25-pounders, while my stupid attempt to join the cavalry had left me unprepared. We learnt about the guns and the complicated mathematics and radio procedures that were necessary to land the shells in the right place. We went on training exercises and I remember the feeling of dread when I saw a fawn coloured Morris drive up; it heralded the arrival of the Major, critical and brusque in manner. We continued to be drilled on the parade ground square; our Sergeant Major was a giant of a man from the Western Isles. If he saw sloppy behaviour the cadet's name was noted in "the book" with a shouted, "You've lost your name, Sir". About a week before we were due to pass out, I was summoned to the cavalry colonel who was in charge of the whole school. He was kind but firm and told me I was not yet sufficiently confident about gunnery – "after all, when you say 'Fire', the damn thing has got to fire!" I felt that that was all he knew about gunnery. So I was relegated, and had to do the final month's training again, while my companions in the squad went on to become officers before me.

We did have some time off; I was still in touch with some of my cavalry friends, and once I was given a lift to London by one of them. There was a long traffic jam in inner London and he was desperate for the gents; there was none in sight, so he hopped over the hedge of a little house and had a pee behind it, only to be chased out by an angry woman wearing an apron and brandishing a frying pan! He courteously lifted his hat and hopped back into his sports car. A clash of cultures. Mercifully the traffic started to move at that moment.

The day of our passing out parade finally arrived, and my parents came to watch me being commissioned. There was an inspection by a very senior officer, and then the Camp Adjutant led the way up the steps, on his grey horse. We followed him, in pairs, and when we reached the top we were officers, at the age of nineteen. We took off the white shoulder tabs to reveal the single pips of a 2nd Lieutenant (N.S. and U.S.(useless) the regular officers would say). How proud we felt, especially when we were saluted by any 'other ranks' who passed us, even redoubtable sergeants who had fought in the War; how bitter they might have felt, but I suppose they were used to it by now.

We were given a fortnight's leave and I hugely looked forward to going with my family to Arran. That year we took a farmhouse up Glen Shurig; we were taken up in an ancient taxi, and when we clambered out, the farmer's wife, Mrs Cameron, came bustling out and asked

"Is there a Lieutenant Maddox here?" I proudly stepped forward, only to be told,

"Ye've to go straight back to Woolwich; I've got the Major's telephone number and ye've to ring him noo."

Dismay; the Suez War was looming and I feared the worst. Mercifully, however, the Major was a Scot and knew Arran; when he heard that we were right up the glen, without a car, he said,

"I don't suppose you can catch the afternoon boat, can you Maddox?"

"No, sir, I can see the boat steaming into the Bay now".

"Of course; and there may not be a boat on the Sabbath, so report to the 20th Field at Woolwich on Tuesday".

So I think a fortnight's activities were squeezed into a weekend. We climbed Goat Fell, played golf and tennis, rowed, swam and danced. The Murray-Brownes were with us, and my young cousins were enchanting. I had quite the feeling of the departing hero as the boat steamed out of the Bay – after all, we had no idea of what the future held.

20th Field was stationed at the magnificent early nineteenth century barracks of the Royal Regiment of Artillery. I shared a room with Pat Ashley, a small, rotund regular officer; he was proud of his Huntingdonshire yeoman background, and only half in joke, held and expressed passionate right wing views – hopelessly politically incorrect in today's world! However, he had a good sense of humour and we got on easily. Unbelievably, we had a batman, who cleaned our kit and made up our coal fire in the morning and last thing at night. It was good to go to sleep by the flickering flames of firelight. I even asked him to help me off with my riding boots by the time honoured method of his bending in front of me, clutching my boot while I used my other boot to push on his backside; the boot would come off and he would nearly fall over. However, Blofield, with his pudding face and shy manner, was bold enough to say that he wouldn't be seen dead in my new suit, specially made for me with its newly fashionable narrow trousers, jacket like a hacking jacket, long waisted, with a ticket pocket, single vent and an Edwardian waistcoat with lapels. I was inordinately proud of it and wore it for forty years until it became impossibly tight for me and I gave it to my son-in-law, Dominic, who still wears some of it with style today.

Our uniforms had already been made for us, the officer's hats, and blues for formal occasions; I also bought a second hand mess kit, skin tight trousers, bum-freezer jacket with red lapels, patent leather boots and spurs which Olive Lloyd-Baker had given me so that I could be her squire. I also bought a bowler and with a tightly rolled umbrella proudly walked along Piccadilly. As I was so young I must have looked rather pompous and ridiculous; but it was the fashion amongst smart young officers at that time. We always had to wear a hat anywhere near the Barracks, so that soldiers could recognise and salute us; we had to lift our hat in reply. At Lloyd Square there are still two rather embarrassing photos of me, one in uniform, and one with a silk scarf, looking rather arrogant. I suppose that when young and lacking in real self-confidence, I needed to belong to a "gang" and put on an aggressive manner.

I tried to prepare for my first duty as Orderly Officer of the Regiment by donning my uniform with great care. I left my room and walked smartly along the parade ground, in front of the long line of white buildings, and round the corner. As I went under the great archway of our own parade ground, I had a mixture of pride and terror. The Sergeant in charge of the guardroom snapped to attention and gave me a quivering salute as I passed – little me! As I appeared, the Sergeant of our platoon guard bellowed,

"Guard, SHUN!!" The whole platoon, 30 strong, stamped to attention, for me to inspect them. I tried to make comments about their uniform with a degree of authority, but not so critical that they would be put on a charge – poor devils. As Orderly Officer, I spent the night in a bare room with only a bed and a chair; I dozed, but had to keep my uniform on. There was a telephone, and when it rang I nearly jumped out of my skin; it was alarming because it might have been a crisis, and as the only officer awake, I would have had to make an important snap decision. Thankfully, the only interruption was a report that a missing soldier, who had gone A.W.O.L. – absent without leave – had been found; I ordered him to be brought to the guardroom where I inspected him and made sure he was alright. Of course, there was always an experienced Sergeant at hand; and any wise young officer would treat him with respect, and would listen to his advice, while at the same time giving the impression that he was in command! I am sure that the Sergeants saw through us, especially as in days of National Service, we came and went with great regularity. If any of us junior officers were in trouble, our punishment was to be given extra duties as Orderly Officer; of course, all the troops knew, and with wicked grins there would be good banter as to the nature of our misdoings!

We were immensely privileged to have the daily use of the Officers Mess; it was, after all, the headquarters of the whole Royal Regiment, with its innumerable regiments scattered throughout the world. The Mess dining hall was particularly impressive, gold and scarlet decoration and handsome portraits of Master Gunners, past and present. Our fortnightly guest nights were unforgettable. We all wore mess kit or blues, many pieces of handsome regimental silver lined the middle of the table, and after the meal, before the toasts, the mess waiters would whip the narrow table cloths off the forty foot long table, in one magnificent movement. The regimental band, as an orchestra, played throughout; the climax was the Posthorn Gallop, a stirring rollicking tune, with trumpets sounding triumphantly. One night my good friend Roger Musker was my guest; after the meal we retired to the bar, took off our jackets and played daft games such as British Bulldog, with much hilarity and rough manhandling. As a cavalry officer, wearing yellow braces, Roger was treated with shocking disrespect. Of course, he responded with equal vigour.

I think there were three Batteries in the Regiment, and two Platoons in each Battery – two with four 25-pounder guns and one battery platoon, or sort of command post. It was commanded by Major Dunlop – pronounced in the proper Scots way - he had recently been transferred from the Indian Army, and had a benign and relaxed attitude to soldiering. I was his junior officer and liked him enormously. One Saturday I decided to go away for a dance instead of playing in a hockey match; the Battery lost by one goal, and on the Monday he called for me and told me he was disappointed in me. Sadly, this was a selfish lack of commitment which I sometimes showed in later life. I felt ashamed. On another occasion, Major Dunlop told me I was to go to a Magistrate's Court and give a character reference for Blofield, my batman; he had been caught stealing women's underwear off different clothes lines.

"It's a case for the trick-cyclist, really" said the Major, "but you had better go and put in a good word for him."

So off I went, aged nineteen, but treated with respect because of the uniform and the pip on my shoulder. I don't know how it all turned out, but it was a strange new world for me; I had never heard of anything like the compulsive need to cross dress. I only hope to God that it was not the beginning of major difficulties or illness for him. I also had to listen to a young woman from the town who complained that one of my soldiers had stopped her and "put his ham up my legs" – a new expression to me. I can't remember what I did, but I probably passed the matter over to the Battery Commander.

But I must go back to the beginning of my time with 20th Field. Col. Nasser, President of Egypt, had seized and nationalised the Suez Canal, and Anthony Eden, our Prime Minister, felt that he must act like Churchill against Hitler and stop a foreign dictator before it was too late. One of our senior officers gave us a political lecture on the necessity of going to war, to recover the Canal and put Nasser in his place. I accepted the official military view, hook, line and sinker. It was only when at Cambridge, that I began to question the wisdom and morality of it all.

When I had first arrived at Woolwich the vehicles and guns had been painted a dull yellow, in preparation for Egypt. Our Platoon Sergeant had fought at Alamein and he gave us instructions on how to survive in the desert, how to cope with the sand, the insects and the lack of water; it was all rather daunting. Our departure to Egypt was postponed, but in the second wave of the offensive our guns were sent to the docks at Cardiff and loaded onto ships, ready for us to embark. Months later, the Adjutant sent for me and told me that he did not know where our guns were, and I was to go and find them! So off I went to Cardiff, travelling first class, as I was in Officers' uniform, although still only nineteen. I went to the docks and eventually found our guns on one of the ships. Quite a day.

At Mons we had been taught how to operate and maintain a radio; we were also shown the workings of the internal combustion engine. The idea was that we should be more capable than our radio operators and drivers; a vain hope. I never mastered the art of twiddling the knobs or understanding a manifold. In fact, when with 20th Field, I was discovered by the Transport Major inspecting my lorries wearing my clean battledress, instead of lying underneath the vehicle wearing my denims. I was on extra Orderly Officer duties next week. It is a good thing we never went to war. I was just not interested in how things worked, and so did not absorb any mechanical information given to me.

After we had been with 20th Field for a few months, we had a new C.O.; before coming to us he had commanded the King's Troop of the Royal Horse Artillery; I had seen them at the Royal Tournament –an amazing display of horsemanship and precision, horses pulling guns at speed in a figure of eight, when a slight miscalculation would have brought disaster. This new C.O. encouraged us to learn to ride. We had the benefit of the Woolwich Indoor Riding School and a Bombardier (Corporal) as an instructor. On the fourth lesson we were jumping without reins and without stirrups. When we fell off and crashed to the ground, the Bombardier shouted, "Who told you to dismount, sir?!!" Military sympathy.

Having watched the four of us, Major Johnson told us that we were now ready to hunt. So a quick dash to London to buy a white stock, a whip to attach to my father's riding crop and a bowler – no reinforced riding caps in those days; they were thought cissy. You can imagine my excitement – it seemed to be a very dashing thing to do.

We were incredibly lucky; the stable staff drove the horses into the Kent countryside about a mile from the meet, while we just drove down in our own car, mounted and were away. There was a great air of excitement and expectancy as we trotted to the meet, the clip clop of the horses hooves ringing out in the crisp, sunny winter air. At the meet there was much drinking of port and doffing of hats, especially to the young ladies, looking very attractive with their white stocks at the neck, bright eyed alert faces and "well turned thighs", as a friend remarked. It was a great moment when we followed the hounds down the road, then hanging around in the cold winter air while hounds drew a covert, the hunting horn sounding 'gone away', the horses pricking up their ears, and we were off, thundering over fields, cantering through woods and jumping gates; sometimes terrifying, but always exciting. Once I fell off – although we called it "being thrown" – while cantering over a frosty ploughed field, but my bowler protected me. Sometimes there was a long hack back to our cars, which was exhausting; our thighs were not so much "well turned" as bleeding; but on arrival, there were the stable staff waiting for us. We gratefully, and stiffly, slowly slid out of our saddles, handed the reins over to the soldiers and drove home to a hot bath. What privilege! I think that even at the time I did not take it for granted.

Major Johnson's wife was a Society hostess. Those were still the days when debutantes held coming out balls; I bought a very well tailored second hand tailcoat at Moss Bros., white tie and waistcoat, and stiff shirts; I needed more than one, because sometimes there were two dances in a week. My father leant me his old Standard 12 and I drove, far too fast, to the West End; a dinner, and then on to a ball at one of the great London hotels. Just occasionally I would dance very close to a girl, cheek to cheek, and her hand gently stroking my hair – very exciting, because I was still so inexperienced. There were also occasional cocktail parties, including one on the river, and country house parties. Sometimes, driving back at three in the morning, I would fall asleep at the wheel, but, thank God, always managed to wake, just in time; in those days no seat belts, of course.

I regularly met with some other officers for Bible study. It was exciting, discovering both the challenges and promises of Christ. One time the padre joined us and at the end asked me, "Why don't you become a Vicar?" At that moment I couldn't think of a good reason why not! Later I did. My income would be about a tenth of what I could earn as a solicitor; I would lose touch with my friends through being busy at weekends, and, thirdly, I feared that if I went into a pub as a Vicar, everybody would stop talking, through embarrassment. Most of the Vicars I had met were rather doddery old men, taking services in almost empty country Churches. There was also the stage parson, a wet, hand-rubbing, ineffectual creature. I did not want to be one of those, and was delighted when at Cambridge people were surprised I was going to be a Vicar – I took it as a compliment! Sadly, after forty years of Vicaring, people can guess my profession just from my voice. I have become one of "them".

Back to my three reasons – when I was training for ordination I had a surprise letter from my godmother, known as Aunt Bobbie, my mother's closest friend from Cambridge days. She was great fun, a senior probation officer and an agnostic. She approved of my preparing to work in the poorest part of Sheffield, and in order that I could have a holiday each year, she gave me shares in her family shoe business, with the value of £4,000 – a large sum in those days. Also, by the time I was an incumbent, Vicar's salaries and expenses had improved; and we did live in good, light Vicarages with gardens, even if none of them were the lovely old houses which I thought would be a compensation for being a Vicar. God smiled.

As for my second reason – yes, I did see less of my old friends, until retirement came; but I have made many wonderful and interesting friends through the job. Thirdly, by the time I was a country parson, and known by everybody in the village pubs, yes, they did go quiet when I came to the bar - and then all offered to buy me a drink!

However, that Army padre did sow the seed of the idea of ordination, in ground already prepared. I struggled with the call, even though I thought it would be a wonderful gift to be housed and paid "to love people"; and my growing faith went alongside my life of hunting and parties. Indeed, I once left home with my whip in one hand and J.B. Phillips' New Testament Christianity in the other. It was noticed and commented upon. Of course, in National Service we did do some peacetime soldiering while at Woolwich – drill, kit and room inspections and, believe it or not, I was the Regiment's Catering Officer! The soldiers said that I knew "sweet f' all" about the preparation of food, so I would get in the way of the cooks in the kitchens, and then wander patronisingly around the eating hall, asking the men, "Food alright?" You can imagine the derisory and good-humoured replies – all good training for parish parties. We always ate well in the Officers Mess.

From Woolwich we would take the guns and lorries into the Kent countryside for exercises. I had my own jeep and driver – sometimes he would suggest a turning in the road and I would say, "Yes, right" and he would turn right, when I really meant, "Yes, left is correct!" Oh dear. In the summer the whole regiment trundled down the A30 to Larkhill on Salisbury Plain. Sometimes we stayed in huts and sometimes in tents, on exercise. After a long day, it was difficult to remember to make sure that all my men were settled and comfortable before eating the food my batman had prepared for me, and was getting cold; but we had been taught that an officer and a gentleman always put the needs of his men before his own; and I did try. It is said of a soldier "he served in the army" and it is true; another good preparation for parish life.

I was not expert at map reading, and once I missed a turning and led my whole Battery up a small road that became narrower and narrower and finally ended nowhere; much cursing and comments about N.S.U.S. officers as the troops tried to turn the massive three ton lorries and guns around!

In my last few weeks, there was a huge divisional gunnery exercise on Salisbury Plain. All the Generals and top brass were in an Observation Post a good half mile from the target. As the firing started, a shell landed fifty yards to the left of the O.P. and a few seconds later another shell landed fifty yards to the right of them. Panic in the O.P. as all the top brass flung themselves on the ground in terror; according to Artillery practice of 'bracketing' the next shell should have fallen on top of them. Immediate order, "DIVISION, CEASE FIRE!" The hundred guns fell silent. Nothing could be proved, but the murderous error was thought to have come from my guns. Mathematics and degrees of the compass were never my strong point. My senior officers just sighed, thanking God that I would be out of the Army in a few days time, and that there were only a few more intakes of National Servicemen before the Army could return to being a competent professional fighting force.

While doing my National Service, I always swore that in later years I would never say that it was a good thing and should be reintroduced. I thought it a deprivation of liberty and I hated being under tight authority and open to rebuke. The years have passed .... and I have forgotten the impact of the bad times, and can't help thinking that some materialistic, selfish, overweight modern young men and women, who have never been physically stretched, would benefit, not only from the abrupt discipline of the forces, but also the need to care for each other and work together as a platoon; but I suppose that is no reason for reintroducing National Service unless really needed. Anyhow, I am getting old and think I know all the answers to modern problems, usually starting with "In the old days............!!" I was proud to have been commissioned, but very glad to be free and leave it all behind before going up to Cambridge.

Chapter VII

CAMBRIDGE - "laid out for those lords of creation,
young men" - parties - praying - Iona - hotel waiter -
Greece

I went up to Corpus in early October 1957, aged twenty.
It is a small and quietly distinguished college. Because I
was an Exhibitioner (as well as an exhibitionist) I was given
a room in Old Court – I believe it is the oldest court in
either Oxford or Cambridge. It is small, grey, intimate and
truly medieval in atmosphere, with low stone doorways
opening onto the staircases, each leading to about six rooms;
mine was an attic, with a good view over the court one way,
and St. Benet's Church and graveyard the other. There
were no lavatories or basins on the staircases, so American
tourists were amazed and delighted to see dressing-gowned
undergraduates, in their slippers, lazily sauntering over the
grass to the washrooms, perhaps at twelve noon, even in the
depths of winter. Sadly, the advent of women
undergraduates (a Good Thing) and modern standards of
privacy and hygiene (a Bad Thing) have led to the abolition
of this healthy, timeless, fresh air method of washing. Alas,

alas. You will notice that we were called undergraduates, and not students, as at the more modern universities.

The heart of the College was the High Table, Master, Dean and Fellows, who conducted research, wrote and almost incidentally, lectured and gave the undergraduates tutorials. Oxford had quads and Cambridge had courts. The Oxford menservants to the undergraduates had been called scouts, the Cambridge men gyps. Both had disappeared in these post war years, but we still had "bedders", women who cleaned our rooms and made our beds; by ancient statute they had to be "venerabila et horrenda" (or some such Latin phrase) meaning "old and ugly". From the earliest days randy young undergraduates could not be trusted with any woman, young and pretty.

We could have all meals in Hall, a mock Gothic part of New Court, of the 1820's, with its high rafted ceiling, High Table and portraits of former Masters. Breakfast and lunch were self service and relaxed, but dinner was more formal – we wore jackets, collar and tie, and gowns (as we had to for lectures, and when in the town in the evenings). We sat at long tables, and to reach the benches by the walls we merrily walked on top of the table to reach our place; the meal started and ended with a Latin grace, sometimes very long and sometimes short and to the point: *"Benedictus, benedicat, per Jesum Christum Dominum Nostrum, Amen."* We had to dine in hall most evenings, sometimes having our own guests, and sometimes dining with friends in their colleges. This was the background to the next three happy years of my life; it included three or four weeks vacation at Christmas and Easter, and nearly four months Long Vac in the summer. My father paid all the fees and also gave me a small allowance; to me it seemed normal, and I am afraid I took it for granted.

I went up to Cambridge with the idea of reading History, and then Law in my third year; I had in mind the possibility of joining my father as a solicitor in his small firm with his office in Gray's Inn. Most of his clients were family and friends and so there were no criminal cases! His wise and kindly advice was often sought and usually followed. In her funeral address about my father, Aunt Eva spoke of his having saved many a young man from wandering the streets of London, having been cut off without a penny by an irate father. It was natural that he hoped I would follow him; but there was no pressure. I remember very little about my study of history. I was enjoying myself far too much in other ways! We often invited some of the Fellows to our parties; it was all very adult and civilised, partly because we were in our twenties, and many of us had been commissioned in the Services; rather different from eighteen-year olds leaving home for the first time.

It is only in looking back on these years that I realise how significant was the change from army to university, where Christianity was in the very stones of the place and where many fine men helped the spiritual side of my life to grow alongside the social side, until finally the trickle of faith became the mainstream – a gradual process, still incomplete!

On Sunday evenings the Dean of Chapel, Roland Walls held open house in his rooms, and usually about twenty undergraduates turned up, talked, laughed and were amazed both at his merriment and also at his wonderfully fresh approach to the man Jesus. Some of the men there were impressive figures – not the wimps and weeds I had feared. Roland was a first class New Testament scholar; but he also talked of his Lord with the infectious simplicity of a child.

It was as if this liberating gaiety set us free from all churchy nonsense and bitter doctrinal disputes, as a child throws off his clothes before dashing into the sea on a hot day. Roland brought me to meet a new, very human, free and challenging Christ; it was like meeting an old friend in new circumstances, revealing Christ's power, his vulnerability and this infectious, inspiring call to follow. A few years later I got to know Roland very well and perhaps I am reading into that first year in Corpus insights which only came to me later? But what does it matter?!

In much of Cambridge there were division and mistrust between different Christian traditions – many free thinking men, brought up in the Church, were very wary of what they saw as the too keen, dogmatic and exclusive group of new Christians, often inspired by Billy Graham's great crusade; these new Christians knew their Bibles very well, especially the Epistles of St. Paul, and seemed to think that every Christian should have a conversion like Paul's experience on the Damascus Road. These men usually belonged to C.I.C.C.U., the Cambridge Inter-Collegiate Christian Union, which had inspired many of the most courageous disciples in earlier generations. They were inclined to think that the more liberal Christians had betrayed the faith, hid behind formal worship, were not committed, weak in belief and had no personal relationship with Christ. Roland always tried to bridge this gap, and in spite of themselves, and in spite of the warnings of their leaders, some of these Evangelicals were captivated by Roland's sincerity and knowledge of Christ; so they responded to his vision of "the Church in the College", and came to the beautiful, formal Eucharists in the College chapel, which I attended regularly. In these services there was a comforting familiar dignity, but also human sincerity and warmth. Once again, I was encouraged and heartened by the regular attendance of some of the very bright and also the very sporty undergraduates. It was O.K. and quite normal to go to Chapel; I hope I would have gone even if it hadn't been!

Looking back I realise that this was the first time that I had really experienced weekly worship of such quality. I also often went to Evensong at half past six on a weekday, loving the readings and the rhythm of the Psalms; all worship was Prayer Book, of course.

I tried to be loyal to the vision of the Church in the College and sometimes went to the C.I.C.C.U. Bible studies and prayer meetings. I learnt quite a lot and was able to join the others in praying aloud in front of everybody; but I still picked up the atmosphere of a secret society, challenging and exciting, of course, but also exclusive and critical of those "not preaching the Gospel" – their version, of course.

Whenever possible I went to a weekday choral evensong in Kings Chapel – it was an unforgettable experience, a privilege to walk the few hundred yards from Corpus on a misty November evening and hear the sonorous great bell toll out the call to worship. In those days the fantastic fan vaulted ceiling had not been cleaned and could only just be seen in the dim candlelight. Something was lost when it stood out sharp and clear years later; a true romantic I am, and proud of it. Some people use phrases like "hopelessly romantic", but it is quite possible to be a romantic and realist at the same time; I feel it is important to be in touch with our feelings, with the past, with beauty, and to give full value to things which can't be measured, not valued only for what they produce. I am not one for the prosaic, superficial, matter of fact, dull approach to life! People, buildings, countryside should be valued for their own sake – time and space given to the things of the spirit - but I do appreciate my motor car!

Once or twice I went to the church of Holy Trinity. One sermon tried to prove the divinity of Jesus by quoting various sayings from the Gospels, but as I listened, I realised each saying of Christ was deliberately open and ambiguous, such as his answers to the High Priest's question "Are you the Son of God?", "You say that I am". Jesus was keen to assert his own humanity, "the Son of Man" and the divinity of all of us. I sensed that from the earliest times the Church was trying to define truths which are beyond definition, an attempt to make dogmatic doctrine from the will o' the wisp, provocative, contradictory sayings and actions of the wandering carpenter. This was a disturbing discovery; but the first Christians had such an overwhelming experience of forgiveness and new life through Jesus that they began to see that he was the uniquely human face of God – His Son. Just lately I have delivered the first of the Purbeck Open Lectures under the title, "Radical Christianity – what can we throw out and still believe?" I gave it to a very receptive audience in a packed room in a local pub. I have included it in the Appendix. My own love for God and His Church grew and was fed by the very good books of daily prayers which I used every night – or at least when I had not been to a party.

Every Sunday evening I would go with a friend or two to the eight o'clock service at Great St. Mary's, the large medieval University Church by the market place. The Vicar was Mervyn Stockwood, a strong forceful character, one of the forward looking clergy, a member of the Labour Party and ready for anything. He would quote George McLeod's favourite story: a stained glass window had these words written on it, "Glory to God in the highest". A boy threw a stone and nicked out the letter 'E', leaving the text to say "Glory to God in the High St" – a neat way of reminding us that Christianity is not just about a man's individual relationship with Christ, but involves housing, employment, in other words, politics – the concern of the "polis", the city; - not just heavenly food for me, but bread in the bellies of the poor.

These evening services at Great St. Mary's were heady stuff: a stirring, often witty welcome by Mervyn, a modern hymn, and then a full address given by somebody of national or international fame; or sometimes Mervyn Stockwood preached himself; I remember one telling comment,

"I often hear some of you say, 'I'm off to stay with my Uncle at Witherington Hall' or 'my cousin's coming out Ball', but none of you tell me that you will be staying with your auntie in 17B Dock Street, Rotherhithe'!".

After the address, a powerful prayer, a hymn, and nearly a thousand undergraduates streaming out, stimulated in mind and stirred in heart. Great days.

Impressive people were doing great things, in the service of the Christ, amongst poor and neglected people, or were giving themselves to stem the tide of dwindling Church commitment.

I soon got to know Sandy Clarke, a Scot, whose mother was Janet Adam-Smith; Sandy's grandfather and my grandfather had been friends in Edinburgh, and Janet and Uncle Moray had worked closely together at the BBC. Sandy had a strong warm bubbling personality, a great sense of fun and a quick wit. I still chuckle at one very Scots story he told. The Church of Scotland is truly democratic, and the Moderator is only chairman, a representative for a year. For the first time in history the Moderator for that year, Archie Craig, went to visit the Pope in Rome, the lovely old Pope John. On his return to Edinburgh the story went round, told in broad Scots, that on the Moderator's departure, Craig had said,

"So long, John,"

and the Pope replied "Arrivederci, Erchie".

Very Scots and typically Sandy.

I soon found that I already had friends in other colleges, men I had known at Gresham's or in the army. One evening, early in the summer term, I was at a drinks party at Queen's. I heard him introduce somebody to "Furse Swann" – now that was an unforgettable name, so I turned and saw the familiar characterful face and distinctive voice I had known in Woldingham days. A few weeks later I was looking out of my attic window in Old Court and saw Furse heading for my staircase. He had come to ask me to join him and another man, on a five week trip to Greece; the third member had had to pull out at short notice. I was "able and willing", and so there began a firm, rewarding life long friendship.

I had to pay for the trip, and so was glad to be asked to join some other Corpus men as a waiter in the Maidencombe House Hotel just outside Torquay. It was quite an experience; I enjoyed serving the families – or, at least, most of them – and they quite enjoyed having Cambridge undergraduates waiting on them. I did not enjoy the greasy washing up, which went on from breakfast until nearly lunch time. It would be romantic to say that I fell in love with some lovely daughter of a family, but it was not so!

Before working as a waiter, I went with our Corpus cell group to Iona, that gem of a little island off the west coast of Scotland, with its fields, rocks and exquisite white sands beyond the machair, the sea green and blue, and sometimes the great waves of the Atlantic crashing timelessly against the cliffs. When that strong and holy man, Columba, left Ireland with twelve men in his little coracle, to bring the victorious news of the Christ to his kinsfolk in Scotland, he landed on Kintyre, and looking back he could see his beloved Ireland on the horizon, as we can from Arran. He knew his heart would always be pulled back, so they rowed on north; they landed in a stony bay on Iona and climbed the hill; Ireland and his past were well out of sight. He sent the brothers throughout the land, and built a church on the island. It was Celtic Christianity calling on the saints, especially Mary and Bridget, as powerful friends; and its faith springing from the earth, sea and sky – very different from Roman legalism with its obsessive guilt and need for atonement; the Celts sang more of Resurrection than crucifixion, with little talk of guilt or atonement. Tragically, centuries later, the Vikings killed the monks who had come to greet them on the shore; and sacked the Abbey.

Years later, in the 1770's, Dr. Johnson and Boswell visited the Island, and so moved was the great doctor that he said,

"What man of spirit would fail to have his patriotism stirred on the plains of Thermopylae or his piety deepened as he stood amongst the ruins of Iona".

There was also an ancient saying "Iona of my heart, Iona of my love, instead of monk's voices, the lowing of cattle; but ere the end of the world, Iona shall be as it was". In about 1900 the Church of Scotland restored the Abbey, and made a magnificent job, but left the other buildings as they were. In the 1930's George MacLeod was the dynamic minister of Govan Parish Church on Clydeside. He was acutely aware of the plight of unemployed workers from the shipyards, and of the gap that separated them from the Church. He took the bold and imaginative step of taking some of them to the Island, along with some men training for ministry in the Kirk, to work together in continuing the task of restoration; he said "The place of worship has been restored, but the place of the common life lies in ruins".

I write in length because both the man and the Island had a long and lasting effect on me. If you want to know more of him, then do read Ronald Ferguson's biography "George MacLeod" published by Collins; it is full of memorable stories. George MacLeod was a large, formidable figure, the descendant of a long line of Highland ministers, some of them Moderators of the Church and Chaplains to Queen Victoria. He was a doctor of divinity, and a baronet; but when I heard an American call him "Sir George", he characteristically boomed "Call me George if you like, or Sir, if you must, but not Sir George, please". He was a colossal figure, a prophet and a man of great foresight, with a brilliant use of language and the telling phrase. He was a passionate believer in the need for community when the spirit of Scotland was being damaged by individualism. He believed that the Kirk must be involved in the grimy business of industrial society, and at the same time he believed in the power of this remote Island to restore true holiness, through the legacy of its past and the powerful spirit breathed out by her very stones. He quoted Peguy by saying "True religion begins in mysticism and ends in politics". In the 1960's he saw the damage we do to the environment; and he preached powerfully against the Bomb. The Church of Scotland was against anything that smacked of Rome, but as a minister of that Church, he used candles in the Abbey, chose a litany for the daily morning and evening Abbey services, introduced weekly Communion, as well as a weekly service of healing and another for commitment.

George MacLeod was a baronet and a Socialist, a holder of the Military Cross and a pacifist, a mystic and a politician; a Scot on the world stage who could be seen at the end of the day, even in his seventies, walking home exhausted, having listened to some young man in personal trouble. It is hard to find words to describe the impact all this made on me. Each week there would be a visiting speaker, of national fame, who would stretch our minds and inspire us, as we met in the small medieval chapter house just off the recently restored cloisters, with the sea visible through a little Gothic window. Heady stuff. I might wander the hills and beaches in the afternoon, and on return, hear the great single bell toll for evening worship; as we came in and prepared for the service we listened to the clear sharp notes of a piano, beautifully played. The members of the community stayed for three months in the summer in preparation for work on the mainland. For services they changed from their working clothes, and wore old blue suits and shirts. The singing was strong, as were the said responses, such as "Except the Lord build the house – they labour in vain that build it". MacLeod's prayers were a fine mixture drawn from the beauty of the island and the needs and suffering of the world. It all led me slowly and surely to live and work in the roughest part of industrial Sheffield. I returned again and again. Many years later I heard that there were four young men on the Island, all strangers, and almost by chance, one was asked how he had first come to Iona –

"I came with our curate, Hugh Maddox"; to their mutual astonishment, the other three said the same, one from Sheffield, one from Folkestone, one from St. Martin's, and one from Sandwich; enormously satisfying!

Later, in the summer of that first long Vac, Furse and I went to Greece. The journey was appalling; we travelled by train, taking three days and three nights in suffocating heat. The lavatories were blocked, the stench was powerful, the carriages crowded and suspicious peasants and their animals got on and off the train. Nevertheless, it was an unforgettable experience to travel slowly through Yugoslavia – it had hardly changed since medieval times – my first glimpse of the grinding poverty of women working in the heat in the fields. In those days the centre of Athens was wonderfully open, a mixture of large areas of ancient ruins, Byzantine buildings and nineteenth century houses; it was easy to wander unimpeded from one to another. The Acropolis and Parthenon were as awe inspiring as I had hoped. About this time the other man left us – it was easier with just two as company. We travelled out of Athens to see the sun setting between the pillars of the temple on the headland of Sunium – surrounded by sea and islands. Often Furse would paint, and having taken some photos I would wander around and then sit for a long time and just look and look. We travelled all over Greece, either hitch hiking – I had done plenty in the Army – or going on the ancient buses. We slept out on the deck of the ship going to Crete, surrounded by Cretans and their hens. Throughout much of the country most of the women wore black. Wherever we went the radios played endless Greek music – a new experience for me – Eastern tonality – very evocative.

The climax was our trip to Mount Athos; we slept on the beach before being taken by small motor boat to this peninsula with its magnificent mountain of Athos rising 7,000 feet, sheer out of the sea. It was a land of nothing but ancient monasteries – at least twenty of them; we would climb up an old stone path, following a donkey carrying a bearded, black-clothed monk, wearing his black stovepipe hat – nothing had changed for five hundred years. Some monasteries were small, perched precariously on the cliffs overlooking the sea, others as large as Trinity Great Court. Their churches were full of the most beautiful icons, each painted with much prayer. The three hour litany, in ancient Greek, was intoned, sung and enacted every day – for its own sake. We would arrive at a vast gate in the ancient wall, pull on the long bell rope, and wait until an elderly monk slowly opened the creaking door and let us in. We ate beans with them in the refectory, day after day, until I became really constipated; one night it changed, and I was about to have violent diarrhoea; in the dark I couldn't find the room with a hole in the floor, and stumbled into a monk's room by mistake; if, in his sexual frustration he had tried anything on, he would have had a very messy experience. Finally, I found relief by sitting on an open stone window sill and letting the muck drop a hundred feet below. I felt better after that This was an amazing week – a visit to a totally different world; the only strange reminder of modernity was a glimpse of Shemara, the Docker's huge yacht, in the bay. Mercifully, the train journey home was cooler and happier. By this time Furse and I knew each other very well, having shared so many extraordinary experiences as well as many thoughts and feelings about life.

In contrast, some time in that long Vac, I had my 21st birthday party. Not long before that, my parents had rented a house in Lloyd Square, in Clerkenwell, on the Lloyd-Baker estate, each house having its own garden, and each square magnificent trees. Renting the house meant that Father could walk to his office in Gray's Inn. The party was a lovely evening; Roger proposed my health with great warmth and sincerity. The only fly in the ointment was Sandy Clarke, who spent too much time dancing with the pretty Gloucestershire girl who had been my partner at the second Hunt Ball, who I had wanted to keep for myself!

What a rich and varied Long Vac that had been.

Chapter VIII

CAMBRIDGE – SECOND YEAR - a Highland lass - Italy

The Christmas vac started with my third and last Hunt Ball, held in Berkeley Castle itself – probably the oldest inhabited castle in England. We drove up to the massive stone walls in Aunt Eva's small fawn coloured windowless baker's van: the owners of the Rolls Royce parked next door were astonished to see us leap out of the back in full evening dress!

Later in the vac, I joined a group of undergraduates on a Mission in the Old Kent Road, led by a Franciscan Friar, Father Michael. It was quite an experience to be visiting in so many poor homes, in a quiet sensitive way, helping the local parish church. We came together in the evening, to swap notes; and I remember the day ending with Father Michael, in his brown habit, leading us in the night service of Compline – a traditional, calming liturgy, handing ourselves over to God for the night. Standing in a circle in a bare church hall, we sang the plainsong hymn:

> *Before the ending of the day*
> *Creator of the world we pray*
> *That with they wonted favour thou*
> *Wouldst be our guard and keeper now.*

It was my first experience of Anglo-Catholic Franciscan worship woven into the lives of people living in wretched conditions – the Brothers have a detachment from many of the wants and needs of the world, and so they are able to go and live wherever they are sent. I was impressed by this challenging obedience. There were about twenty of us on this Mission, and one was Jean Gurney, whom I had met briefly in Norfolk. We became good friends back in Cambridge – she was great fun and a high profile figure with her red coat, fair hair, quick mind, great sincerity and merry laugh.

Also on the mission was a lifelong Cambridge friend, Robert Tollemache. Robert married a very sweet girl, Lorraine, also from a services family, and I went to their lovely wedding. They followed a different course from their parents in their lives, Robert being a teacher, a lawyer, a probation officer, and finally, for many years, a psychotherapist, working in depth with patients and also with those who had suffered torture and were being helped to readjust through the wonderful voluntary organisation, the Medical Foundation. Lorraine was also a social worker and family therapist; they are both still working, and I have a great respect and affection for them. Robert is very tall, aristocratic looking, with a deep voice; and Lorraine is as pretty as a picture. I think they spent some of their honeymoon at High Beeches, stayed with us in the Byre at Gorton Jockie, on Arran, and leant us their cottage for three months at a very important stage of our lives.

While at Corpus, I played hockey and tennis, and even coxed the Corpus hockey boat on the Cam; we were mostly novices to the river, but I greatly enjoyed shouting at these eight brawny friends; although we came nowhere in the Bumps, they didn't throw me in the river. I was probably more at ease standing, long pole in hand, on the platform of a punt, skilfully and smoothly steering it past the Backs. When done well, it all looked calm and graceful. I always tried to impress my passengers, especially any girls, and usually succeeded! I believe Oxford men "do it standing up" from the other end of the punt, where there is no platform – perhaps they are frightened of falling off! Or, have I got it wrong? Was it the other way round? It was fifty years ago! It was the most enchanting thing to do – to go past the ancient colleges, Magdalene, St. John's, Trinity, Trinity Hall, Clare, King's, Queen's and the Mill Pond, looking over the immaculate gardens and gliding under the old stone bridges. Alternatively, we could start above the Mill Pond, and go under the overhanging trees and past the meadows to Grantchester……..

> *Oh! There the chestnuts, summer through,*
> *Beside the river make for you*
> *A tunnel of green gloom, and sleep*
> *Deeply above; and green and deep*
> *The stream mysterious glides beneath,*
> *Green as a dream and deep as death.*
> *Ah God, to see the branches stir*
> *Across the moon at Grantchester!*
> *To smell the thrilling sweet and rotten*
> *Unforgettable, unforgotten*
> *River smell, and hear the breeze*
> *Sobbing in the little trees………*
> *Deep meadows yet, for to forget*

> *The lies and truths, and pain? Oh! Yet*
> *Stands the Church clock at ten to three?*
> *And in there honey still for tea?*

It is for ever poignant to hear Rupert Brooke, writing this in Berlin in1912 and longing for "the water sweet and cool gentle and brown, above the pool, ...in Grantchester, in Grantchester." Only three years later his body lay in "some corner of a foreign field that is for ever England".

Yes, they were happy, carefree days of great and grateful privilege. I believe my grandmother spoke of Cambridge as a place laid out for those lords of creation, young men; all I lacked was a steady girl friend!

It seems strange now, but I really can't remember at what stage I seriously considered ordination: it must have been in the course of my second year, because by the summer term I had decided to read Theology instead of Law.   My father must have been disappointed, but, typically, said very little. On the other hand, when I told my parents of my thoughts of offering myself for ordination, my mother burst into tears.   It think it was partly the feeling of losing her son, and partly the fear of it being difficult for me to find a girl friend and wife: there was some truth in that. Years later, Furse told me that my mother had talked with his mother; they got on very well. I also had a great respect and affection for Nona Swann; although (perhaps because!) she was the daughter of a Bishop and wife of a Dean, she had a strong streak of anti-clericalism! My mother hoped she would put me off the whole idea. In a way I was surprised by my parents worried reaction, as they were both devout people, and regularly attended Church; but neither of them had been brought up in the Church of England.

I was steadily being influenced by the strong, intelligent Christian life of Cambridge, by our Bible studies, by the presence of the merry ordinands in Corpus, and by Iona; and especially by the words of Christ: "the fields are white unto harvest; pray the Lord of the harvest to send labourers into the harvest". I felt that he called me to follow, and that he needed me.

During my second Long Vac we had our family holiday on Arran. On the way I stayed with the family of one of my mother's friends. They lived in Argyll, a truly Highland, almost Jacobean house, with old silver on display, and lots and lots of small Victorian portraits. We were having drinks in the drawing room, when we were joined by their daughter, Isobel. She was slight, with an oval face, skin soft from the Highland rain, large soft hazel eyes and an entrancing smile. I immediately fell in love, especially in those surroundings! She must have been swept off her feet by my open admiration, and happily agreed to go with me the next day on the train from Oban to Glasgow and on to Ardrossan for the steamer to Arran, and join my family for a few days. She was on holiday from Cornell University in the United States. For some reason she and I spoke in soft imitation Highland voices, perhaps as an expression of the gentle, twilight, Celtic spirit of those in love for the first time – for me anyhow; I don't know about her. In hindsight, I suppose it was because I was not used to the reality of such unfamiliar, overwhelming feelings for a girl?

My mother and Aunt Eva were delighted to meet her, and both families made her welcome; we spent the next day happily all together. In the evening I drove her into the hills, and sitting side by side in the heather, I gave her a gentle kiss on those lovely lips. I think I must have kissed other girls before – although I can't remember! – but this was the first time that I had kissed with such tenderness and respect. I was twenty two and a late developer, but I don't think this was so unusual in those days. Sadly, Isobel had to leave the next day, and I irritated my family by constantly singing Gilbert & Sullivan's ditty,

> *"Hey dee, hey dee,*
> *Misery me, lack a day dee*
> *He sipped no sup*
> *And he craved no crumb*
> *As he sighed for the love of a lady".*

Mind you, I did do justice to the Douglas' cooked breakfasts and excellent dinners!

Shortly after this, I went on a trip to Italy, which Furse had planned; we were to join a group of about twenty, going to Venice, Rome and Florence. Unfortunately Furse broke an arm shortly before we were due to leave, so I was on my own with this party of strangers, often feeling lonely and thinking of my new found love, especially on the train going out.

Like every visitor to Venice I was enchanted by the canals, the bridges, churches and paintings. I remembered a forbear who was British Consul in the eighteenth century and had died in his gondola. We were extraordinarily lucky to be there at the time of the Grand Carnival – dozens of huge, colourful gondolas proceeding down the Grand Canal. We also went across the Lagoon in an open boat to the tiny island of Torchello, with its large, austere stone church, reeking with holiness. Strangely, I don't remember much about Rome. In Florence I can picture the lush, leafy shade of the garden of our villa and the sculptures of the great copper doors of the Baptistry of the Duomo. We made an excursion through the Tuscan countryside to Pisa and Assisi. I was over-awed by the great church in the square, and inspired by the little chapel of San Damiano at the bottom of the hill. It was here that St. Francis heard Christ say "Build my Church". With his own hands he restored this ruined chapel and later he was used by God to bring new life, love and faith to the Catholic Church, which had become corrupted by power. Like millions of others before me, I was inspired by the "little man of Assisi". He felt so deeply the agony of the crucified Christ that wounds appeared in his own hands; but he was also filled with spontaneous joy and love for all men and all creation, as in the stories of his preaching to the birds and befriending a wolf. All people and all creatures he addressed as "brother" or "sister" as in his wonderful hymn, "All creatures of our God and King".

The last verse he wrote as he was dying:

And thou, most kind and gentle death,
Waiting to hush our latest breath, O praise him, alleluia!
Thou leadest home the child of God,
And Christ our Lord the way hath trod:
O praise him, O praise him,
Alleluia, Alleluia, Alleluia.

This was typical of his approach to suffering – instead of being embittered by the blows of life, he embraced them, he saw them as being one of the ways to God, even welcoming Sister Death – a most profound and Christlike response to life, the turning of tragedy into triumph, as we offer ourselves to God so that he may work in and through us to redeem evil by bringing some good out of it.

At this stage of my life I was inspired by the call to identify with the poor – probably because my own life was so comfortable and easy: I think that my mother trembled when I told her that I thought I needed to suffer more before I could be a good priest. I didn't know what the future held in store for me

While I was in Assisi I was captivated by the story of Francis who, as a young man, refused to follow his wealthy father into the family firm. Instead, he abandoned his wild way of life, threw off his rich clothes, and as a beggar, chose the way of Jesus. I wrote to Isobel from Assisi; I spoke of the challenge to me to be like Francis and "naked, follow the naked Christ". I guess that she was alarmed by this image of me running through the streets with nothing on! She may also have been alarmed by this streak of intense fanaticism in me. Isobel returned to Cornell, and there was no reply to my 'naked' letter.

Chapter IX

CAMBRIDGE – THIRD YEAR - Theology - rooms
in Old Court - Hospitality - refugee camp -
Oberammergau

Somehow I managed to get a 2:1 in History, so I was
given a fine set of rooms in Old Court for my third and
final year. They were on the ground floor; the lobby had a
gas ring and a sink; the main room looked onto Old Court
one side and the garden and tower of St. Benet's Church on
the other; it had a large, magnificent carved wooden
mantelpiece; there was a separate bedroom, and on the
outside, between the two windows, was a plaque to
Christopher Marlowe. I gave several sherry parties each
term and also the occasional attempt at a meal for three or
four friends, usually scrambled egg and mushrooms. One
meal is still remembered by Jean Gurney; it was in honour
of Sydney Smith, a Canon of St. Paul's about 1800 and a
well known wit. An earnest woman asked him,

"Canon, what is your idea of heaven?" To which he
replied,

"My idea of heaven, Madam, is eating pâté de foie gras to the sound of trumpets."

I had been given me some of this pâté for Christmas, and I played my recording of the posthorn gallop, made at a dinner in the Officers Mess at Woolwich; so we had heaven in Corpus. Most colleges had one or two exclusive dining clubs, and I was invited to two or three of these glittering occasions. Some of my friends gave drinks parties in their College gardens where there were gracious old trees and herbaceous borders ablaze with colour; no worries about drink driving – as all these glorious gardens were in easy walking distance of Corpus.

Through the Theological Faculty I arranged to do some visiting in Fulbourne, the Psychiatric Hospital near Cambridge. It was a vast red brick hospital, set in deep country. I was given a ward full of very mentally ill men, many of them quite old; there was a strange, bewildering, frightened atmosphere, and very sad. The men would either lie motionless on their beds, staring sightlessly at the ceiling, or walk obsessively up and down the ward, muttering to themselves. There was one man, Victor, who was more normal in manner, and he was allowed out of the hospital. He used to come and visit me in the Old Court of Corpus, to the alarm of the College porters.

It was at this time that my father was left High Beeches by Alick McLaren, a first cousin of my grandfather. He had been brought up in Edinburgh and Northern Ireland, but worked as a senior civil servant barrister in London. In the 1920's they bought about a hundred acres of woodland in Ashdown Forest, in Sussex – all around was heather clad open country – Pooh Bear territory. They added on to some farm buildings in a homely 1920s style. It was a wonderful place – but more of that later.

In my third year at Cambridge I read Theology but with the rival attraction of my social life I only got a 2:2. I remember an ordinand at Trinity, Willie Pryor, who enjoyed giving the impression of being an amiable oaf. He told us many stories of his uncle, who had been an Army padre; standing at the altar, surrounded by servers, he was heard to say, "F..k! I forgot the bread!" I often remembered this when anything went wrong. Before the consecration in a Holy Communion service I discovered that, paradoxically, the nearer in time we were to the holy moment, the more kindly were moments of humour; this was gently reassuring for my servers when they made mistakes.

The highlight of the Cambridge summer term was the College May Ball, ending up with breakfast in College and a trip on the river in a punt. My only difficulty was that I had nobody to take as my partner. I had written several times to Isobel, asking her, but no reply. Mercifully a friend found me a partner and we had a great evening – but I've forgotten her name.

One day I was pondering on traditional sexual morality. Of course, it was all based on the need to avoid unwanted pregnancy outside marriage. In the days of Jane Austen, if a man held a woman's hand, it meant they were engaged, as people mistakenly thought about Captain Wentworth and Louisa Musgrove. Holding hands led to marriage and marriage to sexual intercourse, as it was called in the 1950's – the phrase "making love" came in during the Sixties – in Austen's time "making love" simply meant flirting or courting. The basic purpose of sex was, is and always will be, to produce a baby; so on this day in Corpus I made a natural psychological link between holding hands and the birth of a child! Amongst my friends this became known as the Maddox Method of procreation. Naturally, these views had a rather inhibiting effect on me! Even so, they were rooted in tradition and may be nearer the truth about human dignity than the casual hedonistic views of today. "Pompous old git" do I hear you say? To which I reply "Balderdash!".

An ordinand, Paul, had a sweet Japanese girl friend, and they were concerned that I restricted myself by thoughts of the Maddox Method, so one day she flung her arms around my neck and kissed me full on the lips. I was so taken aback that it had no effect whatsoever.

As soon as term had finished I did something very different. John Riches had organised a party of Corpus men to go to Austria and help refugees build new homes. I went with Michael Bayley, another ordinand, with Sheffield connections. We travelled through Belgium and Germany on his scooter, going slowly, taking side roads, and often sleeping in the fields or the barns of hospitable farmers. We usually said a grace over the bread and good German wine, as we sat in a cornfield or by a river – a powerful sense of the presence of God, which is hard to put into words. We went to Cologne, down the Moselle with its romantic medieval castles, and stayed in Wurzburg and saw its vast baroque palace.

We also went to an exhibition which showed the destruction our bombers had wreaked on the city; much of it was still in ruins – superb streets, squares and churches. It was sobering. There was no need for us to bomb Wurzburg as there was very little industry there, but we killed thousands of civilian men, women and children. I believe that Churchill questioned the need for this carpet bombing, saying that there would soon be nothing left, but Bomber Harris threatened to resign if he were not allowed to conduct the raids in his own fashion. Bishop Bell of

Chichester, had a meeting with Churchill to protest at the immorality of bombing civilians, but the war was dragging on, Germany would not surrender; we thought that her will had to be broken, but, as with us in the Blitz, the bombing only strengthened the will to resistance among the people. Tragically, policies considered unethical at the beginning of a war became acceptable after five long weary years of fighting. We should remember this when criticising other nations today; we also have done terrible things.

Eventually we joined the other Corpus men in Austria where we were helping refugees from the war to build their own homes; my job was to shovel sand into the rotating cement mixer. It is a good thing that I was not given a more skilled task like brick laying, or the house would have fallen down before the end of winter.

After the building site I went to see the Passion Play at Oberammergau: the other members of the party were Dr. Simms, the Archbishop of Dublin, and Charles Roderick, the much loved Vicar of St. Michael's Chester Square; it was a good thing that I was planning to go to Sheffield and not arsehole creeping to go up the ecclesiastical ladder; at that stage, any how. As you can imagine, the Play made a profound impression on me.

Chapter X

SHEFFIELD – STEELWORKS - To be or not to be a
priest - living as a Factory worker - praying and studying
with Roland

At some stage I made the first formal steps in offering
myself for ordination and went to C.A.C.T.M. – the
Churches Advisory Council for Training for the Ministry,
rather like W.O.S.B., the Army's selection board. I went
with mixed feelings, interested, challenged, daunted, wary,
as if the net were closing in on me. If I had not been
recommended, or failed, in other words, I would have been
partly angry and partly relieved, knowing that I would have
had the excuse to go away and live a normal life. I was
ambiguous in my feelings about the church and ordination,
and always have been.

Some of the other candidates gave me the creeps; they
were ecclesiastical creatures full of churchy talk. Others
were refreshingly robust, including Jim, a Sheffield working
class lad, who told me he thought I must be a terrible snob,
because of the tweed country suit I was wearing, but after

we had larked about a bit he readily agreed that I was "all reeght", a phrase I was often to hear later. What a welcome compliment! Anyhow, for good or ill, I was recommended for training.

As I was in Sheffield I decided to go and see Roland Walls and the six ordinands who were living, studying and praying with him in community, having spent six months labouring in the city. Among them were John Halsey and John Glasbrook, Magdalene and Westcott men, whom I knew. I was immediately drawn to the whole ethos of the adventure and Roland agreed for me to join him in the new group starting that Autumn.

In September 1960 I went to Roland and the other members of the Sheffield Twelve. Roland's idea was to try a new way of preparing men for ordination. For six months we were to work as labourers in the city, living and spending time with people similar to our workmates; in the second six months we were to share his house, reading radical theology, soaking ourselves in the Gospels and leading a corporate life rather like the Franciscans. Roland had the backing of Leslie Hunter, the prophetic Bishop of Sheffield who had encouraged Ted Wickham to start the Industrial Mission; both men were deeply aware of the gulf separating the Church from working men. Roland had been to Iona; and also to Taize, that remarkable Protestant Community in France, where they had rediscovered the monastic vows of poverty, chastity and obedience, which they lived in a simple, profound fresh way, earning their living in the world and welcoming all to their deep worship. A third inspiration was the community of the Little Brothers of Jesus, another French order, but in the Catholic Church. They followed the vision of Charles de Foucauld, a nineteenth century cavalry officer who had given up soldiering in order to live a very simple life close to Jesus; he started by looking after the garden of some nuns in Nazareth, and then moved to the Sahara to live amongst the Toureg, a very poor wandering tribe. His calling was just to share their life of poverty, to pray and welcome any who came to his tent. He longed for others to join him, but he died alone in the desert, murdered because he was a Frenchman. However, after his death the seeds of the desert sprouted, and under the leadership of Pere Voillaume, the Community of the Little Brothers was founded, and later, the Little Sisters of Jesus. They lived in small communities of three or four, a life of prayer and welcome in the poorest parts of cities of the world. For years I often used his prayer:

> *Father, I abandon myself into your hands;*
> *I am ready for all, I accept all,*
> *That your will may be done in me*
> *and in all men your creatures.*
> *No more do I ask than this, Lord,*
> *Because I love you.*
> *So I leave myself in your hands*
> *With boundless confidence,*
> *And certainty of hope, because*
> *You are my Father.*

So our purpose in Sheffield was not to work in the structures of industry, like the Industrial Mission, or to make converts like Billy Graham, but something different, - just to pray, joining the liturgical worship of the universal church, listen and learn, to absorb into our very being the hardships, the limitations, the attitudes and the hilarity of working people. Unlike the first few weeks in the Army, this was a free choice – to live and learn from people with a different background from our own.

After a weekend of preparation with Roland, we went our separate ways, meeting up again for a day each month to share experiences and to pray, using the set liturgy of the Church, Matins, Evensong and Holy Communion.

I went to live with Mr and Mrs Horton in a council house near the edge of the city. I would get up at six in the morning and catch two buses to clock in at work before eight. Much of the journey was through dark and grim streets. I wore dark blue overalls, a donkey jacket and heavy boots. The Industrial Mission had kindly found me work at Arthur Lee's; it was known as one of the steel works but was not a forge, those very hot, tough places needing skilled workers; they would go straight from work to the pub and drink pints of beer to replace their moisture lost in sweat.

No, my work was in a wire drawing shop, some hundreds of yards long, vibrating with the sound of dozens of machines. I was shown how to operate mine by Lol, a dear, gentle old man who wore brown overalls, and rebuked some of the others for their robust humour. My job was to wheel a large coil of steel, ¼" or ½" wide, fix it on my machine, and cut it into the required lengths. If my thoughts wandered from this boring task, the strips of steel would come out all squiggly! I still have a small metal cross above my desk, made on this machine.

Most of the men accepted me very easily, with typical Sheffield warmth and good humour; I was known as 'Youie'; I don't think that they found me condescending or determined to "convert them". The standard definition of a Christian was somebody who didn't smoke, didn't drink and didn't swear. I didn't smoke. There were also three lads, in their mid teens, Ron, Mike and Sam, who delighted in trying, unsuccessfully, to shock me; they would come up behind me and putting a hand between my legs would touch me up, and enjoyed seeing my startled expression. Mike was a confident young man, with a big grin; he was a great success with the girls. They showed me a photo of him, naked on the grass and his naked girlfriend kneeling over him, while the others stood excitedly around. I had never seen such a photo before, and they whipped it away quickly. There was one moment when Mike, Ron and I were walking through the works at the end of the day and passed a pretty girl going the other way. Mike said,

"Wi' my cock, Ronnie's looks and Youie's brains, we could 'ave 'er!"

I quickly chipped in,

"With my looks, my brains and my cock I could have her thank you very much!"

They laughed. Merriment breaks down many barriers. "All good clean fun" they would say about some performer in the Working Men's Club, singing songs that were certainly not fit for the drawing room.

I had a photo of the three of us walking through the works, in our oily dark blue overalls; but my neatly parted hair gives me away. If a day in the works felt impossibly dreary, or if I were treated roughly, I would remember that I could return to my own comfortable, civilised background whenever I wanted: this was a real limitation to any fanciful idea of mine that I was totally involved with the world of working men.

One of the sad things I often heard in the steel works, and often since, is the view that all Church people are hypocrites; one person in their best clothes on Sunday, and somebody very different on Monday, especially if they were unjust employers. I fear that there was some truth in this, especially in pre-war times, but I honestly do not recognise this description of most of the members of my different congregations. Not perfect, yes; still with the prejudices of their family, yes; but mostly good, kind neighbours giving much to the life of the local community and beyond. Outsiders seem to set us up as people who think we are better than others; whereas I see Christians as sinners who know that we are forgiven.

During the tea and lunch breaks I would sometimes listen to the older men talking bitterly about their hard times in the Depression of the 1930s, the poverty and degradation of unemployment. I wondered how they felt when they saw one of the sons of Arthur Lee walking from his great car to his office in the works. He was a big confident looking man in a dark blue pinstripe suit. Later he was to become a Master Cutler.

Through the Industrial Mission I met Reg Arundel – pronounced in the Northern way. He worked in a factory and his father in a forge. He was about nineteen, and we became firm friends. He was a member of the Young Communists and I learnt a lot from him. I understood the bitterness of the class struggle, the harsh conditions of Northern workers' lives in earlier years, the injustice of capitalism; the grinding work was done by the poor and the profits went to the rich. Reg took me to a meeting of the Young Communists – it was rather like a church service, with rows of chairs facing a speaker, a passionate oration calling for self sacrifice and care for fellow workers, lusty singing of the Red Flag and a collection. I met some fine men there, upright, honest, compassionate and fearless, and I had a real respect for them. I went to Reg's home when a friend from Corpus, Michael Griffiths, was staying with me in Attercliffe. He is tall, dark-haired, broad shouldered and good looking. He still remembers the very first thing Reg's mother said when he appeared,

"Ee, I'm reeght surprised no lass has had thee!"

Sometimes I was taken to a Working Mens Club by my mates. When I first joined the Army I honestly did not know what the word 'mate' actually meant; I would have used the word 'friend'. There were many Clubs in Sheffield and they were enormous, sometimes holding nearly a thousand people. I was taken by some of the men from the works, and would join their families, including children, in this vast room, full of smoke and noise. The entertainment was hilarious and the whole atmosphere rowdy and cheerful. It was quite an experience, and I felt part of it all.

On Saturdays I would sometimes join a Rambling Club and enjoy walking in Derbyshire and the Peak District, fine hilly country, with old stone farmhouses. I would occasionally walk with a girl on these expeditions, but I don't think anything came of it. Many of the grim Northern industrial cities were set amongst wild hills and for many years some steel workers could escape on a Sunday to the moors – a fine tradition and part of the ethos of the early days of the Labour Party.

One morning I got up at six o'clock to go to work. When I am on my own I often form thoughts in my mind, using words and making sentences, but not saying them aloud. On this occasion the words in my mind were all jumbled up and out of order, **"only it's one Thursday more today work at so weekend before the."** It was worrying, but I thought it would get better as soon as I woke up properly and had something to eat and drink. I walked to the bus stop, climbed onto the top deck of the bus and asked for my ticket, "**Brightside at please stop, much how**?" The ticket collector looked at me strangely, but gave me a ticket to Brightside. I got off at the next stop and caught the next bus home. Was I going mad? I left a note for Win Horton and went to bed. I slept deeply from seven till one in the afternoon. When I finally woke I tried forming a sentence in my mind, "Can I speak properly, now that I have had a good long sleep?" "Yes, thank God I can!". I had been utterly exhausted. This word confusion has happened twice more in my life, but never so badly or so alarmingly.

In the early spring of 1961 we rejoined Roland at his Canon's house in Fulwood Road, the West End of Sheffield. I had said goodbye to my workmates with some sadness and bade a fond grateful farewell to the dear Hortons; I kept in touch with them for some time, but sadly lost contact with them after a few years. 393 was a stone semi-detached villa with a garden – nothing very grand in my eyes, but when Reg came to see us, he saw me standing at the foot of the stairs and exclaimed "Youie, yer look like a lord in 'is castle!" And so began the most influential six months of my life.

I shared a room with John Ware; he had ginger hair, an honest open face and a great self-deprecating sense of humour; he was greatly troubled by human suffering and told God so; but he was also one of the most compassionate men I have ever known. I imagine that he was like his grandmother; he told me that if you gave her some good new clothes, within the week she would probably have given them to some woman suffering from the cold. He had done one year of Theological college, at Ridley Hall in Cambridge, and his Church background had been

Evangelical. He was delighted to discover Roland's more open and Catholic way of thinking and worshipping. One of the others was John Oliver, who had already done a year at Westcott. He was engaged to Meriel; she was also highly intelligent, kind and bubbled with fun and delight. I remember her telling me, with mock anger, how cross she had been with John when they had been walking together in a wood and John had seen a couple in the bushes making love, but had not pointed them out to her!

A third member of the household was Kenneth Boyd; he came from Invergordon and was to be ordained in the Church or Scotland. He spoke with a lovely Highland voice, which I envied, and often wore the kilt, Mackenzie tartan. I think it must have been a bold decision for him to come to Sheffield and live an Anglican community life. He much appreciated all Roland was and had to give. Kenneth was also a very good story teller and bubbled with glee. He is now the Professor of Medical Ethics at Edinburgh and much respected for his knowledge and wisdom. Sandy Jackson was the fourth; I think he was also a Scot and came from the Congregational Church. Poor Sandy, I don't think he cottoned on to what we were all about, and rather drifted away; sadly, we lost touch with him before long. We were looked after by Miss Black, who came from the island of Lismore, in Loch Linnhe, north of Oban. She was plump, and spoke with a Highland voice; she was a great character; sometimes she could be very cross with us all – a celibate priest and young men can actually be very selfish. She also had a great sense of fun, and would appear, at most inappropriate moments, with a widely smiling face, all dressed up as a Bishop.

Our day started in the Chapel in the attic; it was plain, with a small window looking onto the sky, white walls and black beams. The altar was a plain wooden table in the middle of the room; on it were simple candles and a rough cross made of two pieces of jagged wood nailed together in the shape of a human form. We knelt in a circle or sat on the wooden stools. It was all very different from a Victorian church, and heady stuff for me. Every morning and evening we said the daily Office from the Book of Common Prayer; we prayed it slowly, often thinking of our workmates toiling away in the steelworks. The Psalms became personal and the lessons challenging and pregnant with meaning. There was also much silence, except when we all collapsed in giggles at some absurd verse in the Bible. We sang hymns unaccompanied. Roland had also chosen words from the Gospels for meditation – things which Jesus had said just to the Twelve, his disciples; Jesus speaking directly to each one of us, "Come, follow me." There was a power and intensity which I had not experienced before; a truly human Christ, ever present.

We spent some time studying, reading way-out thinkers who sincerely challenged the Christian faith, Fuerbach, Nietze, and that amazing Frenchwoman, Simone Weil, a student of philosophy who laboured in the factories. She was a Christ woman, called to live on the edge, never baptized. I also came across The Unutterable Beauty, the poems of Studdert Kennedy, Woodbine Willie. He was a chaplain in the First World War and nearly abandoned God, feeling that God had abandoned him and also the hundreds of thousands slaughtered on the battlefields. He stumbled across the mutilated body of a young soldier, and suddenly saw it as the body of Christ.

A Mother Understands

Dear Lord, I hold my hand to take

Thy body, broken here for me
Accept the sacrifice I make,
My body, broken, there, for Thee.
His was my body, born of me,
Born of my bitter travail pain,
And it lies broken on the field,
Swept by the wind and the rain.
Surely a Mother understands Thy thorn-crowned head,
The mystery of Thy pierced hands – the Broken Bread.

And another poem, **High and Lifted Up**:

Seated on the throne of power with the sceptre in Thine hand
While a host of eager angels ready for Thy service stand.......
God, I hate this splendid vision – all its splendour is a lie,
Splendid fools see splendid folly, splendid mirage born to die.
As imaginary waters to an agony of thirst
As the vision of a banquet to a body hunger-cursed,
As the thought of anaesthetic to a soldier mad with pain,
While his torn and tortured body turns and twists and writhes again,
So this splendid vision turns within my doubting heart,
Like a bit of rusty bayonet in a torn and festering part.
Preachers give it to me for comfort, and I curse them to their face.
Puny, petty minded priestlings prate to me of power and grace;
Prate of power and boundless wisdom that takes count of little birds.
Platitudinously pious far beyond all doubts and fears,
They will patter of God's mercy that can wipe away our tears.
All their speech is drowned in sobbing, and I hear the great world
groan,
As I see a million mothers weeping all alone.
See a host of English maidens making pictures in the fire,
While a host of broken bodies quiver still on German wire.
And I hate the God of Power on His hellish heavenly throne,
Looking down on rape and murder, hearing little children moan ...
"Thou who rul'st this world of sinners with Thy heavy iron rod,

Was there ever any sinner who has sinned the sin of God?"........
God, the God I love and worship, reigns in sorrow on the Tree,
Broken, bleeding, but unconquered, very God of God to me ....
On my knees I fall and worship that great Cross that shines above,
For the very God of Heaven is not Power,
But power of love.

I have quoted so much of this searing poem because it opened my eyes to a new and profound vision of the God who is like Christ. It moved me then and it moves me still. I believe that God does not, cannot, interfere to save us, but he does suffer in us and with us. He is the Suffering God, suffusing us with His love, if we will accept it and absorb it; then we can have the understanding and strength to support others who are suffering now.

This is the Gospel for me; it is a vision that inspired me then and inspires me now, a vision for which I have tried to give my working life.

Back to Fulwood Road – after an afternoon of shopping for Miss Black or working in the garden, we met to study a passage in the Gospels. Roland make it very real and immediate, and bubbled with glee at some of the absurdities of the religious folk in the story. One day Jesus was seen banging his head against a tree. "Master," said one of his disciples, "Why art thou banging thy head against a tree?" "Because I have seen what you lot are going to do with my message!" – a favourite make up story of Roland's. Sometimes in the middle of our Bible study there would be a knock on the door and some piteous wretch would be standing there asking for food and help; the Gospel study was abandoned and the Gospel lived in practice as the Christ was fed and found shelter. If only the Theological Colleges could have the same freedom and priorities!

99

Sometimes the Christ at the door was Roland's brother, who was on the road; very painful and difficult. I asked my parents to come and stay, so they could meet Roland and my friends and see what we were up to – I don't think they were reassured!

How did we manage for money? Roland had his stipend as a Canon of Sheffield Cathedral, where he sometimes preached; he was also available to many of the clergy who came to him; one was Kit Howell-Thomas, a man in his fifties, the Vicar of Attercliffe, the vast industrial end of the city. He struck us as being one of the most natural, human and unchurchy of all the clergy who visited the house. We all contributed to the expenses of the house with the money which we had carefully saved from our meagre wages. When this money ran out we ditched our studies and worked as labourers, throwing up bricks on a nearby building site – good theological training.

We went with Roland to Iona; in those days we travelled all the way from Oban by sea, in the lovely 1930's King George V. As we sat on the deck, waiting to disembark, a seagull was squawking loudly near us. "Sister gull, please be peaceful," said Roland, blessing her with his hand. She stopped squawking immediately. Much merriment.

While we were on Iona a man told Roland about a strange experience he had just had. He was alone at the back of the Abbey; he felt himself compelled to move forward, and kneel at the crossing; then he was led to move slowly to the great High Altar, and lie flat on his face, with his arms outstretched. He heard himself saying strange words in a language unknown to him. He asked Roland what it all meant? Roland was dumbfounded – the man had felt this irresistible compulsion to follow the actions and say the Latin words of the liturgy for that particular day in the year – a liturgy which had not been performed since the Reformation four hundred years ago. There are many such stories on Iona, where the veil between earth and heaven is thin. We also went with Roland to the Taize Community in Burgundy. This was in the early days when there were only about thirty Brothers and we worshipped in the 13th century village church, stripped of all its nineteenth century vulgarity. We stayed in a honey coloured stone guesthouse in the village, and had our simple meals under a vine in the courtyard. It was all very compelling and challenging; I felt a strong urge to offer myself to join the Community. I mentioned it to the French guestmaster who put it all in perspective by saying with his French accent,

"Do not make any decision just after passing seed. Is that how you say it?"!

I gulped and agreed; I no longer felt the need to become a Brother; but I had offered – sort of.

Not long after we had left Sheffield Roland founded the Community of the Transfiguration, living a life of prayer, work and welcome in an old reading room in Roslyn, just outside Edinburgh. If you want a fuller taste of his bubbling humour, learning and sense of proportion, read "Mole under the fence - Conversations with Roland Walls" by Ron Ferguson, St. Andrew Press.

And so our year with Roland in Sheffield ended, and I returned to Cambridge a rather different young man; it had been an amazing year, with many powerful experiences.

Chapter XI

WESTCOTT HOUSE - training to be a priest -
thinking - laughing - praying - Sussex - and a girl

In the autumn of 1961, aged 24, I was back in Cambridge.
Westcott House was opposite Jesus – not spiritually
opposite, I hope, - but across the road from Jesus College.

In my first term Ken Carey was the Principal, a good,
modest, traditionally devout man of the Old School; he
obviously believed in the tradition of Westcott which
included men of different backgrounds and
churchmanship; but he was accused by the irreverent of
trying to turn them all out as Christian gentlemen – no bad
idea, I think! Occasionally Ken would wear the scarlet
cassock of a Chaplain to the Queen. After a term or two of
mine at Westcott he left to become Bishop of Edinburgh.

He was followed by Peter Walker, whom I already
knew, as he had followed Roland Walls at Corpus. Before
he came to Corpus we heard that he was a man of prayer;
also that on his last day off, at his mother's house, he had
spent the day asleep, recovering from staying up all night

with a dying parishioner. He was a shy man, and seemed rather bewildered by all the changes required by the students in the radical days of the Sixties; but he soon won the respect and affection of us all. Our first Vice-Principal was John Habgood, who had a first class degree in both science and theology. He was another rather shy man, but an excellent lecturer and tutor, with a delight in the paradoxes of life. Later he became Archbishop of York. He was followed by Don Cupitt, also a colossal egghead with an enthusiastic questioning mind. He became a television personality through his searchingly honest programmes, the Sea of Faith. Those were the days of Honest to God, a slim Penguin book that did no more than bring together the more radical thinking of established theologians over many years, but because it was written by John Robinson, Bishop of Woolwich, it hit national headlines. He reminded us that we cannot talk of God as a person, as God is beyond our imagination; he told us of Bultmann, the German theologian of the 1920s who tried to make the Christian faith acceptable to the young scouts and guides in his parish; his main attempt was to "demythologize" the Bible so that its basic message could be more easily heard by today's questioning youngsters. All this was heady stuff and I thrived on it, combining traditional liturgical prayer with radical thinking.

During my two years at Westcott I spent much of my time with the family at High Beeches. It was south of Forest Row in Sussex, on the quiet top road through Ashdown Forest, from Wych Cross to Coleman's Hatch. There was a large old stone lodge; in one half lived Woodams, a wonderful old man with a true Sussex country accent, rarely heard today. He looked after the garden and the woods. At one stage Father employed a forestry firm to do some planting; previously they had criticised Woodams for wasting time, because he planted each little sapling lovingly by hand; but a higher proportion of his trees survived than those planted by the machine. He probably talked to them; Prince Charles would have approved. Woodams would also tell us that he had seen a hedgehog milking a cow. Mrs Woodams was a lovely old lady, crippled with arthritis; she accepted it with dignity, and spoke in the sweetest and most gentle manner imaginable. I used to pop in and see her whenever possible; she called me "Mr Hugh" which I rather liked – and Carola was Mrs Colin; perhaps feudal and sexist, but logical! In the other half of the lodge lived their daughter and Davidson, who worked in the woods with his father-in-law, doing the more basic jobs – an old fashioned hierarchical set up. Their daughter, Christine, did some cooking for Mother; she was more modern, and there was none of this Mr and Mrs Hugh nonsense with her.

There was a fairly short drive through the beeches and rhododendrons, and the house was smaller than the rather grand lodge suggested. We spent most of the time in the library, with Alick's wonderful leather bound books, comfortable leather arm chairs and a large fireplace; beside it was a cupboard which housed a big metal wheel with a handle. When you turned the wheel a draught blew up under the logs in the grate; when children whirled the wheel, sparks flew everywhere. Off the library was the logie – years earlier, Alick's cleaner had got muddled with the 1920's word loggia. 'Logie' sounded more basic and more Scots, and it stuck. It was a happy place, with old stone and brick walls, and a low open wall, framing the view over the stone terrace with its roses, sloping paddock, a bank of rhodies and a distant hill. Alick had kept a pony in the paddock and hunted in his eighties. Near the house were a hard tennis court, croquet lawn, pond and a superb large magnolia whose flowers stood out against a large Scots pine. In the wood there was a spring and natural stream. As a birthday present to Alick, Ethel had it dammed and an oval shaped swimming pool made in the valley. Up the steep banks were a mass of yellow azaleas, and above them the pale green of larches in the late spring. The water, of course, was cold, but warmer, even if very green, by August. You can imagine the many happy bathes we had there, with all the guests who stayed over the years. My father and mother were very hospitable, and had many friends and relations to stay, especially those who were troubled, or led a lonely life in London.

Round about this time Jean Gurney asked me to join a party going to the Northern Meeting, the Inverness Highland Ball, and to stay with them in their house on Speyside.

The Northern Meeting in Inverness was unforgettable; the ladies wore full length ball gowns, often in white or pale blue, with a silk tartan plaid over their shoulder; most of the men were in Highland evening dress. Although I had my McLaren kilt, sadly I could not afford a velvet doublet and ruff, or black jacket, so I was one of the minority in a dinner jacket. The reels and strathspeys were danced perfectly, but not with the wild abandon of Arran's Glaswegians.

By contrast, I used to help out in a youth club in the poorer area of Cambridge, where the boys and girls tried to shock me with accounts of their sex life. I wasn't shocked, just rather envious. Sometimes I had two or three of the boys to my rooms in Westcott; they brought their own records with them, to play on my record-player. Sadly, it disturbed the studies of my neighbours! I had been inspired by a visit to Westcott of Father Borelli, a tough little Italian priest who worked in a very poor part of Naples. He wanted to make contact with the Scunizzi, the street kids, but they ran away when they saw him coming in his black cassock. He dressed as a vagrant, and hung around at the edge of their fire; finally, he became part of the gang, would warn them when the police were approaching, and even get involved in some of their illegal activities. Once he had won their trust he was able to bring them back to his presbytery and organise a better way of life for them. The famous author, Morris West, stayed with him to write his story. Sadly, I heard a rumour that Borelli went off with his wife.

At Westcott each of us was given some activity in the town, to give us experience of parish life; we also went on parish placements for a few weeks to learn from good Vicars. I was given charge of the Leper Chapel, a small, unspoilt medieval Church on the outskirts of Cambridge; it was a reminder of the centuries old tradition of the Church caring for those cast out of society; today, it draws its congregation from the nearby housing estate, where I would visit them in their homes, as well as taking the services and preaching.

Life at Westcott was good; I formed life long friendships; as well as the stimulating lectures, discussions and the visits by interesting priests, there was much teasing, laughter and fun. The main rhythm of the day was the three liturgical services in the chapel, all Prayer Book of course; Matins, Evensong and Compline, last thing at night, followed by silence, which I loved. As the gentle words and plainsong of Compline died away, I loved to linger in the quiet, not thinking, not using words, but looking at the cross and the gentle candlelight on the altar. Images from the day would float through my mind, memories of other people's suffering or joy, and I would see Christ in them all, part of his crucifixion or resurrection; for All is One.

When I went to Westcott my sister Alison started her training as a physiotherapist at the Middlesex Hospital. In the summer holidays she had a group of her friends from the hospital down to High Beeches for the day. As always, I was on the lookout for a girlfriend, and I noticed a gentle girl with a lovely smile, and talked with her a bit. The following weekend there was a party back in Woldingham and I asked Alison if she could invite this girl down for the weekend. I hoped that I was asking the right one, as I wasn't sure of her name! I went to Forest Row station to meet her, and it was a great relief when I saw the right lovely girl getting off the train; it was quite brave of her to come. All went well and she became my girlfriend for nearly a year; she often stayed at High Beeches and came to Westcott many times. I stayed with her family but did not feel at home with them. I felt her parents disapproved of me. Julie and I canoodled a lot, especially one time, when having taken a service in the Leper Chapel I drove us to a hayfield, still wearing my black cassock; taking it off made me feel delightfully wicked. During the summer before ordination I took Julie to the Church in the wood at High Beeches; we said Evensong and then lingered. Apparently back at High Beeches, Father said to Alison, with his gentle smile,

"Evensong seems to be taking a long time tonight"!

We were both inexperienced and, with great difficulty, very controlled – in my situation as an ordinand, sex was out, sadly!. One weekend we drove down to Devon to stay with some friends; in their invitation letter to her, they mentioned the creaking floors in their old house which would warn her if I came to her bedroom. In fact her virtue was quite safe, but her parents saw the letter and feared that she was being invited to a licentious household. Julie told me that she had to work hard to persuade her parents that she would be good and to let her go – she was nearly twenty. Later on, her father sent her a newspaper cutting which said that men were only interested in sex; perhaps he was right, and perhaps he knew himself well. In my last term he wrote to Peter Walker, the Principal, asking whether my intentions were honourable. It was rather embarrassing for poor Peter, but he talked with me and wrote a reassuring letter to her father. I suppose her parents were right to be worried; indeed, I had to ask myself whether I wanted Julie as my wife; lovely though she was, and very good for my confidence, we did not really have a meeting of minds; reluctantly, I ended our friendship. I felt bad about turning her away, but I believe that she returned to her previous boy friend and moved abroad.

At about this time, a few months before my ordination, I was very smitten with another girl; she was a strong character and was going up to University in the autumn. After we had met she went home by coach; she wrote and told me that she had felt angry with somebody who had taken the seat beside her, because I had sat there a few minutes before! She was tall, with the Celtic mixture of black hair and blue eyes, and a lovely aristocratic face. She rang High Beeches, and I believe that when I heard it was her on the telephone I went quite white. Just before going to Sheffield I showed my love for her. She said,

"I must love you, or I wouldn't have let you kiss me like that!"

Mind you, she didn't have much choice! So I went to ordination in a state of some confusion and excitement. After I had been in Attercliffe for a few months she reluctantly agreed for me to visit her at University, and while there I soon realised that a few weeks at University had put an end to her fancy for a curate in Sheffield.

Chapter XII

SHEFFIELD – ATTERCLIFFE - dreaded dog collar -
immersed in the lives of the people - "The Duchess",
Hague & Wilf - difficulties - Alan Eccleston

Attercliffe was the industrial end of Sheffield, a vast area
of enormous steelworks, lying each side of the river
Don, between Sheffield and Rotherham; it had row upon
row of cobbled streets and small Victorian houses. Many
had been back-to-backs, with just two or three rooms for all
a large family, no yard, and, of course, no lavatory. They
were built during the booming years of the industrial
revolution, when millions of people poured into the cities
from the surrounding countryside, in search of work; with a
growing population and with the use of machines on the
land, not so many "farm hands" were needed. I always
think that is a very significant phrase, farm "hands": men
and women are sometimes only valued for the work they
do, for the extra profit they can bring to the farmer. When a
machine can do the job better than a man's hands he is no
longer wanted, he loses his job and the cottage that goes
with it, and drifts into the harsh world of heavy industry.

churches, St. Alban's and St. Andrews. It was the era of church statistics; with four churches, three clergy and two church workers in a parish of 36,000, we should have had a combined congregation of about five hundred. We had thirty seven; and proudly considered ourselves the greatest failure in the Church of England.

I think that both John and I found it difficult working for Kit as Vicar; but we had respect for him – he was a man of integrity. He had served in the Indian Army, and then was a teacher; it was not hard to guess! He offered himself for ordination, and went, in early middle age, as a curate to Attercliffe, and then as a Vicar in a parish in the north of the Diocese. Attercliffe then needed a new Vicar; thirteen men came to look, but the hopeless task was too much for them all, and none accepted. Finally, reluctantly, Kit was prepared to return to the parish; he knew the Vicarage and the grim streets which surrounded it, and yet, when nobody else was willing to take up the challenge, he accepted it. This earned our respect. In spite of his Establishment background, he was a committed Socialist, and in his retirement in Hertfordshire he was the Secretary of the local Labour Party.

During my last year at Westcott I went to stay with John in Carbrook Church House. Already he was finding Kit difficult, but even so, I knew that I must go to Attercliffe, that God was calling me there, if you like. However, the Vicar was by no means sure that God was sending him a curate, whom he should welcome with open arms! Because it was such a tough job, in such a tough place, I assumed that it was rather wonderful of me to offer myself. I took it for granted that Kit would be glad to have me; but not so. I think, in hindsight, that he was irritated by my assumption that I would be offered the curacy. I guess that he was also switched off by my enthusiasm, and suspected that I was just doing the fashionable thing of "slumming it". At the time though, my concern for the people of Attercliffe was genuine.

It is a pity that we were not ordained deacon at Westcott, alongside all our friends with whom we had been trained; commissioned together before being sent to our different parishes.   Instead, I found my ordination a depressing experience.   The 3-day retreat was in Whirlow Grange; some of my fellow ordinands were irritatingly churchy, seemingly more interested in ceremonial than in people.   The addresses were given by the new Bishop of Sheffield, John Taylor; I found him rather narrow in theology and formal in manner.   The ordination itself was in Doncaster Parish Church, vast, and unknown to me; the only familiar faces were my family, Kit and John.   Even before the service I put on the dreaded dog-collar; in those days it was the whole thing, which cut off your head from the rest of your body, as if your brain were to be separated from your heart and balls; a coldly rational control of feeling and life-giving desire, leading to an unrealistic and suppressed character; whereas I have often noticed that the heart is the motivating force in a person's life, and the brain is used to justify the consequent reaction; for example, two brilliant professors, or politicians, argue fiercely, using their theology or political theory to support the belief learnt in childhood.   To understand that other person, we need to listen to what his heart is saying.

In Church life the significant moment is when a man or woman is made a priest; some say, "priested" which feels like "castrated" – ugh! When going by train to Edinburgh I often see Doncaster Parish Church dominating the town - and shudder.   In practice, being made a deacon makes a greater difference to the outward circumstances of life than being made a priest. I was now a Rev, wore a dog-collar, was employed and paid £40 a month by the Church, and under the discipline of ecclesiastical authorities.

A year later, on St. Michael's Day, 29th September 1964, I was ordained priest in Sheffield Cathedral. This was a much better experience. There were fewer "creepy ecclesiastics" on the retreat; I met Richard Hanmer who was being ordained deacon to serve on a vast housing estate near Attercliffe; we kept in touch and he was my best man at our wedding. He had also been at Cambridge, at Peterhouse: at the gathering after the ordination his parents talked with mine, and it seemed normal after the artificial atmosphere of Doncaster; Richard's father was a brigadier and hunted with the Portman. Richard is somebody of great integrity, inner strength, with a gentle smile, and a warm, self-effacing courtesy. He and his wife Sheila have remained genuine friends over the years. When he was chaplain to the Bishop of Norwich he visited every house in the Cathedral Close, canvassing for the Labour Party. It was good having him with me at the ordination, and it was good having members of the Attercliffe congregations and Youth Club there in the Cathedral, at the heart of the city. These were now people I knew and loved, and I was being ordained to serve them. It made sense.

One of our churchwardens was a remarkable man, Tom Strodder. He had been in strict training to become a top athlete; he worked in a forge, and one day a small piece of molten steel flew out and severed an artery in his thigh. He was rushed to hospital nearly dying. Constant prayers were said for him in Attercliffe Church; very near death, he was given new life, and this made a profound impression on him. He knew that God was real, powerful and life giving;

also that He had work for Tom to do. As he recovered, he became more involved in the local church. He had a gentle wife, Lily, and two lovely daughters; Elaine was an idealistic student, with long flowing hair, a sweet smile and a lovely singing voice; amongst other folk songs of the day, she sang "Dirty Old Town". One night, coming home on her scooter, there was an accident, and she was killed. Tom and Lily were shattered, devastated and empty. In her hopeless misery Lily said, "I wish that Elaine could give us a sign that she is alright". At that moment Elaine's shoes jumped off a chair onto the floor. Not long after, a gate which only Elaine used, suddenly banged open; and other signs followed.

Both Tom and Lily became involved in the world of psychic healing and had some remarkable stories to tell. With prayer and the laying on of hands he was able to relieve severe headaches and stomach pains, and probably did much more. Sadly, the Vicar was very wary of all this, which left Tom and Lily feeling misunderstood, discouraged and rather bitter. In those days I was more open to the world of the spirit than I am now. One time, Tom was with us on Iona; we were in the small and very powerful tiny chapel of St. Columba. Tom asked for the protection and guidance of God, we both said the Lord's Prayer, and then Tom moved into a kind of trance. He had told me that people had spoken to him, or through him from "the other side". After a short time he began to speak in a voice that was hardly recognisable; his face was pulled into a shape longer and thinner than his own. I can't remember his exact words, but they were from a French doctor, of the sixteenth century, telling Tom that he must continue with his work of healing. For me it was a powerful, timeless experience, transcending the barriers of time and death; it was not eerie, spooky or evil, just remarkably normal. It may have come from Tom's deep collective subconscious, (Jung) released by Elaine's death and frequent continuing communication, or it may have been nearer a mystical encounter. What is the difference? And who can tell? Both for Tom and for me it was a real experience.

Many of the Old Testament prophets, as well as Jesus and Paul, had powerful, life changing mystical experiences; and, of course, they are common in all the great faiths, especially in the East. In the West we like to think that we have open scientific minds, but, in fact, we have closed our minds to the world of the spirit and so suffer from the self-inflicted wounds of doubt and disbelief, cutting off part of human nature and our ability to receive at a deep spiritual level. "Because of their disbelief", even Jesus "could do no works of healing" for the people of Nazareth: they could not see beyond a return visit of the carpenter's son. We westerners have much to unlearn.

On Mondays we went to the Vicarage for breakfast, provided by Kit's wife, Grace. She was a winner – warm, classy, relaxed, untidy grey hair, a cigarette dangling out of her mouth; she had a good mind, sense of humour and proportion, and a quick perception in personal matters; I think she understood our difficulties; these breakfasts were some of our more normal and natural times. They were followed by our weekly staff meeting, when we went through a list of the congregation, swapping information as to who we had seen in each of the churches the day before and whether any visits were needed – a good pastoral discipline. We then discussed wider issues affecting the church and theology. On Monday mornings we were usually joined by Dick Evans who ran the Youth Club, where I spent many noisy evenings, playing table tennis and mingling. Once I was chatting with a girl who had large brown eyes and a lively personality. One of the boys said,

"You fancy her, don't you?!"

I could have killed him. He was right, of course, but what could I say, except a hurried "No", as I blushed and lied. We also ran the Sunday Club for Church youngsters, where we had more serious discussions and outings, sometimes helpful, sometimes discouraging.

Much of my time was spent in visiting. In those days hospital chaplains sent the clergy the admission notes of new patients; there were too many to follow them all up, so we guessed, from the ward and the patient's age, whether we should try to visit, either in their home in the parish or in the hospital itself. It was often a relief to drive away from the grey streets of Attercliffe. Back at Westcott we had been solemnly told about women's ops – "the major", "the scrape", etc – all completely new to us naïve young students. We visited in homes to arrange christenings and weddings; once I had to do four weddings in an afternoon; it was a good thing that I could act, as all genuine emotion had been exhausted by the time I came to the fourth. I also had to give them marriage preparation, which was rather ludicrous! I think that from my complete ignorance I gave them advice on sexual matters. Mind you, in those days few engaged couples lived together, so perhaps some of them were as ignorant as I was. Most were fairly young, often in their teens, and would have lived with their fathers and mothers up to the wedding day. Marriage for them was a major upheaval, with many false expectations that a young husband would be like a girl's father, and a wife like the boy's mother. Christenings would often follow and over the years I sometimes came to know young families quite well.

My first funeral visit was to a tiny house in a grimy street. As I passed the window, I saw the family sitting round the table; I noticed glasses and a half-full bottle of whisky. After I had knocked on the door and was let in, the bottle had gone, so I immediately said, "Come on, where's the whisky?!"

With sheepish grins, they reached under the table where they had quickly hidden it; needless to say, they gave me a hefty dram. After I had heard the gory details of the husband's death I tried to encourage them by talking of the Resurrection. It was neither the right moment nor their way of thinking; I soon noticed that instead of saying, "Dad died last year", Sheffield people would say, "We buried Dad last year" – a typical, down to earth (!) Yorkshire matter-of-fact saying, even if they did have some vague idea of the after life. It was not long before I dropped talk of the Resurrection; as I was trying to connect with the mourners, even to me it sounded forced and false. Instead I would say a short prayer of thanks for the person who had died, leaving him in God's hands. It was only years later that I hit on the liberating thought that as Vicars we are not paid to "bring hope" in any distinct, dogmatic sense. Instead representing God, we are to be with the bereaved family in their grief; our physical presence in their own home speaks more loudly than any words.

Most of the Attercliffe funerals were arranged by the Co-op Funeral Service, and even in those days they had great, shiny, black limousines, and it was poignant to see them dominating a small, blackened side street, each car being as long as the width of two houses. It was good to see this dignity in death; for a few hours, even the poorest family were treated like royalty; most had saved up for their funeral over many years. Many of the burials were in one of the windswept cemeteries high up in Sheffield, and every graveside was a preparation for the death of my own father and my own mother – mind you, she was still alive nearly fifty years later! It was also, of course, a reminder of my own death; so is every Christian service; all speak somewhere of death and eternal life; the rhythm of liturgical daily prayer gives us a wholesome, fundamental view, mental, emotional and spiritual, of life on earth in the context of eternity; for I believe life and death, earth and heaven are All One. I must admit that it was sometimes hard to believe this as I took a burial in this bleak, cold cemetery, of some coarse, drunken brute of a man, who had given his family hell. Then, it just felt to me that we were disposing of his corrupted old body; that it was the end of him, and that was all there was to it. It was with difficulty that I tried to hold on to the belief that God loved this sod as much as He loved me.

Once I had to take the funeral of a sixteen year old, whom I knew slightly; he had been drowned when mucking about with his mates by the filthy canal. He was a cheerful lad, but always in real trouble, and none of his broken family or neighbours had a good word for him, until he died, and became a loveable angel who could do no wrong. For me, in my sheltered naivety, it was all very strange – the open outpouring of grief at the graveside, mixed, I guess, with guilt, followed by the laughter and then blame and quarrelling in the pub afterwards. Every now and then I had to do a day's duty at the City Crematorium; this meant taking up to eight funerals in a row, all for families I had never met. By the end, I was emotionally drained, but a few quick words with each undertaker and looking at the faces of the sorrowing relatives made it possible to take even the final funeral with a degree of genuine sadness.

I visited one dear little seven year old, Garry, while he was in hospital; and then continued to see him regularly back at home, where he lived with his Dad, Mum and two brothers. He had some form of cancer; even so, we had hopes of his recovery, and prayed for him regularly and earnestly, both in our clergy prayers and in his home. He slowly lost strength and looked paler and paler; he died at home, and I went to see him in the local funeral parlour, his beautiful little face, white and cold. It was the first time that I had been involved in the death of a child, and it was a heavy, heavy burden. I took the funeral, and kept in touch with the family; I only hope that I was of some help to them. I had the smallest glimpse of the effect on the family, the father, the mother, the brothers or sisters, of the loss of a beloved son or daughter, brother or sister. Thank God, it is not so common these days, but in years gone by it was all too frequent, and many families had to live with this bereavement for the rest of their lives. Most of the spiritual writing down the ages was written with the heartfelt experience of life and frequent death; it gives an important perspective on eternity.

On the day of Garry's funeral I also went to an evening service in the Week of Prayer for Christian Unity. The thought came to my mind that there was a profound, almost mystical link between the disunity of the Church, the fractured Body of Christ, and the death of this little boy; not a logical link, of course – Richard Dawkins might scoff, - but my spiritual, emotional response to those two events in the one day. I am told that mystics in most spiritual traditions have a simple message, that ultimately All is One, so man's sin, (pride, selfishness, cruelty etc.) flows from the same pool as man's malfunctioning body, pain and untimely death. To my mind the story of Adam and Eve is a

121

profound story about man belonging to the earth, at one with it. Break the bond and we will bring disaster upon ourselves, whether damaging our lungs through smoking, our livers through excessive drinking, or the earth, sea and sky through pollution. An individual's genetic disease is not the result of his own wrong-doing, of course, but, rather, may be the result of the random, destructive nature of human biology. George MacLeod was a mystic, and it was his belief in the spiritual nature of matter that led him into industrial politics; later he thundered with poetic majesty against the blasphemy of splitting the atom, the basis of the structure of matter, to destroy men, women and children in Hiroshima and Nagazaki, with a bomb named Trinity, on the day of the Feast of Transfiguration; blasphemy indeed, and far worse than calling God names.

Hinduism and the old African religions share the same view of the spiritual nature of all created beings. Jonathan Pollit knew the spiritual basis of the Friends of the Earth – what a title!

During my time in Attercliffe I bought an open bright blue second hand Triumph Herald, which I usually drove with the hood down; exhilarating, especially in open country. It was not a sports car, but I pretended it was, and once I cornered fast through the cemetery gates and nearly crashed into a hearse. After a Bible study in somebody's home in the parish I would sometimes drive the members to their homes. On one summer's evening the last passenger, sitting beside me, was the pretty young mother of some of our youth club members, and I drove her, hood down, right up Attercliffe Common, for all to see – not really very wise; I often found myself in this dilemma, caught between good manners and the need to avoid scandal – one of the many pitfalls of clergy life. Years later, in Sandwich, I remember a P.C.C. member being horrified by a gentleman's kind offer to drive her home, after a church meeting, in his great gleaming Jaguar – what would the neighbours have thought as he drew up outside her home?!

During our time in Carbrook Church House we were looked after by Mrs Wood, a jolly, plump grandmother whom we lovingly called 'the Duchess', which tickled her. She shopped, cooked and cleaned for us; for months after our arrival the house stank of cats; the previous tenant had had fourteen; and all our clothes were stiff from the dirt in the air from the steelworks. When I left I burnt them all. A frequent visitor to the House was Wilf; he was scrawny, shabbily dressed, and suffered frequent bad epileptic fits. We were all fond of him, and he could be good company; we regularly gave him small amounts of money, which sometimes led me into difficult negotiations with him; he would get very distressed, ending in his having one of those awful fits. John would sort it out. The dear Duchess was also very good with him. Another visitor was Hague. He had probably suffered shell shock and was mentally very ill; he lived rough, had a black beard, a long filthy overcoat and a shabby beret. He would talk to himself, and the children would throw stones at him; he would then walk up the Common, waving a clenched fist and shouting fiercely. Kit gave him one meal a day, and we another, leaving the food in the outside coalhouse of our backyard, as instructed.

At one stage, we shared the house with an out-of-work Methodist minister, David, a lovable but rather intense figure; he was horrified that we fed Hague like a dog, outside. He wanted Hague to live with us; Kit was very concerned as to how it would work out, but reluctantly agreed. Hague joined us; he had a bath and put on the clean clothes we had ready for him; we burnt his old ones. While he was having his bath, we crept along the corridor and standing at the door, heard him singing – one of the most beautiful sounds I have ever heard. We cut his hair and he shaved off his beard; when we came back from visiting, we would find him sitting in the rocking chair by the open fire, peacefully smoking his pipe, quietly chuntering away to himself, and ready to join in some short simple conversation; a truly rewarding sight. Sometimes he would come back from his daily walk in a fearful state, shouting fiercely again; children would have been tormenting him once more, which made me very angry; but we did not know who they were, and there was nothing we could do. For a few weeks we had an Indian priest staying with us, Alban; he was a very jolly fellow, and came back one day, wreathed in smiles, very pleased with himself and told us, in his Indian voice, that he had seen an advertisement which said, "Don't be vague, ask for Haig"!! I believe that shortly after I had left, Hague was back on the streets again – Kit's worst fears justified. However, I heard that a Pakistani family had given him a home in their attic, believing him to be a holy man.

About halfway through my time in Attercliffe John Ware met and married Phillada. She was a Child Care Officer and met John through a mutual friend and later they worked together to help an Attercliffe family. She is tiny, hardly taller than my mother, and I still think of her whenever I sing George Herbert's hymn, 'King of Glory, king of peace' because Phillada pointed out to me that the last line says, "E'en eternity's too short to extol thee". She is very professional and totally dedicated to helping people in trouble. A more genuinely compassionate pair it would be hard to find in the length and breadth of the land. They also bubble with self-deprecating mirth whenever we meet.

They are now retired, living in Bristol, near some of their four children. Even in retirement John worked as a part-time prison chaplain as well as helping in the parish. He is highly critical of the prison system, which wastes the golden opportunity of educating the prisoners, and giving them real fundamental training to help them sort out their own problems. Phillada has only just retired from a senior post guiding social workers, and also is involved with the World Development Movement. What a couple!

The Vicar of Darnall, our neighbouring parish, was another truly remarkable man, Alan Eccleston. He came from a poor background, was a double first in English and Theology, shy in manner, but delighting in the absurdities of life, and strong and confident in his beliefs and public speaking. His horror at Capitalism and its crushing injustice led him to be the Secretary of the local Communist Party, outstripping in his socialism many of those fine Anglo-Catholic priests working in slum parishes. He had married Delia, sister of Furse's mother and daughter of a Bishop, she spoke in an upper class voice, but was totally committed to Alan's vision of Christian Communism. She was good friends with Grace Howell-Thomas, both grey haired, no make up, heavy smokers, tough, warm hearted and caring. Delia burnt with anger at the false assumptions of her childhood and at the pompous uncaring Church which totally failed to recognise Alan's gifts until near the end of his life. In fact, Alan was one of the most outstanding post war priests of the Church of England, highly intelligent, deeply prayerful, widely read, and totally committed to the people of his grim parish.

Alan was steeped in a highly disciplined spiritual way of life and was also far ahead of his time in his radical theology. There was only one Church meeting in the week, the

Parish Meeting, so that Church members could serve in local affairs and politics, instead of endless Church business. About a dozen or twenty people came, week by week, most with little formal education, but highly perceptive and confident in their views. One Franciscan monk came to talk to them and was wary of their theology of Christ, "it sounds as if you are making him merely human". They jumped on him, "What more do you want, than for him to be truly human?!" Poor man, he had some thinking to do.

Alan and Delia were very kind to me, and I often went to their house and heard him speak. He warned me not to be "too pious"; he thought I was not tough, realistic enough, and not involved in the real world of political life. After his retirement Alan's gifts were, at last, recognised by the Church, and he was often asked to speak at Theological Colleges. With a twinkle in my eye, I asked him what he told them? With infectious delight he said, "I told them to read the whole of Shakespeare every year!" He and Delia retired to a tiny cottage in Cumbria. Delia spent the last years of her life in hospital and Alan went to see her every day, travelling on three buses. I believe that when he celebrated a short, simple Eucharist at her bedside, the whole ward was transfigured.

Amongst other things I started a small discussion group in the Staniforth Arms, in my part of the parish. We were usually about half a dozen men, and over pints, or in my case, half-pints, of beer, we would discuss matters of moral, political or religious interest. One regular attender had ginger hair, a little moustache and was faintly spivish. He was a painter and decorator, and regaled us with regular stories of the countless luscious women, dressed only in a negligee, who waited for him to appear in their houses; or, if they were not ready for him on his first visit, they would be on his second – according to him! I will never know if there was any truth in those lascivious accounts; I guess there was; but probably exaggerated. All a new world to me. He was a regular attender, and seemed very grateful for my friendship. When I left he came to the station to see me off, weeping openly.

Most of my time was spent in people's houses, meeting the families of our youth club members, engaged couples and young parents before and after a baptism; and, of course the visits before and after a funeral. Also Kit gave me a long list of lonely elderly people to see; after I had left he kindly told me that it was only then that he realised how many people I had seen, and how much my visits had meant to them.

I also went into the old people's clubs; I think they enjoyed their merry flirting with the young curate, with cackles of Yorkshire glee. Not many people came to the services in our four churches; in fact, once I went to Carbrook Church, built in Victorian times to hold a thousand, and nobody turned up; and it wasn't because I was in the wrong church; so I went and met people in the pub. Wonderful training – after all, church attendance couldn't get worse than that, could it?! No, our calling was to pray and be with the people in times of hilarity, in times of grinding misery, and mostly in times of comradely friendship and family life.

Most of the poorest families spoke in the Yorkshire dialect amongst themselves. Sometimes one of the kids would welcome me to his home,

"Hey, Mum, Yughie's 'ere".

"What's tha doing 'ere, Yughie? Can I get thee sum tea?"

His mother would tick him off,

"Thou can't say 'tha and thee' to t'curate".

To her, it was too familiar, and showed a lack of respect for one of the clergy.

John Ware told me of other phrases he had picked up. A widow said to him,

"We buried our Jack last year, and I do miss me bit of cumfort."

John was a married man, you see, and would understand. On another occasion, a woman told him how she had fallen in their back yard, and twisted her ankle. Through the kitchen window she could see her husband sitting contentedly in his chair, smoking his pipe; she desperately shouted for him to come and help her, but her cries were drowned by the sound of the television. She thought,

"It's funny 'ow yer can luv an' 'ate at t'same time!"

Very, very true, and it is a help for some people to know that it is quite normal to have conflicting emotions at the same moment.

The normal greeting from any woman was,

"Allo, luv" – warm and friendly.

The men and boys would say,

"All reeght, Yughie?" and in answer I would give them a thumb's up.

The Grayson family were always in difficulty of some sort; I think there were four boys and two girls living in the usual very small house; the boys were little monkeys, but I was fond of the family; the father was out of work and very pale and poorly; the mother struggled on nobly. Finally, Mr Grayson died, and they kept the open coffin in the front room, as often still happened. Their grief was awful, and their fears for the future great. The whole wider family was close in Attercliffe, and even distant cousins would be referred to as 'our Tommy', or 'our Liz'. I saw Reg Arundel quite often, and also a friend of his, John Robinson, a good-hearted, plump, bearded young man who would join us walking on the magnificent hills and moors of the Peak District. One day I took all the children I knew out into the wild moorland of "Wuthering Heights". I think there were about a hundred kids, and only two mums and two teenagers to help. We went by train and then walked. When I saw them rolling boulders down the hill at each other, I felt like Moses and the disobedient children of Israel. For many of them it was their first trip into the country; they had a great time, and I got them all home safely – I think. Health and Safety!?

Shortly after I had left Attercliffe, Ann Sapcote married Reg, and they had a son, Thomas, but, sadly, they split up some years later. Ann became an academic, and amongst other things, wrote a very nostalgic book about Carbrook and Attercliffe in the past, carefully researched, lamenting their destruction. As a girl she was a secretary in the steel works where her father and brothers were employed, and I vividly remember her indignation as she told me bitterly how she resented the days when she typed out the envelopes to the firm's shareholders, colonels, titled people and clergy living in the South of England. They lived well on the profits created by the men of her own family amongst the sweat and danger of the blasting heat of the forges. Listening to this burning sense of personal injustice from a girl I respected had a far deeper and more lasting effect than any amount of political theory. Naturally I voted Labour for years. We heard of a conscientious employer who set up a well-equipped medical centre for his men who were often wounded by the machines in his factory; but what was really needed was expensive new machines. We were told that the Church is not only a hospital for the wounded, but also God's servant for basic change in men's hearts and the structures of society – his kingdom on earth, for which we pray.

Most of the teenage members of our Sunday Club were very keen on folk music and the songs of Bob Dylan and Pete Seeger; and I sang along with them; they gave purpose and dignity to the grim struggles of working class life. I particularly remember one of the songs of a play we saw in Sheffield, "There are few that know such hardships as we poor grinders do"; it was based on one of the bitter attempts of the grinders to strike, in the middle of the nineteenth century.

I often think that without the slow growth towards universal suffrage combined with the hard won right to strike, started by the Tolpuddle Martyrs near us here in deepest Dorset, we would still have the utterly appalling working and living conditions of the great mass of the poor, as in the days of my grandfather's birth.

I watched Churchill's funeral on the television, the enormously uplifting service in St. Paul's, the silent crowds thronging the streets and the cranes dipping in salute as Churchill's coffin was carried in a barge up the Thames, unrehearsed and unknown to the authorities. Mind you, I had heard some working people say that it was not Churchill who had won the war, but the soldiers who had fought and died. Even so, he was a great, great leader who knew the hearts and minds of the British people. As I walked the cobbled streets of Attercliffe that evening I felt uplifted and inspired by this man, and very close to the people who lived their hard lives in this Northern industrial smoke. A great man, in his death as well as in his life, makes us all one.

It was while driving my sister Alison from the station at the start of a short visit that I heard that John Kennedy had been shot.

One day in Carbrook Church House the telephone rang. It was the Vicar, very angry, "The funeral family is waiting for you in the Church. What on earth do you think you are doing? Get down there at once!"

It was unforgivable, of course, to forget a funeral, but his anger was very demoralising; Whenever the telephone went, my hand shook slightly in alarm at the thought of some impatient criticism to come.

Poor man, he found me difficult – even when he tried to smile at me I felt that it was forced! I only saw the really gentle side of him when he was nursing his dog after an operation; he was probably just as kind with sick or sad parishioners, but we were never there to see it. When John had married Phillada I was his best man, and wore the kilt. The good John was perfectly happy, but Kit made it very clear that he disapproved, as it was drawing attention to myself. He was probably right, but I resented his schoolmasterly manner. However, he did take the wedding service in that natural human way that I had admired at first.

John and Phillada had a baby girl, Ruth, and they asked me to be her godfather. At the christening, in one of our churches, I wore my Corpus tie instead of my hated dog collar, as I was there as godfather and not as curate. The

131

next morning Kit told me off and demanded to know whether I thought I was a priest or not. I exploded. I swore at him and stormed off, feeling he didn't begin to understand or appreciate me. I think I was a little deflated when later on I heard that he had gone to Grace saying, "Thank goodness, Hugh has lost his temper at last!" In my mind that rather took from the drama of my great moment! A few weeks later he criticised me for some minor mistake and I shouted, "What the bloody hell does it matter?!" Before long we both agreed that it was time for me to leave.

So what were John and I doing in Attercliffe? What was the Church for? These were questions we often asked ourselves. I hope we helped a number of people individually; we probably helped a few reach their potential, but we were not able to increase the tiny congregation or have grand schemes for improving the whole community instead of just aiding a few to escape from it. I returned to our original vision of living amongst the people, offering the Eucharist on their behalf, and being available.

Chapter XIII

MAIDSTONE - what a change! - a thriving parish -
love, at last

John Ware and I were approached by a Vicar in Warrington
to join his team. Based on the Parish Church, we were to
visit in local industry and take the apprentices to the Lake
District, keeping in touch with them afterwards through the
local church; it avoided the usual split between the local
parish church and industrial mission, the first being
primarily concerned with individuals and the second with
people and structures. It was a good way of working, I
visited Warrington, met and admired the Vicar, and agreed
to go; John and Phillada went to a church on the edge of
Sheffield.

In the summer I had my usual week on Iona and then
went to join my parents who had taken a lovely old house
on the shore of Cromarty, an enchanting eighteenth
century town of fine houses and fishermen's cottages, by
the sea; and we had a happy family holiday. Clunes had
been the factor's house for the Ross estate and was near

perfect, unchanged over the centuries, long, low, natural, comfortable, every inch had character, with that loveable air of faded gentility which always makes me feel at home! There was an old fashioned kitchen, with a stone floor, old wooden cupboards, well scrubbed deal kitchen table and an Aga. The china, glass and the pictures were all of old quality; the upstairs drawing room, with its open fire and gold framed pictures, overlooked the sea. My parents had taken it for five years, and we had many happy times there; Cromarty is on the Black Isle, just north of Inverness; the North East was new territory to me. Through Robert Tollemache I had met a Magdalene friend of his, with the lovely Highland title of John Shaw of Tordarroch the Younger: he wasn't at all grand and pompous in manner, but rather fey and arty. His family home was Newhall on the Black Isle, but when I asked him if he had many relations nearby, he sadly said, "No, most of them were scattered after the '45"; there were relics of Bonnie Prince Charlie in the house when I called there. I am not the only one who lives in the past.

At the end of the holiday I drove south, passing Warrington on the way. I was daunted at the thought of moving to a new grim town, knowing nobody, and having to share a house with strangers. It was not like going to Attercliffe which had been on my heart for three years, and where I would be joining John. I feared I would be lonely and wrote to the Warrington Vicar saying I had changed my mind. Strange.

I had told Peter Walker, Principal of Westcott House, that I was looking for a second curacy, (the normal pattern in those days) and he put me in touch with Niel Nye, the Vicar of Maidstone, and one of the finest parish priests in England. In the war he had been a chaplain with the RAF in the desert; his jeep was blown up, his driver killed and he was reported missing, believed killed. A memorial service for him was held in St. Martin-in-the-Fields. Many months later, Budge, his young wife, was working as a nurse on the ward of the hospital. She was told that somebody wanted to speak to her on the telephone. Breaking all rules, she ran down the ward and spoke to Niel. She just knew it was him. He had been blown out of the jeep, crawled away, but was captured and sent to a prisoner of war camp for officers in Italy. With the help of others, he led a massive break out, and made his way over the mountains and back to England.

When I arrived at Maidstone Vicarage there was a lovely blonde lying on the lawn, the Vicar's daughter – so I took the job! Her father was, indeed, a fine man, with a distinguished ascetic face, committed to his God, the Church and people. He offered me the post, and I gladly accepted. His daughter, Mary, had been convalescing after a time in hospital for kidney trouble, and decided to go back to London the next day; and so, of course, I suggested that we go on the train together and that we go to lunch at Lloyd Square. She agreed, and we talked all the way; she was very gentle in manner and told me of an anti-war demonstration she had joined, and also of her Uncle Mark, Dean of Pretoria Cathedral in South Africa. He had been imprisoned for giving support and accommodation to the relations of those who were in court for the infamous Treason Trials of Nelson Mandela and others. We went to Lloyd Square, where Minnie Simpson, from Jamaica, was another guest. Mother gave us kidneys for lunch; Mary and her family were vegetarians, and she was recently out of hospital for kidney treatment, so she really struggled, but managed to get them down! keen to make a good impression, which she certainly did. Very content, I returned to Sheffield and prepared to move a few weeks later.

Shortly after this I had a letter from Niel saying that the Archbishop of Canterbury was worried about Niel's health and wanted him to leave the demanding post of Vicar of Maidstone and Rural Dean, and become the Diocesan Tait Missioner, a free, roving post to help the clergy and start new initiations; a much lighter work load. Niel was disappointed, but wisely obeyed. In his letter he told me that I was free to break our agreement and not come as his curate, as he was leaving soon, in a few months. You can imagine my reply. I gladly said that I would still come, not adding my main reason, which was that if I went somewhere else I might never see Mary again.

I said my goodbyes in Attercliffe, to the four congregations, the lovely elderly people, the Autumn Leaves clubs, and the boys who often came round to our house and had become part of our life; also to the Duchess, Wilf and Hague, of course. I drove down to Maidstone in my little Triumph, laden with cases and boxes – my furniture came later, on the back of a lorry.

For a few days I stayed at the Vicarage; they were a lovely family, and I felt at home with them; they were gentlefolk, as my old relations would have said, but with that attitude to life which came from their working together, helping people in all kinds of trouble. Mary was at home again after another bout of kidney trouble.

As Mary was at home, with nothing else to do, she helped me decorate my house and we spent much of our time together, in a very easy, unselfconscious way; and, remember, I only had a few weeks to win her! After five days I declared my love. We both needed to adjust. I had grown up in the fifties, and she was a teenager in the sixties; a lot had happened in those ten years; and she had to cope with my wanting to be both a country gentleman and a slum priest. She wore a mini-skirt, but felt that I wanted her to wear a twin-set and pearls!

Christopher was her much younger brother; she had helped bring him up as a little boy; he was thirteen at this time, cheerful, friendly and uncomplicated. He has remained one of the closest of my genuine friends to this day. He still remembers my seeing his family off on the train for his brother Mike's first wedding. He turned to his mother with impish younger brother glee, "Mummy, look, Hugh is kissing Mary!"

After a few months she agreed to marry me.

All Saints, Maidstone, was the church of the town; it is a magnificent medieval building, on the bank of the Medway. Niel was an efficient and inspired leader, worship was of a high standard, with a good robed choir, and there was real lay leadership and involvement; it was my first experience of a thriving parish. It all meant a major adjustment for me; for six years all my theological and spiritual formation had been grounded on the centrality of the Christ, both eternal and very human, and his involvement in the life of the "wretched of the earth", through the circumstances of his birth in a stable, his life as a homeless and much reviled prophet and his ghastly death. For me, to follow him meant being with the working people of Attercliffe. My family, my social life and my holidays had been in a different compartment.

Now I was in a pleasant county town, surrounded by the beauties of the Kent countryside. In Sheffield, the crematorium had been set in a bleak, grey, grim cemetery, overlooking the factories and the city. Now, I was taking funerals in a pleasant modern building, set in lovely gardens surrounded by cornfields – a different world. Friends and members of the congregation included well educated leaders of the community, headmasters, lawyers and the like, and Niel was Chaplain to the Mayor. I was now with the people who made decisions affecting everybody else, instead of being with those on the receiving end. Also, we were not far from High Beeches. Before, I had been leading a split life, now all my thinking, praying and visiting had to be integrated with my officer class way of looking at things. There were council estates in the parish, and it was a true test of my sincerity to see how much of my time I spent there. In Attercliffe, a one class industrial parish, there was less real temptation to drift towards the well off and the intellectual.

There were also, of course, major adjustments in my own life. For the first time ever I had to look after myself – shopping, cooking, cleaning, washing; it seemed to take up a lot of time. Mary was vegetarian, and each time she came down from London I gave her potatoes, fried egg and sprouts. I couldn't think of anything else.

Shortly after our engagement was announced I had a letter from the Archbishop of Canterbury, no less. He wasn't begging me to be his Chaplain or take up some key post in the Church of England; instead, he told me that I must leave Maidstone, not because of any terrible misdemeanor I might have committed in just a few weeks there, but because it would not be fair for a new Vicar to inherit a curate married to the old Vicar's daughter! Fair enough, so I went to see the great saintly, scholarly, shy Michael Ramsey in the ancient palace at Canterbury. He greeted me at the front door, benign smile beneath his enormous bushy white eyebrows, both hands raised in warm welcome, and led me to his cosy book lined study where he suggested that I go and see Victor Kingston, the new Vicar of Folkestone Parish Church, as he was looking for a curate. After this we sat together in the deep comfortable chairs, but it seemed that the Archbishop was at a loss for words, and did not seem to know what to say. I gather this was normal! So I rose to go, he blessed me and bade me an affectionate farewell.

As Mary's father was a Canon of Canterbury, we could be married in the Cathedral. To establish a residential qualification, Mary lived for the statutory fifteen days with one of the married Canons living in the Close. I don't think there was too much gossip about this beautiful blonde creeping into his house late in the evening, and slipping out in the morning. We decided to be married in the Crypt, or the basement, as we enjoyed calling it, a wonderful endless space of heavy Norman arches. We were married by Mary's godfather, Bishop Stanley Betts. The reception was in the nearby Roman Catholic St. Thomas' parish hall; my father provided the champagne. We drove off, far too fast, in my open Triumph, had dinner at the top of the Post Office Tower, and then joined the night train for Scotland.

I had read of the overlapping realms of sex and religion! Yes, loving sex and religion are really two aspects of the same experience. I am told that the Hebrew language, like Elizabethan English, has the same word in both sentences, "He knew his wife; she conceived and bore him a son," and, "Thou shalt know the Lord thy God, and obey Him." The Hebrew religion is earthy, basic and wholesome – a man and woman are experiencing the love of God when they make love and create a child. They are God to each other.

In the Prayer Book, when the groom gives the bride her ring, he says, "With my body I thee worship"; and a man can pay no greater honour to a woman than wanting her to be the mother of his child, and a woman can pay no greater honour to a man than wanting him to be the father of her child. It is all a very wonderful, great and loving mystery.

The Song of Solomon in the Hebrew scriptures of the Bible is the most beautiful love poem about the enchanting bodily love between a man and a woman; it is typical of false religion when it is described as an allegory, talking about Christ's love for His church – typical of the irritating false spiritualisation of the body, typical of the Greek influence affecting the early church, separating body and soul – very harmful.

Religion is not about heaven after death; it is about heaven on earth. For some it can be <u>on </u>the earth as well as in bed!

I was tickled by the fact that among our presents were two prints, one from the Archbishop and one from the M.P., one of the cathedral and one of All Saints, Maidstone; all very different from Attercliffe! It was good to see a party of friends from Sheffield at the wedding, members of the congregation and the Sunday Club; and Richard Hanmer was my best man.

On our return from Scotland we went to our flat in Folkestone.

Chapter XIV

FOLKESTONE - a great Vicar - a youth Passion Play - tragedy - motorbikes - Jamie

Victor Kingston was the Vicar of the fine medieval parish church of Folkestone, dedicated to St. Mary and St. Eanswythe; it is set on the cliff top, overlooking the Channel. He had Irish blood and had boxed when he was in the Army. He was a big man in every way, with a large frame, a large heart, a big belly and a big family, six children. He used to say that whenever he slipped off his braces another child would soon pop out. His wife, Sheila, was a gem; her kitchen was full of washing up piled high; there was always food, drink and a warm hearted welcome for anybody coming to her door – a wonderful woman; slight in stature and strong in character, she was comfortably at home as wife and mother, and content to appear to play second fiddle to her husband. Victor had been Chaplain to the 3rd Carabiniers and Chaplain to the Guards Division, Assistant Chaplain-General, with the rank of Colonel, and Chaplain to the Queen. After leaving the Army he was the Dean of Bulawayo Cathedral, in Rhodesia, as it then was; he was treated with great respect by the whole community there, was addressed as Mr. Dean, and knew and highly respected Sir Humphrey Gibbs, the Governor, who had a very difficult job to do.

Victor had an endearing habit of calling almost every man, "old boy", and almost every woman, "love". He had only arrived in Folkestone a short time before me, and after his time in the Army and Bulawayo, he did feel many of the congregation were locked in a formal, lonely correctness, so he would put his arm around the old ladies, saying, "Hullo, love, how are you?" They were startled, but soon came to miss this warm greeting, if he were too preoccupied to give it. In my imagination I can see him greeting the Queen formally, "Good morning, your Majesty," and then forgetting himself and putting his arm round her, and saying, "Hullo, love, how are you?" It would have been a foretaste of Barak Obama. Although Victor could look quite smart, in a dark suit or red cassock, his normal black cassock was shabby with age, and covered in soup stains, with his belt sagging beneath his belly. After all the difficulties of Sheffield, and the upheaval of Maidstone, I felt reassured by Victor's approval of me and his encouragement.

After celebrating the Holy Communion, the priest, in his vestments, walks solemnly to the clergy vestry, reverently holding the silver chalice and patten in his hands, suitably covered in a glorious cloth. Victor would wander from altar to vestry, humming a tune from the latest London musical. Somehow this delighted me, and seemed to be symbolic of his love for his Lord, his love of life, lived to the full, and his love for people, with no distinction or difference between them, all flowing from the one source. His family remember how he loved to talk about "my wonderful sermon on modesty"! One day I was in our flat and the telephone rang; it was Victor, "Hullo, old boy, how are you?"

"Well, thanks; and you?"

"Fine, old boy. By the way, there are some funeral cars at the church and I'm not taking the service. Is it yours, by any chance, old boy?"

"Gosh, yes! Sorry! I'll be straight there."

"Good; - all right, I'll tell them you're delayed, but are coming".

All said in his usual relaxed voice, taking my failure in his stride – worse things happen in love and war; a big man, and what a leader! I would have followed him anywhere. He was also disciplined with his correspondence and his care for people; he set me the example which I have always followed, of taking a white pot plant to every family at their first Christmas after a bereavement. He pointed the contrast between two parishioners; one a prissy old member of the Church who quoted the Bible at him. One of his merry teenage sons was in trouble in the town; she wrote Victor a letter, referring to St. Paul's letter to Titus, which said that an elder in the Church "must have one wife, his children believers and not open to the charge of being profligate or insubordination". When he told me about it, Victor was spitting with anger; he had Irish blood, and could be quick tempered; usually about people, rather than with them, face to face. In contrast, he gave encouragement to Barbara, a new member of the congregation, a warm hearted, relaxed former nurse who discovered that one of the rather grand old ladies in the congregation was ill and on her own. Barbara went round to give her a bath, leading the old lady to say, "I didn't know that that is what Church is all about".

My main responsibility was as priest-in-charge of St. Augustine's, the daughter church near the harbour. I enjoyed taking the services, bur rather clashed over one or two small issues with the elderly couple who really ran the church – rather unwise of me. I was also responsible for the youth work from both churches; they met in the cellar of the Vicarage. I then asked them all to our flat; they began to take it for granted, so we moved to a small room in the Church Hall. Once they became too rowdy; I lost my patience and turned them all out. I was glad that I could be brisk and impose discipline when necessary; previously I had been inhibited by a desire to appear to be always patient and loving! I did not want them to see me as one of the kill-joy Vicars. We did a short sketch for an informal service in the parish church, which included somebody being shot, in front of the High Altar. I am sure that it made some important spiritual point, but what, I can't remember. It did not go down well with the elderly members of the congregation.

During those years there were often press reports of battles on the beaches, between the Mods and the Rockers. The Mods wore parkas, rode motor scooters and were of the student type; the Rockers wore black leather jackets, rode powerful motor bikes and feigned a violent approach to life, copying the American Hell's Angels. There was a well known vicar, Bill Shergold, who rode a bike himself, got to know the Rockers on their own ground, and founded the 59 Club, to befriend and help them, and also to channel their love for speed in a creative way, such as delivering rare blood to a distant hospital. With this example in front of us, Mary and I hung around in the Sunshine Café, where the

Rockers met. We got to know some of them, including John, a tall, bearded man, a little older than the others, perhaps a bit more responsible than the rest, and possibly their natural leader. They seemed surprised and gratified that we took some notice of them, that we did not judge them because of their threatening appearance. Victor was somewhat wary, but gave permission for me to start a club for them, in the basement of St. Augustine's Church; we called it The Dungeon. For some months it went well and the bikers and their girl friends seemed to settle down. One day there was an alarmed telephone call to the Vicar from an old lady living near the Parish Church; she was worried because she had seen a "band of ruffians invading the Church," and she feared that they were there to wreck the place. They were our Club members coming to a funeral. I was rather proud to have them there, in their uniform; many of them had never been in a church before. Unfortunately, some of our church teenagers started to go to the Dungeon, drugs were passed and their parents were getting very worried. Sadly, I agreed that it was time to end the experiment. We tried to keep in touch with the bikers, as friends, but it was never quite the same – mutual trust had been broken on both sides.

Some of our Church teenagers were fine young people, singing in the choir, serving at the altar, planning to go to University to lead worthwhile lives. Four of them were in a car, driving back from a church gathering in Canterbury; there was a crash and two of them were killed. It was devastating; I had never been involved like this before. The whole town was shaken. Victor and I went to see the mother of Roger Morgan, one of the two killed, a member of our choir and our youth group, which included Victor and Sheila's two youngest daughters, Tina and Alison. As soon as Victor saw the heartbroken mother he took her in his arms and held her. Never before had I seen such warm, human, unclerical behaviour, and was profoundly impressed and inspired. As the years went by, I tried to help people in something of the same way. The Parish Church was packed for their funeral with the coffins of the two young men, lying side by side in the chancel, where they had sung and served.

Before we came to Folkestone, Mary and I were given the chance to choose a flat for ourselves, and the Church would pay the rent; we chose one near the Esplanade. Whenever I walked to the Parish Church or the Vicarage, I looked out to sea. How different from Attercliffe, and much appreciated. Even from the start it was not easy for Mary; it was a different life from London. She was not really keen to be a curate's wife. Sometimes I would be walking in my cassock with Mary beside me in her jeans, and it did feel very odd. You know the old jibes, "there are three sexes, men, women and priests", and also, "in that marriage, she wears the trousers". Yes, it felt very odd to both of us, and we avoided it whenever possible.

A few months after we were married I was thrilled when Mary told me that she was going to have our baby. I do not use the phrase, "fell pregnant", which was still in common use, and almost implied that it was a disgrace. In fact, when I shared our good news with the wife of one of our Churchwardens, she said, "Oh dear…. But I suppose it can't be helped!". Victor and Sheila were much more encouraging; and of course, the four prospective grandparents were delighted. Niel and Budge were living in Canterbury, and we saw them quite often, as well as occasionally going over to High Beeches.

A joyful and memorable day was when I took the wedding in Coleman's Hatch of my beloved sister Alison and the good and kind Foley Goepel – they were so happy together. The reception was at High Beeches, where a piper, Bruce Taylor, led us through the wood to the swimming pool where we drank champagne as we floated in the warm green water.

Because of her kidney trouble, Mary put on a lot of weight in pregnancy, which, naturally, she found very difficult. Finally she went into Canterbury Hospital, where she had an appalling time – three days in painful labour. I was with her as much as possible, reading to her, but I did whiz back to attend a P.C.C. meeting; I would never have done that today. Finally, and only after much persuasion, they operated, and a baby boy was born by lower-section Caesarian. Mary stayed in hospital for some days, in no fit state to feed him or care for him; so when they came home I looked after him for much of the time. After a few weeks we took him to High Beeches, and during most of one night, I could not stop him crying; I tried everything – feeding, winding, changing his nappy but with no success. I think all he needed was a long, long cuddle. He was a beautiful baby – naturally! – and Mary and I were very proud of him. He was christened James McLaren at a private service in St. Mary and St. Eansewythe's, with both families present; Roger Musker and Chris Nye were his godfathers and my sister Alison was his godmother and I wore the kilt. In the summer we took him on his first visit to Scotland. We drove to Dover in our little green mini van, which we put on the overnight train to Perth. We called on the Queen at Balmoral, but sadly she can't have got our message saying we were coming, and was out, probably stalking. We then went on for a very happy holiday at Cromarty, and have a photo of Jamie being bathed in the old kitchen sink.

Although there were some difficult and depressing times in Folkestone, most of my memories are of happy sunny days by the sea and the lovely unspoilt Kent countryside. My work brought me in contact with a wide variety of people, the posh and professional, worthy citizens, musicians and resting actors, the fishermen and the motor cyclists.

I produced our own home made modern Passion Play, which we performed in the Church. It was in the early days of such youth drama, following the example of Ernest Marvin in Bristol. Jesus, his enemies and his followers, were all in jeans and sweaters, and the music was folk songs accompanied by a guitar.

Some weeks after the Passion Play our telephone rang; it was the Bishop of Dover – he could be a touchy prelate, and he could also be very astute and encouraging. He told me that Austen Williams was looking for a curate at St. Martin-in-the-Fields and would I contact him? I was tremendously excited at the thought, and Mary and I went to see him in the Vicarage overlooking Trafalgar Square. He talked at length about St. Martin's, and without asking anything about us, he offered me the post. So ended a happy two years working with Victor and Sheila; he had done me a power of good, and I shall always be grateful to him.

Chapter XV

ST. MARTIN-IN-THE-FIELDS - The Crypt -
homeless - great occasions - Alive! - Anna

I still can't believe how lucky I was, to have been offered the job of Senior Curate at St. Martin's; there was no other position in the Church of England which I would have preferred. The church itself was built on the corner of Trafalgar Square, in 1725, before the homes of the poor were cleared from the area to make a grand memorial to England's naval hero, Admiral Lord Nelson. From the steps of the church you can see his monument soaring into the sky; the National Gallery is on one side of the Square, South Africa House to the left, then Canada House opposite, Charles I looks down Whitehall, the Admiralty, Horse Guards, the Cenotaph, the Ministry of Defence, the Scottish Office, the Foreign Office, the Treasury, Westminster Abbey and the Houses of Parliament, while Admiralty Arch leads down the Mall past St. James Palace, St. James Park, Clarence House to Buckingham Palace. To the north of the church were Soho, the theatres, and the Peabody Buildings, Victorian charity flats. It is called St.

Martin-in-the-Fields because the first place of worship was a chapel-of-ease of Westminster Abbey, for the nuns of the Abbey to say their midday office when working in the convent garden – the market garden of later years. Today, St. Martin's is at the very heart of London. When I was at Westcott I had been to a service at St. Martin's and remember the Vicar, Austen Williams, using the phrase, "Let us each pray for any one person who is on our hearts" – wonderfully personal in the midst of the anonymity of London.

St. Martin's had been transformed by Dick Sheppard, its Vicar during the First World War. He had been serving as an Army chaplain and came to London to see for himself the Church which he was being offered. Having done all the official business during the day, he spent the evening and much of the night exploring the parish. He wandered amongst the evening diners, the theatre goers and actors, and when they had all gone home, he sat with the homeless trying to keep warm under the railway arches. He realised that he was being offered the care of the most extraordinary square mile imaginable. He accepted the offer.

There were only eleven people at his institution service; he told them of a kind of vision he had been given when he had returned to the trenches. He saw himself standing on the steps of this great church, in the great square of the greatest city in the world, and hosts of the ordinary people of London were streaming past him into the church. He stopped one of them and asked him, "Where are you going?" He replied, "I am going to the place of my Christ, which is warm and light, and where nobody will push me behind a pillar because I am poor". Within a few months Dick Sheppard made this vision come true. He was very aware of the plight of the soldiers coming home from the front, arriving late at night, at Charing Cross Station, and having nowhere to stay. He let them sleep in the church. Some of the grand people objected to finding mud and blood on the seats of their reserved pews, for which they had paid. Some of them left, but their places were taken by hundreds of other people who came to listen to Dick, and to help him in his work. He ended the tradition of having numbered, reserved pews; he opened them to everybody, so that you no longer had to pay to sit in the body of the church. He cleared the six burial vaults under the church, removing and reburying the dead and using the vaults to provide the soldiers and the homeless with somewhere to sleep. He shared the outlook of Studdert Kennedy, who joined the staff at St. Martin's for some months after the war. They both believed in a human and very compassionate Christ; both were so firmly grounded in the worship of the Church of England that they could be confident and free to reach out to everybody in new ways. Dick was known as the People's Parson. There are many stories told about him in his biography, "H.R.L.Sheppard, Life and Letters", by R. Ellis Roberts, published by John Murray in 1942. It also tells of many times of self-doubt, depression and struggle with crippling asthma. One night he came home to the Vicarage, wearing white tie and tails, as he had been to some function at Court. He found a girl sitting on his steps, crying. He sat beside her, and discovered that she came from a poor part of Edinburgh, had had a row with her strict parents and had come down to London, knowing no one, having no money and nowhere to go. He hailed a cab and they set off at a rattling pace to catch the late night train to Edinburgh – an incongruous looking pair. They arrived at Waverley Station early in the morning, took another cab to a poor house in Leith, and leaving the girl in the cab, surprised her parents by knocking on the door, still dressed in white tie. He explained the situation, persuaded them to welcome her home, fetched her from the cab, returned to Waverley and was back in London for lunch and an afternoon meeting.

The BBC were wanting to broadcast live church services and offered the opportunity, first to Westminster Abbey, and then to St. Paul's, but both were shocked at the idea, "Why," they said, "a man might be listening to divine worship on the wireless, while standing in a public house, with his hat on." Dick Sheppard leapt at this chance of speaking to people in their own homes, talking directly to people who never came to church. He spoke regularly on the Home Service, living up to his name of the People's Parson. St. Martin's was known as the Church of the Unbaptized.

We left Folkestone with some sorrow, and were touched by the sadness of many friends, old and young, who came to our farewell service; but we were very excited to be moving to Trafalgar Square! We were given a modern, three-bedroomed flat, tucked away behind the Vicarage and Parish Office. The windows looked out onto the offices barely twenty yards away, and to leave the flat we had to walk down an outside metal staircase, but once through the great door by the Vestry Hall we were right next to the church, and near the Square. What a position! And what privilege! We even had a parking space for our car under the building, as the Vicar did not drive. This was my fourth curacy, which was very unusual, but I was only thirty two; and I was paid a Vicar's salary. Shortly after our arrival in the summer, the Vicar, Austen Williams, went for his holiday to the Summer Isles, off the west coast of Scotland – he loved the peace and the birds. The other curate was Ted Stopps, a former teacher, recently ordained, married, with three daughters. He was seriously ill, and died within a few weeks of our arrival. I went to be with the stricken family in their flat in Stockwell. As well as their terrible grief, I remember going and returning by taxi – a different experience from Attercliffe. Austen came from the Western Isles, took the funeral, and immediately returned to finish his holiday. Officially, the Church Wardens were in charge while he was away, but I was the only priest, and had to respond to all the immediate crises and demands. I had to learn very quickly! One Sunday I took all the seven services, including a Folk Service in the afternoon, and ending with another quiet Communion at 7.30 in the evening. I looked in at all the different activities, the Brownies and Guides, the P.M. Boys Club, where young waiters played football in the courtyard, still in their chef's overalls, the Alcoholics Anonymous, Thursday Night at Eight for student types, the International Club, the old people's clubs, the choir practice, the lunchtime discussion group, the canteen, the Soup Kitchen and anything else that might be going on. It was an unusual experience, and most helpful, as few curates had such involvement right across the board.

It was humbling, working at St. Martin's, being carried by the long tradition of caring. Austen was good to work for – he gave me great freedom, maximum opportunity and minimum responsibility. He shared responsibility with the Wardens and the Committees, where he would often sit at the back, doing the crossword. Austen was a fine-looking man, immaculately dressed, usually in collar and tie, with a lovely voice; he was an arresting speaker, an experienced broadcaster with a good command of the English language and a special wit; he often used delightful understatements to describe and defuse crises. He was widely loved, admired and followed. He regularly gave time to troubled individuals. He said that if there were two doors, one for people who were succeeding and one for people who were failing, he hoped that he would go with Christ through the door for the misfits. He was a Chaplain to the Queen, and I saw him one Christmas time, standing in the portico wearing his scarlet cassock; a rough looking old man stood beside him, with his filthy hand on Austen's arm, saying,

"Why are yer all dressed up like Farvver Christmas?".

"Because I am one of the Queen's Chaplains".

"Corr, you've spoken to 'er, 'ave you?".

He went away, at least a foot taller – he had touched a man who had touched the Queen. In his own person Austen had incarnated all that St. Martin's stood for, bringing dignity to the wretched of the earth.

St. Martin's was world famous for its work among the homeless: the Council would no longer allow people to sleep in the Crypt, as it had no facilities up to modern legal requirements, but hundreds of men came to the soup kitchen every Sunday. The Social Service Unit would try to find them proper accommodation elsewhere. The S.S.U. worked in the basement of the Vicarage, with ten full time workers, often untrained, but very experienced, helped by a hundred volunteers. It was led by Norman Ingram-Smith, urbane, beautifully dressed, a bald head gleaming above his horn-rimmed spectacles and his warm smile. He avoided labels, saying, "Bill has just spent some time in prison, Andy is having trouble at the moment with drugs, Ernie rather prefers other men to women, or George thinks he is Georgina;" kindly, understanding descriptions of friends of his, avoiding phrases like ex-prisoner, drug addict, homosexual or transvestite. Those friends were around and with us all the time. Norman went to see a friend who had been in prison for many years, taking his Christmas card with him; in his pleasant encouraging voice, he said "I'm glad to see you've had several cards already." "No, Norman, those are the cards you've brought me over the last seven years". Norman White, a big Eastender, could write about "our Saviour, the Lord Jesus Christ" but could also be uncouth, threatening violence and ringing up our flat at all hours of day and night, incessantly repeating terrible threats and ecclesiastical manipulations; but we couldn't help being fond of him. Years later, when the Bishop of Sherborne instituted me as Vicar in Dorset, he told the congregation that he had come into the clergy office at St. Martin's only to see Norman White about to break a chair over my head! Another man, Michael, returned to St. Martin's, having been in prison for murder. He was short, but wide, and very, very strong. One day he saw me walking from our flat to the church, wearing my black cassock; he put his great arms around me and held me up for all the tourists in the buses to see, and laugh. I did not dare to struggle, in case his powerful arms crushed me. On another occasion I was carrying our baby daughter, Anna, across the courtyard, and Michael asked if he could hold her. What was I to do? Say yes, and he might crush her, say no, and in a fit of frustrated anger he might grab her and hurt her. He took her, ever so gently, cuddled her and looked at her with love in his eyes. Later I remembered that trusting God <u>means</u> trusting people, for God is in people; God is Life; if I trust life, I am trusting what I call God; if I hate life, I hate God, and if I love life I love God – I am only beginning to see this!

One of the Churchwardens was Sir Trenchard Cox, a truly distinguished, shy and humble man; he was the

Director of the Victoria and Albert Museum, and knew the names of the children of the staff, even if some of the administration rather baffled him. He was gentle in manner, and sometimes I would go to the Crypt at the end of an evening, and find him sweeping up the fag ends left by the members of Alcoholics Anonymous, clumsily wielding one of those very long brushes; he was quite short sighted. He really believed in AA and the help they gave to desperate people. He also made friends with the West Indians, Africans and Indians who came to St. Martin's. I believe that one night he and Lady Cox were at a very smart dinner party, where other guests started telling unkind racist jokes. Trenchard quietly remonstrated. They ignored him and carried on. He made a gentle signal to his wife, they stood up and quietly left, without another word; let's hope that their departure was followed by an embarrassed and repentant silence.

Another typical story of this remarkable man: St. Martin's needed a big injection of money to carry on its worship and caring work. The Vicar suggested selling the eighteenth century silver. Trenchard was horrified. The next day he agreed; God and troubled people were more important than keeping antiques where they belonged, even though this care of antiques was his passion and his life work. He lost the respect of many of his colleagues – but he won ours. Lady Cox was the writer of detective novels. She used to sit in a pew at the back of the Church; during one service a hand holding a knife was moving towards her stomach; she gently removed the knife, replaced it with a hymn book open at the right page, and carried on singing.

Christmas was an amazing experience at St. Martin's; it began at the beginning of December, with Carol Services nearly every night, for different schools and societies with

St. Martin's connections, as well as several of our own. Again and again I would climb up the many steps of the Grinling Gibbons pulpit to welcome seven hundred people in a packed church. There was a huge Christmas tree opposite the pulpit, and round it were beautifully wrapped coloured parcels brought by people from all over London and beyond, to be taken to children's homes and hospital wards throughout the city. I arranged one broadcast Carol Service using modern hymns sung by Nadia Catousse and Johnny Dankworth. At the Christmas Eve Midnight Mass the nave was full of nurses in their uniforms and coloured capes. As December wore on, the tension and distress became greater, as lonely and edgy people became more agitated than ever. One day a poorly dressed old woman asked me, in a Cockney voice,

"Where's the Vicar?"

"He's resting, before the big service".

"I gotta see 'im".

"Why?"

"I got summfink for 'im".

"Well, can you give it to me?"

She looked suspiciously at me, and fortunately, for once, I was wearing my cassock. "Well, I s'pose you'll do. Me ole Mum took this from under 'er bed, and said I waz ter give it to the Vicar, for the poor, like".

She handed me a dirty envelope, and when she had gone, I opened it – a hundred pounds in crumpled bank notes (worth about £500 now). While I was still standing, bemused, in the aisle, one of the vergers sent me a woman and child, who were desperate for food. I gave them one of the notes. Again and again St. Martin's was the meeting place of those in need and those who had been moved to give. St. Martin was, of course, the Roman soldier who ripped his cloak in half to give to a shivering beggar; in a dream that night the beggar was revealed to be Christ.

One of our Carol Services started beautifully. After a moment of candlelit silence, the scarlet robed choir of the Royal Parish Church processed up the aisle, singing plainsong; the whole congregation joined in the first triumphant carol and then sat in respectful anticipation as the first lesson was read, from the first chapter of Genesis .... "and God saw everything that He had made, and, behold, it was very good." "Rubbish!" came a loud disgruntled northern voice from the back of the Church. From his own bitter experience he couldn't let such a statement go uncontradicted. One of the sidesmen escorted him out; whenever possible, somebody would go out with such a man, would listen to him and try to help.

Emmy was one of the troubled members of the St. Martin's family; during a service she would often walk in front of the altar from one side of the Church to the other. At one Carol Service my wife was reading about the Archangel Gabriel's message to Mary, - that she would have a Son. Mary asks Gabriel

"How can this be, seeing I know not a man?"

"GET LAID!" shouted Emmy as she crossed in front of the choir.

From the beginning of December it was a joy to go into Trafalgar Square. Nearly all day it was uplifted by the joyful singing of carols, sung by the members of different charities; they stood around the Christmas tree, an annual gift from the people of Norway; I loved to stand at the far side of the Square and see the soaring spire of St. Martin's framed by the flying, glittering drops of the fountains, and the many white lights of the tree – magic. In mid-December Austen broadcast the St. Martin's Christmas Appeal, a long established tradition, started by Dick Sheppard. The money raised could be given away entirely at the Vicar's discretion – a rapid response, without bureaucracy, for a great personal need, usually backed by a local social worker. A whole team, mostly elderly ladies, opened the envelopes which came from all sorts and all places – sometimes handsome donations, and sometimes a few stamps and an apologetic letter from an O.A.P.

The Vicar also broadcast a monthly act of worship from St. Martin's for the World Service; there was a special little room off the crypt, for the sole use of the BBC and their equipment. Years earlier, the Vicar had spoken of Jesus' healing a blind man. A mother wrote to him from India, asking for help for an operation for her daughter; she had been born blind. The Vicar cabled a donation, and after a simple operation the little girl began to see for the first time. Whenever the Vicar broadcast, the family would gather round their wireless in India, and the mother would say to her daughter, "That's the man who gave you your sight." The girl grew up, married and had a child – a little girl – born blind. In despair, she wrote to the Vicar who again contributed for another operation, and all was well.

People would often come to St. Martin's from all over the world, and having heard the broadcast services all their lives, they would say, "It's like coming home." Austen loved to travel; once he visited a remote house in Nigeria, and was greeted with a joyful cry, "It's the Vicar!".

159

I usually looked in at the monthly social run by the International Committee. I enjoyed asking "Anybody here from the West Indies?" Wide smiles of gleaming white teeth in ebony faces; and many uplifted hands as I went through lots of countries in the world. "Anybody here from Nigeria?" Up went a hand. A few minutes later, "Anybody here from Biafra?" Up went the hand of his neighbour, with whom he had been chatting happily – their countries were locked in bitter war. We enjoyed shocking some white South Africans coming to Evensong by having a large black West Indian, Ben, carrying the processional cross at the head of the Choir, robed in the Queen's scarlet. The Dean of Johannesburg Cathedral, Gonville ffrench-Betagh, was in prison because of his support for black South Africans. I stood outside South Africa House with a large placard, "Free the Dean."

I enjoyed working in the Office – it adjoined the Vicarage, was on the first floor, and had large windows overlooking the courtyard and Church. There were two young secretaries, Margaret, and Fran from Canada, totally dedicated to the ethos of St. Martin's, and great fun. Once an Indian came to the Office and when told my name, exclaimed, "I heard you in Delhi yesterday!" I had done some broadcasts for the World Service and used stories about the life of St. Martin's. I went to a BBC training day for priests who were broadcasting and did several Prayer for the Day talks, and also some television. I was also a member of a group producing a religious magazine programme for Radio London; I sometimes wondered whether they were worth the time involved; but I suppose that it made me feel important!

Our weekly staff meetings were informal, relaxed, amusing and profound. We arranged a service rota at our equally relaxed clergy breakfasts (where I learnt from observing Austen that it must be OK to heap marmalade on your toast). Sometimes we would discover that we all had accepted invitations to preach elsewhere, on the same day. We negotiated in a most calm and adult manner. We had two part time members of the clergy staff, Trevor Beeson, editor of New Christian and later Dean of Winchester and Colin Hodgetts, tall, bearded, free, be-sandalled, organiser of the London School of Non Violence, which met, with Satish Kumar, in one of the vaults. This was a Ghandian version of Dick Sheppards Peace Pledge Union, which had encouraged its members to vow never to fight again, after the horrors of the First World War; - profound, visionary and surely in the spirit of Christ, but, sadly, it only encouraged Hitler. S.Y. Lee led the Chinese congregation.

I was joined by other curates, successively, Mark Moreton, steady and wise, John Kirkham, Cambridge, Westcott friend, who shared his time with St. Margaret's Westminster, became Chaplain to Archbishop Ramsey and later Bishop of Sherborne, and Ron Swan, whom I had also known at Cambridge. I am afraid that I rather played the Senior Curate with all of them. Occasionally I would take an Assembly at St. Martin's High School for Girls; it had moved from Trafalgar Square to Tulse Hill. For some minor drama I had in mind, I needed the sudden unannounced appearance of an unknown man, to be the beggar, or the Christ, or something. As poor Ron toiled up the Hill on his bike on a hot summer's day, to surprise the girls, he wondered if this was really what he had been ordained for?!

We often worked with Ken Leach, Rector of Soho – a true academic and true Anglo Catholic Socialist; he told us horrifying stories of the drug world; he seemed to know personally all the infamous characters of the seamy side of London's life – as well as all the famous of the theatre. Quite a bunch we were; and I did feel that we were at the heart of London life; but all the time we were surrounded by the sad, the lonely and the dirty. Whenever I came out of our flat I would be approached by some swaying Scotsman or Irishman. I rarely wore a dog-collar, was bearded, and sometimes scruffily dressed, so I would occasionally forestall their demands for money, by saying "Jock, (or Paddy) can you give me a bob or two, I've had nothing to eat?" Surprise, disgust as Jock or Paddy turned away, swearing loudly! Of course, if any man, woman, boy or girl was in trouble and needed help, we could take them to the S.S.U. where Norman and his staff would do what they could.

These were the days of Vietnam, the anti-apartheid movement and the Civil Rights marches in Alabama. I was standing on the steps of St. Martin's when I heard of the death of Martin Luther King. I showed a series of newsreels of his life at a weekend away which I had arranged for Thursday Night at Eight, a gathering for students, nurses and young office workers. The film profoundly moved and inspired me – the Bible based courage and nobility of the man, the horrific contemptuous violence of the baton-wielding police thugs, the heartening sight of black and white, priests and nuns marching arm-in-arm and kneeling when confronted by the police; and after the newsreels had shown us much of the long struggle, to see and hear, in full, Martin Luther King's tremendous speech to a vast crowd who needed fresh inspiration and renewed courage to win: "I've had a dreeeam……." "I've beeen to the mountain top, and I've seeeen the Promised Land……." After the lynchings of "Negroes" and the spark that lit the flame of Civil Rights, when weary Rosa Parks refused to give up her seat for a white man, only forty years later we have Barack Obama; but the descendants of those police thugs and their supporters are still very much alive.

These were heady days, when student revolt in England was idealistic; we sang "We shall overcome ……. Black shall walk with white ……. For deep in my heart, I do believe, we shall overcome some day." Many of our young people were angry left wingers and hated the police, "the fuzz"; it was a temptation for me to take sides with them, while at the same time remembering I was a Christian priest called to love all. I was also an official of the Established Church and used my status to visit a student arrested at a demonstration when he was in Pentonville – it is always paradoxical and a delicate balance.

At the weekend away for Thursday Night at Eight there was a very dedicated young married couple; they marched for peace and hated the fuzz. I organised some role plays with off-the-cuff, spontaneous dialogue. The young wife played the part of the wife of a police officer, anxiously seeing him off to police a demonstration. Later one of his colleagues came and awkwardly told her that her husband had been badly injured. She was distraught, and angry with the demonstrators who had attacked her kind and conscientious husband. I haven't forgotten the stunned expression on her face when she came out of role, a changed woman.

I sometimes visited our more wayward young people where they were living, in dirty, overcrowded rooms, up several flights of stairs, sharing lavatory and bathroom with lots of others – the days of Rachman landlords – degrading poverty far more depressing than the back streets of

Sheffield, where there were families and a sense of togetherness.

The steeple of St. Martin's soared high into the sky above Trafalgar Square. While it was being repaired there was scaffolding near the top, and a very long ladder up to the weather vane. To my horror I saw a man climbing up, threatening to throw himself off; suddenly we saw him start to fall. It was just his coat which he had thrown down. A young policeman, on duty nearby, climbed the ladder and coaxed him back to safety. The policeman had no training for such a task; he was not a steeplejack, but just an officer on the beat with a strong sense of duty, compassion and courage. He would have had a story to tell his grandchildren.

Our little green van had packed up and we bought an old Morris 1000 traveller, a small shooting brake. One day we were driving down to see Mary's parents in Canterbury; Jamie was sitting on Mary's knee, and when she had seen to him, she put him in his baby seat in the back. I pulled out into the middle lane to overtake, saw a big lorry coming fast the other way and braked to pull back to our lane. The road was wet, and instead of going left we skidded to the right and just hit the lorry coming up the hill. There was an almighty crash, and my eyes closed in horror. When I opened them I expected to find myself dead – I can put it no other way. I seemed to be all right and unhurt. Trembling with dread, I turned to see if Mary was alive. She was, but had broken some ribs and damaged her knee. We must have been wearing safety belts or it would have been fatal; but they had only recently come in; this was1970. With equal dread I turned to look at Jamie. He was crying, but all right. My next terror was that other cars would crash into us, as the lorry had stopped in his lane and we were in the middle one; but, mercifully people came to help, called police and ambulance and diverted the traffic.

Much of our luggage was scattered over the road, including our family coloured slides. The ambulance took us straight to Canterbury Hospital, where Mary stayed for two or three days. Thank God that we were all alive, and that Jamie had been put in his baby seat only a few minutes earlier. I remained in a state of shock, until I used it as a basis for my next sermon at St. Martin's. I think I talked about a renewed sense of wonder at the miracle of the gift of life. As soon as the service was over I realised that I was free of the numbing, unreal state of shock. It helps to talk – especially if you are ten feet above the two hundred people listening.

I think Mary enjoyed the buzz of living at St. Martin's with its community of staff and volunteers, but also felt trapped living up a fire escape, with a toddler. Often I would take him out for an hour in the afternoon in "Jamie's Park", going through Trafalgar Square and up the Mall; the Park looked lovely in spring and autumn and he enjoyed feeding the ducks in the lake. He was a very good looking and endearing little boy, eager and loving. My father and mother adored their first grandchild, and also had him to stay at High Beeches. Once, having put him to bed, they finally sank into their chairs by the library fire, exhausted. "Granneee, Granneee," came a little voice from upstairs. Up my mother would toil, "Yes, Jamie?", "Grannie, I'm hungry". Down to the kitchen and back up with something to eat, and sink back in her chair. "Granneee, Granneee", she heaved herself up the stairs, "Yes, Jamie?". "Grannie, I'm firsty" – down to the kitchen and back with a drink. Collapse. "Granneee, Granneee." This time my father leapt up the stairs, flung open the door and briskly asked,

"Yes, Jamie, what do you want?" "Oh, I haven't thought yet!" He still loves to tell the story against himself. As a child he was pleased that we said he had a "sense of humyour".

Londoners love a coach outing and so I took a party from St. Martin's for a day trip to High Beeches, in Ashdown Forest in Sussex. As they climbed out of the coach and heard nothing but the singing of the birds they exclaimed "Oh how peaceful!" My father and mother greeted them, one by one, gave them tea, strawberries and cream, in the logie, overlooking the paddock and the hill opposite, clothed in rhododendrons; they talked and listened to them so gently. It was much appreciated, and talked about years later. In traditional fashion, on the way back we sang all the old favourites – Mebbe it's because I'm a Londoner, Doing the Lambeth Walk, Daisy, Daisy, - happy days.

After our car crash my mother paid for us to have a short break at the Grand Hotel in Brighton. While there we bought an MG Magnette saloon, with wooden dashboard, leather seats, smooth gears and suspension fit for a racing car. It was already ten years old and stood out amongst the modern cars, as having character. It had only done 20,000 miles and cost £600. We loved it.

Once Mary and Jamie were invited to tea at Buckingham Palace – not by the Queen, but by her Chambermaid, the daughter of a Vicar, and a member of St. Martin's. On their way back, Mary and Jamie were stopped by the police, because an IRA bomb had just exploded down the road. I was enormously relieved to see them coming home safe and sound. (Where does that phrase come from? – a Saxon word meaning robust, or healthy, Dr. Johnson.) Once I strolled down the Mall to see the

Queen riding in a state coach, flanked by the Horse Guards, on her way to open Parliament. Nobody cheered or waved. I was sad and disappointed, but only managed a few quiet words and a slight movement of my hand. Once she had gone by I realised I should have given a loud, loyal shout, "God save the Queen", and waved vigorously – but the moment had gone. The silence of a crowd can dampen a person's enthusiasm, as much as an angry crowd can make him lose his serenity and join in the loud shouts of the tumult.

We had met the Queen's Chambermaid at the Shrove Tuesday Parish Party in the Crypt, given for everybody actually living in the parish, Cockneys from the Peabody Buildings and top advisers of the Queen from the Palace. We ate, drank, sang and played daft party games – the favourite was the 'hat game' when a box of widely assorted hats was produced, both men's and women's; we stood in a circle, all but one of us wearing a daft, inappropriate hat. We moved round to music, the hatless one grabbing the hat from the head of the moving person in front, who would then lunge forward to grab the headgear of the person in front of him. The Vicar, in his scarlet cassock could look especially ridiculous in a Cockney woman's close fitting hat. It was such fun, and wonderfully homely for country people who had come to London and were lonely. I feel sorry for people who have never known this uninhibited corporate togetherness, all ages, all classes, typical of any lively mixed parish.

St. Martin's is in Trafalgar Square and while taking a service we often heard the scream of police sirens, or ambulances outside. If I was leading the congregation in prayer I would try to help them understand that the sound was not an interruption of our prayers, but a reminder of the people we were praying for. Most Sunday afternoons we could hear the amplified shouts of angry speakers addressing crowds of demonstrators. We were never far from politics and the issues of the day. I believe that The Lordship of Christ leads us to care for broken people; but it also means that we are to be the servants and agents of his rule of love at the strong centre of national life, matters of racial justice, world poverty and housing.

St. Martin's had two hostels – one in Clapham and one in Taunton. If Austen had an unencumbered day he would make a spontaneous decision to go to Somerset to see them, much to their surprise and delight. In later years I tried to follow Austen's example and make a long spontaneous journey for a brief visit to somebody in need; it was always much appreciated. Different charities, church societies and international pressure groups would sometimes ask to meet at St. Martin's, hold a service, or make a demonstration. There were sometimes difficult decisions to be made, but there was a general assumption that we should encourage any movement which sought to help the oppressed; I suppose you could say that we were a mildly left wing bunch, on Biblical authority!

The world famous Crypt was used for the soup kitchen on Sunday mornings and for occasional parish functions, but for the rest of the time it lay empty. To make contact with young people, I started a Folk Club. My idea was that the members would sit, cross legged on the floor and sing from printed song sheets – hopelessly old fashioned and churchy. Ken Leach put me in touch with Judith Piepé, a short, plump, strong, motherly Jewish lady who worked in the East End and knew the folk scene. Thank God she helped me! We brought in chairs and a platform. Just for the opening night, Judith brought along a delightful

American couple, Doris Henderson, a petite black lady with long hair who sang most sweetly and powerfully, and Ron, a gentle man with black beard and long black hair, who gave us his liquid light show, psychodelic colours thrown onto the ancient stone arches of the Crypt by a projector with different coloured oil on the slides, changing and bursting in time with the music. The rest of the Crypt was in semi-darkness; he created the most amazing and exciting atmosphere. He came for the opening night, and stayed for five years.

Before we could open I had to negotiate the security details with the vergers and the Administrator, Colonel Searle; he always wore his Signals tie and was very particular – necessarily so, in keeping an eye on the fiancés – mistyped, should be finances! - and the smooth running of such a lumbering, ramshackle organisation. Whenever I went to see him in his little office in the tower, I felt like a schoolboy going to ask permission from the Headmaster. He would occasionally appear in our Parish Office, and one day Margaret told me that it was soon to be his birthday. I bought a bottle of champagne, and when he turned up, we toasted him. That helped.

The Folk Club ran for nearly thirteen years, and its profits paid for my whole salary. The audience, of about 200, was of all ages, but most were in their twenties, nurses, students, and office workers; they came from all over the world, especially America and the Commonwealth countries. Judith Piepe helped me run and compere it, but after a time I felt she cramped my style, and our committee were getting fed up with her promotion of her own particular singers. Reluctantly, and with a bad conscience, I asked her to leave. I felt I had used her, but it was easier when we were free to run it our own way.

These were heady days for me. As you can imagine, I hugely enjoyed being on the stage, introducing the singers, relating to the audience – many came every Sunday – aiming at a blend of sincerity about the more idealistic songs and light hearted merriment. I told them of Sir Peter Howard, Chairman of the London Rubber Company; he was charging more for his products, and so was the first man "to raise the cost of loving!". I had a good team of helpers, drawn from the Church, members of the Club and Thursday Night at Eight, the more respectable gathering for the young. With the name of St. Martin's, I could ask almost anybody to come on a Thursday. Many courteously declined the invitation, but, amongst others, we did have Spike Milligan, David Steele, then leader of the Liberal Party and the son of a Scot's minister, and also George MacLeod. That was a rather sad evening for me; he was getting old, seemed less in touch with the young; they had never heard of him and were not concerned with the issues that he was still so passionate about.

The Folk Club followed the Sunday Evensong, usually the best attended service of the day. It had a powerful atmosphere all of its own, with a mixture of loyal members of St. Martin's and people who had come from all over the world, with high expectations. I tried to make it personal by greeting people as they came in and shaking them by the hand as they poured out into Trafalgar Square. It was a daunting experience, climbing the steps of Dick Sheppard's pulpit, and preaching instead of Austen Williams. It was all right if I had some moving, thought provoking story to tell, but all too often my sermon was ill prepared; it was alarming to hear "the bells of St. Martin's" peeling out to summon people to worship in the centre of London, when I really had little to say!

My final duty, at the end of a Sunday, was to check and lock the whole Underground of Crypt and vaults. Sometimes I would find some wretch huddled up in a corner, trying to sleep. Normally, the vergers would see to the security and I had to promise the Colonel that I would be equally conscientious, or the Folk Club would never have got off the ground. So my final act of the day would be to turn this poor man out into the night. It seemed a betrayal of all that St. Martin's stood for.

These were the days of Jesus Christ Superstar and Godspel, which we saw in the Roundhouse, a converted railway shed. I found it very moving and felt inspired to create another modern Passion Play. I booked the Church hall in Folkestone for a weekend and took down about twenty people to see if we could fashion something together. We arrived late on Friday evening and went straight to the Vicarage where the good Victor and Sheila had soup and a great pile of sandwiches ready for us. One of our number said, "I never knew Vicars were like that!" We slept on the floor and then did numerous role plays based on incidents in St. Luke's Gospel. We only got as far as Chapter Five, but it was enough to give us the confidence to continue.

I gathered together a cast of about thirty, mostly from the Folk Club, but it also included sweet elderly ladies from the congregation and two distinguished looking men in city suits. Two Jewish girls were amongst the most creative, right from the start. We also had a stylish young Old Etonian, who wore long boots and flowing black hair; we were a richly assorted bunch. In the rehearsals we made it up as we went along, leading to an amazing fresh insight into many well known stories - and much of the rest I wrote myself. Jesus was played by one of the youngest of the cast, long dark hair, a fine sensitive face and a remarkable quiet confidence and detachment. He knew nobody, came from nowhere and disappeared when the first round of the play was finished. We assembled a music group from the Folk Club and used a variety of songs. We went to town on the publicity; we called the play 'Alive'! and showed large posters, had it announced on Radio London, and I took leaflets to a meeting of the London Diocesan Synod. I held out the leaflets to the members going into Church House but many ignored me, thinking I was protesting about some issue of life ecclesiastical – far from it!

The suspense before the opening night was awful, but the Crypt was full. Without any welcome or announcement, and there was no curtain to raise, one of the audience flung himself on the floor of the aisle, in a terrible fit, and a young man came from his seat, calmed and healed him – and so the play began. It was electric. One by one Jesus gathered his friends, a tough, bearded Canadian was Peter, black haired Bernie was Mary Magdalen, and a swarthy hefty Cypriot was Matthew, the tax collector become disciple. He sang "Amazing Grace" with incredible power and feeling – even though he did later seduce one of the girl disciples. Several of the twelve were girls, which surprised some. The Lord of the Dance was part of Jesus' challenge to them all.

> *I danced for the scribe*
> *And the Pharisee*
> *But they would not dance*
> *And they wouldn't follow me.*
> *I danced for the fishermen*
> *For James and for John*
> *They came with me and the dance went on.*

Stanley had distinguished grey hair and wore a smart suit. Somebody was sitting at a table, collecting money for the Church; with a flourish, Stanley wrote a cheque for £1,000; he was followed by Bundles, a wizened little old man in scruffy clothes and a filthy cloth cap. He banged down a 10p piece, saying, in a Cockney voice, "That's all ah got!" and shuffled off. From the sidelines, Jesus turned to his friends and said, "That old bloke has given more than the posh guy – he's given everything he had". The old man in the cloth cap had a council flat, but it was so full of rotting bundles of newspaper that he couldn't move into it; so he slept on the streets; a tragic, poignant reminder of the danger of filling not only our homes with things, but also our lives with the clutter of prejudices, bitterness and regrets. We always tried to be kind to Bundles, but it was hard to get through to him; I sometimes fear we used him.

After he had shuffled off, Jesus sang Ralph MacTell's **'The Streets of London'**.

Have you seen the old man
In the closed-down market
Kicking up the papers,
With his worn out shoes?
In his eyes you see no pride
Hands held loosely at his side
Yesterday's paper telling yesterday's news.

So how can you tell me you're lonely
And say for you that the sun don't shine?
Let me take you by the hand and lead you through the Streets of London
I'll show you something to make you change your mind.

Have you seen the old girl
Who walks the streets of London

173

Dirt in her hair and her clothes in rags?
She's no time for talking
She just keeps right on walking
Carrying her home in two carrier bags.
So how can you ....
In the all night café
At a quarter past eleven,
Some old man is sitting there on his own
Looking at the world
Over the rim of his tea-cup,
Each tea lasts an hour
Then he wanders home alone.
So how can you ....
And have you seen the old man
Outside the seaman's mission
Memory fading with
The medal ribbons that he wears.
In our winter city,
The rain cries little pity
For one more forgotten hero
And a world that doesn't care.
So how can you ....

One of the best scenes in the play was when the top religious clique in the town asked Jesus to dinner, probably more out of curiosity than kindness, so that they could boast to their friends about having snubbed him; he was in the public eye, and everybody was talking about him. When he arrived they ignored him and denied him all the usual courtesies, continuing talking amongst themselves. A tart, a pro, turned up and wept with gratitude and devotion at his feet; in rebuking his host, Jesus told him, "her sins, which are many, are forgiven, for she loved much; but he who is forgiven little, loves little."

This is, perhaps, my favourite story in the Gospels. At times I see something of myself in the woman – "a priest is like a teacher and a whore; we're all paid to love" – and like her, I am in need of forgiveness. I see something of myself in the self righteous religious somebodys.

In Jesus' time Jerusalem was the sophisticated, international political and religious capital of the Jews. In the Hebrew mind, of course there is no division between faith in the sovereign God and the affairs of the nation. God rescued a whole people from slavery, and God demands that aliens be welcomed and treated with respect, "for were you not, yourselves, slaves in Egypt?" God also demanded that an employer pays his labourer proper wages, and pays him on the day. So Jesus, the carpenter from up North, has to proclaim the kingdom of God, the overwhelming power of his Father's love; and it is channelled, focused, starkly challenging in his own person; and in this 'xairos' this X, this single moment in human history, everybody is confronted with the choice to be with him or against him in all he stands for, crazy generosity, being willing to break tradition to reach to a person in need, freedom from people's opinion, forgiveness rather than judgement, being ready to take colossal risks in trusting people and trusting life and, above all, being prepared to suffer, even die, out of love for others.

So, in our play, the tension mounts, Jesus is alone, ahead of his friends; they sense his heaviness of spirit; they are afraid and do not understand. Christ, the carpenter, knows the risk and probable outcome of his shouting aloud his challenge and acting it out himself – the risk of an excruciating death. But he <u>has</u> to shout and he <u>has</u> to put it into action. So we had tables where the City Bankers and the Mayor of London and Canons of St. Paul's Cathedral

175

were working. Today, they would have had computers with them. In anger, the carpenter crashes their tables over and drives them out of the Crypt; a challenge to the shoddy, profit-driven materialism of all of us today. Earlier, at some point in the play, to show his freedom from the controlling power of money, he tore up a pound note (worth £5 today). This always provoked criticism – the money could have been used to buy food. Yes, it was provocative, and was meant to be – people argued about it. This incident has no basis in the Gospels, except, possibly, the waste of very expensive ointment poured over Jesus' feet; but it was in the tradition of the prophets – they were good PR men in their day. It was meant to provoke, and it did.

We acted the Last Supper in the style of Leonardo da Vinci, and in movement copying Godspel. It was the Passover meal, the family celebration of God's saving act in delivering the children of Israel out of slavery in Egypt. Dan Brown would have approved, as we had women at the table. You could have heard a fly buzz in the far corner of the Crypt while Jesus knelt and gently washed the feet of all his followers – later they said it was soothing, consoling, relaxing, comforting. The audience watched with total attention. Sometimes the silence was broken by the urgent wail of an ambulance in the Square. "If I, your Lord and Master have washed your feet, you should also wash one another's feet." Jesus took the symbolic bread and wine of the Passover meal and gave it new meaning, his body would be broken on the cross and his blood would seal the New Covenant between God and man, unconditional forgiveness – in everyday terms, Jesus was willing to stick by everything he had said and done, even to death. With guitar accompanying them, to the tune of the House of the Rising Sun, the cast sang

"There is a green hill far away without a city wall,
where the dear Lord was crucified who died to save us all.
We may not know, we cannot tell, what pains he had to bear,
But we believe it was for us he hung and suffered there.

He died that we might be forgiven, he died to make us good;
That we might go at last to heaven, saved by his precious blood.
O dearly, dearly has he loved, and we must love him too,
And trust in his redeeming blood, and try his works to do."

As the last words died away, the Christ stood, bread and wine in hand, and said to everybody in the crypt, "Will you join me in this meal?" His friends took the bread and wine to everybody in the Crypt, no ecclesiastical questions about ordination or church membership.

Then Jesus and followers walked round the Crypt, through the audience, to Gethsemane, where Jesus, on his knees, desperately tried to face down the temptation to cut and run, return to Nazareth, take up his carpenter's tools, marry and have sons and daughters. It was his final moment of decision; this temptation to take the easy way out had been with him from the beginning. He made the grim decision to go through with it and not betray all that he stood for; this decision made, he staggered back to his friends. He had begged them to watch and pray, to be with him in his terrible, lonely agony. They were fast asleep. All his doubts surged over him, nearly drowning him. Very human. Three times he had to endure this exhausting swing of emotion and willpower, before he was ready to accept what would probably happen to him. He was betrayed by Judas. In the play Judas was always played by a strong character who had looked Jesus in the eye at the Passover meal, daring him to be a national hero? This was not written in the script, but just emerged naturally, spontaneously – fascinating.

Jesus was arrested, falsely accused and flogged, off stage; but the 39 lashes could be heard throughout the Crypt. With the single notes of a guitar, a girl sang Handel's "He was despised, despised and rejected, a man of sorrows and acquainted with grief.......".

How to stage a modern crucifixion? The whole cast hemmed him in and, hidden from the audience, killed him, lynched him as the "Negroes" were by the Ku Klux Klan. On the shoulders of his friends his dead body was carried out.

Heavy, heavy silence…………..

The unaccompanied voices of the cast sang Bach's hymn.

O sacred head, surrounded by crown of piercing thorn!
O bleeding head, so wounded, so shamed and put to scorn!
Death's pallid hue comes o'er thee, the flow of life decays;
Yet angel hosts adore thee, and tremble as they gaze.

Thy comeliness and vigour is withered up and gone
And in thy wasted figure I see death drawing on.
O agony and dying! O love to sinners free!
Jesus, all grace supplying, turn thou thy face on me.

In this thy bitter passion, good Shepherd, think of me
With thy most sweet compassion, unworthy though I be:
Beneath thy cross abiding for ever would I rest,
In thy dear love and confiding and with thy presence blest.

Heavy, heavy silence ………………………….

Half the cast were behind one set of massive Crypt pillars, and half behind another. They spoke to each other – a whisper,

"He's alive!"

"Where is he?"

"He's in you!"

"Where is he?"

"He's in us"

and a louder and louder shout

"He's alive!"

"He's alive!"

"He's alive"

The last shout echoed round the Crypt; it was heard in the Square, and the whole cast broke into singing, "I danced in the morning when the world was begun......" They danced joyfully round the whole audience till they all sang the choruses and the last triumphant verse,

> *"They cut me down, and I leap up high,*
> *I am the life that will never, never die;*
> *I'll live in you if you'll live in me;*
> *I am the Lord of the Dance, said he."*

On the second night, quite spontaneously, and without any encouragement from the cast, the whole audience joined in this dance of the Resurrection.

Nearly every other performance ended the same way, but with the cast taking the initiative. That first, spontaneous outburst of life could never be repeated, but it still lives in my mind and the memories of everybody there that night.

After each performance I went with many of the cast to the Duncannon, just over the road, and some of the audience always joined us; there, in the pub, night after night, we talked with complete strangers about the Christ.

We had planned on four performances, but both cast and audience wanted more, so we did another four, and then another eight, and finally it ran for nearly two years, twice a week and sometimes at weekends. I would often take two or three group bookings from schools or churches, and we usually had about a hundred and fifty attending. There was sometimes a reaction from within the audience. As Jesus was saying, "If somebody takes your coat, give him your shirt as well….. give and it will be given to you ……" a poor disturbed man began to argue, "That's all bloody lies – nobody fuckin' gives anything to me!" The man playing Jesus was startled, but spoke gently to him and introduced him to a friend who went out with him and listened to him. Powerful, spontaneous, street theatre – and real. On another occasion, a man who was an alcoholic took his sip of wine at the hands of Jesus; he was so shaken, that, for the first time in his life, he acknowledged that he needed help, and staggered off to the Unit next door. After the next performance he told me about this. Who knows how many hundreds of others had felt themselves addressed by God, but never mentioned it?

Invitations began to come in to take the play to other churches, schools and colleges. Two of the cast bought old ambulances and with the help of a few cars, we became a travelling circus. The cast slowly changed over the months. After eight performances Jesus left, disappearing as quietly as he had arrived; others moved out of London or left the country; but after many a performance eager members of the audience asked to join us. If one of the actors failed to turn up, others would spontaneously take their place, probably adding their own interpretation in both words and movement. The play was fluid, responding to different needs. I stood at the back of every performance with my heart in my mouth until the moment when the Dance of the Resurrection broke out and I could join in. Of course the members got to know each other very well, especially when we travelled, and slept on church floors. I think two marriages emerged from the play, and by now there are probably children and grandchildren of Alive! as well as one of the disciples who became a priest. I took a full wedding blessing of two members of the cast at a party in a flat on a fifth floor. The wine had already flowed, we gathered in a tight circle round the bride and groom while they reaffirmed their vows – the warmest, most natural wedding I've ever taken.

We put on a performance at St. John's Kennington, playing to a full church. Two drunks were there, one in each of the opposite side aisles; one of them started interrupting Jesus and the other shouted out, across the audience, "Shut up, you bastard, let 'im finish!" Verily, an angel in disguise. We stayed overnight at the Education College in Chichester, and performed in their immaculate hall –Bundle's sudden appearance from a side door came as a shock. I am afraid that, somehow, we had hidden him until that moment; I don't think he minded; he enjoyed the spirit of the thing, and was a hero of the students once the play was over.

We took Alive! to several churches around London, by invitation of members of the play; sometimes the audience was no larger than the cast, which was frustrating, but we hoped that it helped those who did come. The Curate of Great St. Mary's asked us to perform there, so we went to Cambridge and shouted, sang and danced in this magnificent University Church where I had been inspired and learnt so much when I was an undergraduate. I could hardly believe it. One day I met John Oliver on the steps of St. Martin's; he had been with Roland and at Westcott with me, and was now one of the Chaplains at Eton, where his wife Meriel's father had been a housemaster. He asked me to come and preach next half. On the spot, I thanked him and asked if I could bring Alive! instead. I tried to give him an honest description of its merits, and he agreed. So off we went, ambulances, hippies, Bundles and all, and were courteously put up by members of staff. Once again, we performed our provocative scenes, sang and danced in the limited area of the main aisle of the ancient chapel; if there were any angels in the roof, they would have looked down in mild surprise; they would never have seen anything like it there before. I then had drinks with the Headmaster, Michael McCrum, who had been Senior Tutor at Corpus, and later returned as Master of the College. He was as charming, tall and quietly powerful as ever.

We also performed at the College at Winchester, where I knew the Chaplain. Our most memorable visit was to Wormwood Scrubs. I can't remember whether this was by invitation of the prison chaplain or whether I offered to go – I certainly felt that we needed a different audience to Eton and Cambridge. One night we rehearsed in the vast empty Victorian chapel and the next night were ready to recreate the life of Christ amongst the wretched of our day. A vast crowd of prisoners was marched in, many hundreds – no voluntary occasion was this; many were old lags and many were pathetically young. They were talking and complaining loudly. A senior warder thundered, "Shut up!"

and sudden silence fell upon this mob of men. Awesome and eerie. They were intensely interested in the first few scenes, but when the girls came on, they broke into cat calls and wolf whistles, which startled the girls; this had not happened at Eton; but they tried to carry on regardless. In the play Jesus talked to the multitude about the chains of religious or social snobbery and the love of money. "So I have come - to set you free!" Wild cheers and laughter from the prisoners. Jesus grinned, and managed to carry on. When Judas appeared for the second time, they booed and hissed, like kids at a pantomime; they were loyal to Jesus; but when the crowd moved in to kill Jesus, I heard the prisoners should "Go on, finish 'im off – put the boot in!" And the shouts grew louder and louder; the hysterical anger of a mob of violent men. I suppose their pent up frustration and suppressed anger burst through at the first sight of violence, and they wished it were their own boots thudding into the innocent victim. Terrifying.

It is possible that there has never been such a similar spontaneous reaction to the crucifixion in all Christian history. I don't know. Audiences in the Medieval Mystery plays, or Oberammergau will have been moved to love and pity, but shouts of genuine, gut anger? I doubt it. When the play finished, heavy silence was imposed once again, and the prisoners were marched out. Back in the changing room all the girls broke down in tears – released of the tension of continuing to act in the presence of such wild emotion. I shall never forget it. I went back the next day to have a discussion about the play, as I always tried to do. I went to the Scrubs branch of the Church of England's Men's Society; twenty or thirty prisoners turned up, many of them well educated men, and we had the most profound and insightful discussion of what the play was really about, issues such as our need for forgiveness and our need to forgive others, and this from the depth and bitterness of their own experience.

There were very few funerals at St. Martin's, and when I did take one it always involved a trip to Golders Green. I took the occasional christening – I use that word instead of 'baptism'; it was the way we talked when I was a child, and I still have my christening cup. The word 'baptism' only came into my vocabulary later on and was often used by those who wanted to make a clear distinction between 'Christians' and everybody else. A young couple would often meet at St. Martin's, marry there, and have their child christened there, continuing to belong to St. Martin's and remain involved, even if they lived in the suburbs.

Weddings were more frequent, and often they were of naval officers – the Admiralty was in the parish and we flew the white ensign. They were typical Navy officers, clean shaven, confident, but not pompous – subtly different from the Army. A few years later I met one of them again, and he reminded me how I had given him and his best man a Polo mint as we stood on the steps before the service. There were some Nigerian weddings, both men and women looking very dignified in their colourful robes; the effect was rather spoilt for me by seeing lots of people standing on the pews, taking photographs to send home. Once I took a Chinese wedding and was alarmed when one of the vergers showed me the Banns form, with the names of the bride and groom. At the rehearsal I anxiously hoped that there was a different, Chinese, way of pronouncing the groom's name, but no, the next day I had to stand in the church and say, "I, Fook Yue............"

There were also memorial services for national figures, actors, politicians, top Admirals and the like; I would help organise them and would take the service; usually those would be taken by the Vicar, but if he was away, or busy, he would be more than content to let me do it all. I was also asked to preach at St. James' Piccadilly and St. Margaret's Westminster where I saw Lord Hailsham, the Lord Chancellor, sitting in the front pew. I used, as the basis of my sermon, Mary's desperate cry, "Oh God!!" as she struggled up dangerous scree on Holy Isle, off Arran. What I said about it I can't remember!

The annual St. Martin's Fair was a great occasion, always held near St. Martin's Day, 11th November. The whole of the Underground, Crypt and vaults were used for dozens of stalls, each run by a different organisation of the Church. By tradition, the curates always ran a hot dog stall, and I would go to Berman's, the theatrical costume company, to collect the chefs' white uniforms and tall white hats. We did not have to pay for them – the name of St. Martin's led to much generosity. I also went round to all the pubs in the parish, asking for bottles to be raffled at the Fair; for this I always wore my dog collar, and, as you can imagine, it took me a very long time! I only dreaded going into one pub, the Salisbury (?) which was all silver and mirrors and where there were no women; the men all turned and looked at me in a hungry way which made me very uncomfortable. I was glad to get out. Very different were the wedding receptions, often held in famous hotels, the Dorchester, the Hyde Park Hotel, the Savoy, just up the road. I thrived on it all, and if I felt I was being undervalued at a party somewhere else in London, I just had to ask somebody, "Where do you live?" They would tell me, and then ask where I lived? "Trafalgar Square". For a few minutes I would bask in the glory of St. Martin's - manipulative. I was very full of myself. ("Was?!" said a voice from the kitchen). There was always the danger of false pride in being part of such a wonderful, famous church, talking more of St. Martin's than of God.

Towards the end of our time there we were overjoyed at the arrival of our daughter Anna, a lovely baby. Jamie had been longing for her and was very attentive to his little sister. She was christened by Austen in the oval, marble seventeenth century font where King Charles II had been baptized. As we now had two children, the fire escape to our flat became increasingly difficult; I had been at St. Martin's for nearly four years and it seemed time to move to a house with a garden. The Provost of Southwark Cathedral came over the river to see us in our flat; he asked me to become a Canon of the Cathedral and bring young people in. This was a great honour – I was only thirty-five, but I hardly considered it. I feared that it would be like St. Martin's, but without the glamour; we also wanted to get out of London. As I say, I was very full of myself; but it was truly difficult to go anywhere which would compare with the opportunities I already had.

We were asked to go and look at a daughter Church of St. Mary's, Wimbledon. It had an intelligent and committed congregation, who were doing imaginative things like giving overnight accommodation to people visiting seriously ill family in hospital; but it had a modern Vicarage, with no fireplace, and a small, dull garden; it was still in London. Earlier we had been approached about Sandwich, the Cinque port on the East Kent coast. I had gone through it in the train on a visit to Folkestone; from the train it had looked very remote, dull and poky. I had asked for the opinion of another clergyman who had already been offered the living, and he confirmed this opinion – his daughter had been alarmed by the roar of motorbikes through the narrow, dirty streets. So I did not even look at it – on very little evidence – what town does look good from the railway line?

That year we spent the days after Christmas with Mary's family at Charing in Kent; her father was now Archdeacon of Maidstone. Mary's brother, Michael, told me how much he had enjoyed wandering along the Quay at Sandwich, looking at some of the old boats. This chance remark suddenly made me think of the town in a new light. We were free the next day and went to look around Sandwich for ourselves, and discovered what a fascinating historical town it is. We liked the Rectory and its surroundings and realised how foolish we had been to turn down the offer; we rang the patron of the living (the parish) and asked if we could be given a second chance.

Some livings are in the gift of the Crown, exercised by the Ecclesiastical Secretary to the Prime Minister. At one stage I walked down from Trafalgar Square to 10 Downing Street, was admitted through the famous shiny black door and waited in the little room to the left; shades of "Yes, Prime Minister"; I was shown along endless corridors to the attic room where the Church Secretary worked. I was not impressed with anything he had to offer. Whether the good Lord wanted me to go to any of those parishes I will never know, in this life, anyhow; but I just couldn't see myself adjusting to any dull parish after St. Martin's.

The patron of Sandwich was the Archdeacon of Canterbury, Michael Nott, and the responsibility stayed with him, personally, even when he was no longer Archdeacon, until a new Archdeacon was installed. It was a joke in the diocese that when the new Archdeacon introduced himself to his predecessor he said, "I'm Pawley",

- "and I'm Nott", said the other. At this time Michael Nott was Provost of Portsmouth Cathedral, where my brother, Colin, had married Carola, daughter of an Honorary Canon. I rang him and he gave me a second chance and we went to meet the two Sandwich Churchwardens. We liked everything we saw, they approved of us, and so we had two firm offers, Wimbledon and Sandwich. How on earth to decide?! Direct approach to the Almighty seemed to provide no answer, so I wrote a letter of acceptance to each patron and went round the corner to the Post Office in Trafalgar Square, said a simple prayer, and after a few moment's indecision, popped Sandwich in the box and returned to our flat to write a letter declining the kind offer of Wimbledon. So the next nine years, and all that followed was decided by a chance remark about boats and the picture in my mind of Jamie going round the Rectory on his trike – it had garden both back and front; that image stood for a different way of life, not in a London suburb, but in a market town near the sea. I thanked God that I had made that decision, and I still do.

I went down to Portsmouth to meet Michael Nott; he welcomed me warmly, encouraged me and told me of the people of Sandwich and their need to be loved. He had heard of what I had tried to do at St. Martin's, and expressed the hope that I had not peaked too early in my priesthood – a wise comment.

To compensate for my failure to get a parish near Rugby, which he had recommended, Eric Abbot asked me to preach at Westminster Abbey. I told them about Alive! and how I had taken it to Eton and Wormwood Scrubs – two similar institutions. The American visitors looked puzzled.

Shortly before we left St. Martin's I had an interesting talk with a young man who was much involved with my work there; he went to the services, regularly attended Thursday Night at Eight and was also on the committee of the Folk Club. He was a great supporter and I thought I knew him well, but apparently he had found me hard to approach and too quick to move on to the next person; I suppose I was too much like the host at a drinks party who is always looking around to make sure everyone is happy. At a deeper level, I suppose I was too controlled, holding in my hurts and disappointments and so not finding it easy to be genuinely open. I think he found the other curate, Mark Moreton, more approachable, slower, quieter. I was somewhat surprised and hurt, as we had done so much together, but I was grateful to know the truth.

Almost my last duty was to introduce a concert. Standing in the pulpit I told the packed church that I was leaving the next week, but how good it was to be welcoming the London Bach Choir to sing St. Matthew's Passion, as it had inspired me more than any other music. I offered the concert and the work of St. Martin's in a prayer and returned to my seat for the opening chords ....

So ended the most stimulating, rewarding and humbling years of my life, carried by the tradition of Dick Sheppard and carried by the community of all the people who had committed themselves to St. Martin's and all it stood for, the caring, suffering, redeeming love of Christ, lived out in the centre of London.

Hugh Maddox

Posing "cool command".

At the Corpus May Ball.

With Jean Gurney (now Jean Mayhew), in a punt on the Cam
(from Cambridge Daily News).

With the lads and lasses at the steelworks.

Combined success with a pretty girl?

Unwinding at Arthur Lee's.

"Me mates".

The Duchess and Wilf at Carbrook Church House.

Hague (Before).

Hague (After).

The Grayson family.

With Mary at Canterbury Cathedral – my father in the background.

With Mary, Jamie, Anna and Sir Trenchard
Cox at St Martin-in-the-Fields

The Holocaust Museum, Jerusalem.

"Helping" Richard Gulliford on the farm.

George Bridle at West Morden

Holy Isle and Lamlash Bay from the garden of Gorton Jockey

On Green Island. Sarah MacLeod, Ellie King, Adam Carter, Wendy Carter and Don MacLeod

My mistress "Catherine"

"Oh, Shit!"

My 60th Birthday, with Mary Sabben-Claire and Jo Pope, of Green Island, at her swimming pool.

*With Bruce Randall, Restoring Corfe – he looks pleased at a crack
he has just made at my expense – No respect*

With Jamie, his friend Linda and my mother at a mere 103

Anna, Nooka, Casper at Jenny Goepel's Wedding

With Vici and St Martin's Overseas Club at Winterbourne, Kingston

Vici, daughter Catie & grandaughter Charlotte.

With Gary Bushett – now 18.

Chapter XVI

SANDWICH - my own Parish - Cinque Port - St.
George's Golf Club - difficulties - happy days - good
friends - Gorton Jockie - Israel

Sandwich is a fascinating town of about five thousand
souls. One of the Cinque Ports, in the thirteenth
century it was one of the great ports of England, second
only to London. It was always in danger of being raided by
the French, so its ancient streets zigzagged, so that no arrow
could be fired any distance. It was raided by a fleet from
Honfleur, and the mayor was killed; to this day his
successor wears black robes, a crow amongst the bright
plumage of royal scarlet at the annual garden party at
Buckingham Palace. It has three magnificent medieval
churches, and any number of fine merchants houses and
cottages; intriguing patterns of ancient red tiled roofs and
picturesque walled gardens. By the seventeenth century the
River Stour had silted up and Queen Elizabeth finally
refused help to clear it, in spite of many petitions; before
long, the great times of the port were over; by the

nineteenth century Sandwich had become a small, drab inwardly looking market town on the remote east coast of Kent, far from London.

Members of the prestigious Wimbledon Golf Club wanted a links course, so two members walked the south coast and chose the land lying between the town and the sea – now the Royal St. George's Golf Club, a Championship course. It had a very upper crust membership including the Astors and the Prince of Wales in the 20's and 30's, so by the time I became Rector in 1973, living in the big houses of Sandwich Bay and the Georgian fronted medieval houses in the town, was the court of St. James, weekending and retiring by the sea. There were so many members of the House of Lords that they were not even a rarity; also judges, diplomats, heads of famous schools, actors, journalists and well known sportsmen. There were also the townsfolk, shopkeepers, teachers, people working in all the usual jobs, and families living in the large council estate on the edge of the town where many of the old Sandwich families lived, serving the community and supporting the church. On the north bank of the river were three large industrial firms, Petbows, Haffendens and Pfizers which brought the families of bright young chemists into the area. All in all, it was a fascinating rich mix of humanity. It had a primary school, a secondary school and Sir Roger Manwoods, a part day, part boarding boys Grammar school. Sandwich still had its own Town Mayor and Town Council, was one parish, and apart from members of the Roman Catholic and United Reformed Churches, everybody in the town was my pastoral responsibility and every spiritual need came to my door and our church. It was a good parish, my first living, and I should have been very proud: but it seemed a quiet, distant corner of England after the vigorous, varied international life of St. Martin's, in the heart of London;

and, to start with, I was still feeling bereaved, but it did not take long for us to feel deeply at home with such lovely people and very grateful for living in such an amazing town.

St. Clement's is the magnificent medieval church set in the churchyard next to the Rectory, and has one of the finest Norman tower arches in England. I loved it. It was there that the Archbishop of Canterbury instituted me as Rector, with all the dignity of the Church of England service. Before going over to the Church he and Mrs Ramsey had a meal with us and the children in our new home.

Marjorie Graves had been brought up in Sandwich, went to London to learn typing and ended up teaching at Hosters. While there, she occasionally worshipped at St. Martin's. She retired to Sandwich and during the interregnum prayed earnestly for a new Rector who would bring more young life into the church. She was overjoyed at my appointment and gave me unqualified help and support, working as my secretary. Elderly Bertha Luckhurst was another gem; tall and thin, she knew what church life was really about. Peter Cranfield was a troubled teenager; occasionally he came to church and I would guide him to sit beside Bertha. She understood him and looked after him wonderfully. Even in her eighties, when there was a working party to tidy the churchyard, there was Bertha, with a little pair of shears in her hand. Every parish has a saint.

I worked closely with the town undertaker, Dave Collins, a chubby, cheerful and kind man. He had a small old Austin hearse, and as we wound our way to the Crematorium through the lanes of the East Kent countryside, I couldn't help thinking how different it was from St. Martin's, where a fleet of gleaming black limousines took us to Golders Green. Soon, of course, I came to enjoy the gossip with Dave as we went along; or I slept. Rather incongruously, in the middle of the farming countryside, were the pits and villages of the East Kent coalfield, where, in the twenties, unemployed miners from Scotland and Wales found work. Several times Sandwich benefited from the magnificent lilting Welsh voices of the Snowdon Male Voice Choir.

There was another moment when I was amused at the contrast with my former life on the staff of the Royal Parish Church on Trafalgar Square. It was when I was hiding in a cold dark brick outside lavatory of a country school, itching from the beard of my Father Christmas costume. Ho! Ho! Ho!

We had arrived in Sandwich shortly before Easter. I had changed the garage into a study, with a large window looking onto the garden. I was sitting at my desk on Easter Eve, trying to think of something to say for the following morning. The telephone rang; it was the mother of a friend. She told me that his seven year old daughter had died. I sat for a long time in heavy blackness of spirit before I wearily picked up my pen and tried to find something to say about Easter. It couldn't be anything trite and superficial, a happy message for Easter. I had to speak with integrity, thinking of my friend with every word I wrote. I can't remember what I finally struggled to say, but I know it was wrung out of me, slowly and with great difficulty. I hope that it was more profound than my original ideas; and I also hope that it may have helped some in the packed church next morning – people who were struggling with some tragedy or bereavement in their family. The following week I went to the funeral – heartrending.

Every Sunday evening I had a gathering of young people, sitting on the floor of my dimly lit study, some from the town and some from Sir Roger Manwoods, including a tall, fine-looking African boy who spoke perfect English. I noticed that colour of skin might seem to divide people, but a similar accent bonds even more strongly, whether public school or Brummie; I suppose it is a sign of a common background. After a few Sunday evenings the Head Boy of Manwoods and the Mayor's daughter started going out together – isn't that what the Church is for? Love, and all that sort of thing!

We had a Youth Service in the ancient church, and we danced up the aisle accompanied by guitars, drums and tambourines. St. Mary's was a redundant Church, a vast medieval space, with timbered roof and thin wooden columns. I got permission to run a Folk Club there and about a hundred and fifty young people came each night, from all around. I had my old friends from the Crypt Folk Club down to sing; but after some months they couldn't be bothered to come. Also, the rumour went round Church circles that drugs were being sold at St. Mary's – almost inevitable with a large gathering of young people in those days. Under pressure, I decided its days were over and we closed. Even so, the Club had given me a good reputation with the young. Bob Callaghan became a very involved and helpful teenage Church member and went on to ordination and is now national secretary for Inclusive Church

In my first few weeks at Sandwich, Mary had told me that she had heard some Manwood's boys commenting on our washing line – "The Vicar's knickers!" I was strangely hurt; they didn't yet know me, and I was no longer the hero curate of St. Martin's, but in their eyes, probably a pompous Establishment figure; but after a few meetings of the Folk

Club it was different. As Rector I was an ex-officio governor of Manwoods and at their Speech Day I filed in with the other local worthies to sit on the platform. The film 'If' had just been showing; it told of a rebellion in a boys boarding school where the Chaplain ran the Corps; the boys had seized the rifles and started firing at the self-satisfied old fellows on the platform. I scanned the hall for any sign of hidden weaponry; but when the Chairman formally welcomed me, the boys broke out into spontaneous applause – very gratifying; but as the years went by I merged naturally into the gang of worthies; the new boys had never heard of the Folk Club or the Head Boy and the Mayor's daughter.

I also used St. Mary's for a Nativity Play, acted by adults in full costume, showing that the story is not just "for the children"; with some really lovely music and the great space for slow moving processions it was impressive. The children gathered around the Christ Child to sing Away in a Manger, "no crying he makes" – but the real baby we had in the crib let out some lusty bellows. "Tears and smiles like us he knew" is better theology. When Good Friday came we had a traditional Passion Play with a large wooden cross, and Roman soldiers in full armour – by courtesy of Bermans, but now I had to pay for them. Again and again I tried to start another modern Passion Play, like 'Alive' but I just couldn't get motivated; but I did produce a few Gospel scenes role played by a cast of mixed ages, in modern dress. When we performed in St. Clement's Hall and the epileptic fell on the floor, Major Michael Archer started to go to help him, but Molly Barrett, sitting beside him, restrained him; she guessed it was part of the play. They were total strangers, but ended up getting married. Next door to St. Mary's was the King's Arms, and there, with the help of the hostess, Mrs Ann Bliss, we planned a Harvest Supper in the great church – a wonderful sight.

I tried to visit regularly on the estate, and always called immediately when I heard of a death. Before he retired, my predecessor had been old and ill, and had not had the strength to do the same, so these visits were much appreciated. One heart-rending funeral was for a baby – a burial in the churchyard; I shall never forget the wild sobbing of the young mother. Another time I heard that a teenager had been killed on his motor bike; I went straight round to the family; they were all gathered together in stunned silence in their council house sitting room. I hugged both father and mother and then listened to the horrifying details. Thank God, I didn't try to say anything, - because there was nothing to say. After some time the mother said, "But you know, Hugh, everybody's been so kind, not only the family but the neighbours as well". Over again, I realised that if I did not try to inject hope, somebody in the family would find love in themselves, and this hope was their Resurrection; but it took courage and patience for me to hold the silence ....on and on ....

When we arrived in Sandwich we took Jamie, then aged six, to the local primary school. I felt awkward standing at the school gates waiting for him. Was I a fellow parent, friend or Rector? Jamie was not happy there, and after some weeks we took him away and he went to a small prep school in the neighbouring village. It was difficult for me, as the Head Teacher of the primary school was a lovely man, Ralph Sage, a grandfather figure to many in the town and a member of my congregation. One of the estate mothers, also a churchgoer, told me that they all thought I was one of them, until we removed our son and sent him to a private school. Jamie's happiness was more important than parish strategy. Later we found him an even more imaginative school, where he sang in their very good choir. Some years later he became a weekly boarder, which was a mistake; quite apart from his feelings, I hated driving away from the school after taking him back on a Sunday night.

Mary was finding life difficult and was away for some weeks, searching for help with the difficulty of living with me (I won't be nauseatingly confessional, but even some of my good friends think that I might not be easy to live with!), she was also trying to find her own adult personality, not an Archdeacon's daughter or a Rector's wife. We went to Taize and Brother Roger suggested that we should have a time apart, and we agreed. It was a devastating and lonely time for both of us. Mary went regularly to the Westminster Pastoral Foundation, and I went to Austen Williams at St. Martin's for help. When I was working with him we would often arrange to meet at a certain time in the evening, and almost by tacit agreement, we would usually both be several minutes late. Now, I was waiting at his door ten minutes before the appointed time. I found it humbling. He also helped me find my own being, independent of my parents, who had come to the Rectory to help with the children. So began many years of seeking counselling, both for myself and for the family. Of course, as every priest hears confidences or confessions, we are all meant to have our own confessor, spiritual director, soul friend or whatever name is given by different church traditions. My nerves were often stretched to breaking point, trying to run the parish, going to London and looking after two small children, and uncertain of the future. Mercifully, at this stage I learnt again to weep, the natural and helpful release of pent up emotion, just as necessary for a man as a woman. In the eighteenth century a Frenchman wrote "There is no nation on earth so bellicose or lacrimose as the English." I imagine that it was Prince Albert who brought the harmful notion of the stiff upper lip – useful for running an Empire, but inhibiting in family life.

Several members of the congregation were of enormous help, bringing food and looking after the children. The wife of one of my friends had to stop taking them out, as town gossip said she was having an affair with me! Depressing. When driving, on the worst days of worry and lowness of spirit, the thought would occasionally flash through my mind, either in Sandwich or later in Dorset, that by just turning the wheel and crashing into an oncoming lorry, I could end it all. Thank God the thought passed quickly, but it was useful for me to have had a glimpse of that dark place where so many people live. The most helpful moment was when celebrating the Eucharist with my congregation; I offered the chalice to God, carrying all my worries with it. It must also have been sad for church people, who had had such high hopes of us. On the other hand, several parishioners loosened their stiff upper lips and shared their similar experiences. One day I was at a gathering at Canterbury Cathedral and was talking with a friend. He introduced me to the man next to him, who said,

"THE Hugh Maddox?"

With a grin, my friend echoed,

"Yes, THE Hugh Maddox!"

I nearly hit him. I did not feel I was a well known success any longer. At the end of the session, outside the Cathedral West door, a Canon told me of various liaisons of ecclesiastical people we knew well. It was bizarre, unreal and very disturbing. During those weeks, and at other bad times later, I couldn't settle to any work; I didn't have the heart to call on anybody, even if that would have put my own troubles in perspective. Instead, I would just walk aimlessly along the ramparts and return home feeling no better. After some weeks away, Mary made the brave decision to return to family and parish. With great relief we set off for our family holiday on Arran.

I could always talk confidentially with our doctor, John Greaves; he was also a member of my congregation, and we shared our difficulties very openly with each other: but I didn't want to bother him too often. We also worked together in trying to help his patients, my parishioners; he would often stop his open Peugeot to tell me of somebody he had just seen who needed some support and comfort. It was a good trusting, natural way of working together, doctor and parson, body and soul

I called him one night at four in the morning after Mary had been in agony. He was with us in minutes, and got her to hospital in an ambulance straight away, - for an emergency gall bladder operation; no keyhole surgery in those days. With recurring complications she was in hospital a lot at this stage; also a few years later she slipped a disc, through helping me move furniture, and was in traction for weeks. Once again, parishioners and family came to the rescue, but it was bewildering for the children and exhausting for me, as well as being painful and depressing for her; and, of course, she missed them desperately. Sometimes I was so tired that after I had driven to Canterbury for my long awaited visit, I would fall asleep in the chair by her bedside. Next time I tried to leave Sandwich early enough to have ten minutes sleep in the car before going into the ward as soon as visiting was allowed. One year Mary was in hospital for most of December. Jamie was about seven and, poor little boy, had to come with me to several Carol Services. The Church glowed with gentle candlelight and I announced the first carol; in the hushed silence which followed, a little voice from the front was heard piping up,

"Not once in bloody David's city AGAIN!"

Suppressed laughter throughout the Church.

We continued to stay with my father and mother at Broich for our annual holiday on Arran, but we longed to have our own home there. Much of the island and many of the houses were owned by the Hamilton family. In those days there were no estate agents in Scotland; houses to be sold were advertised in the local paper and went to the highest bidder in a system of closed bids in sealed envelopes, all to be opened on a specific date. We looked at Gorton Jockie, it had been a croft, with house, a byre for six cows and twenty acres of fields, all rented from the Hamilton Estate.

It was a typical white washed Highland house in a superb position, right on the shore, overlooking Holy Isle to the front and the village and hills to the right, and it was just two hundred yards from Broich; the fields had already gone back to the estate. The byre was probably the oldest building in Lamlash, long and low, built of stone; the slate roof came down to the top of the doors; it had probably been a dwelling for both the family and the cattle, before the house was built in the early 1800's. The house was damp, and people told us that on a rough night, the sea would come down the chimneys. Peter MacArthur came and looked at it for us; he immediately saw that all the damp was caused by a blocked rune, or gutter, so water had been pouring down the walls of a bedroom and kitchen beneath – repair the rune and all would be dry. We fell in love with

it and I went to the Factor and made "an offer of over
£7,000"; we really wanted it, so thought of £8,000, then
feared that somebody else might have had the same ides, so
I offered £8,050; the verbal offer was accepted, we shook
hands on it, I confirmed it in writing, and that was that.
There was a lot to be said for the old Scots system.

We returned home with great excitement; at last we had
a home of our own, a little part of Scotland. In the autumn
I enjoyed going down to the auction rooms on Sandwich
Quay to buy interesting second hand furniture. We hired a
good sized van, left the children with grandparents, and
after all the excitement of Christmas, set off North; Mary's
brother, Chris, came with us, bringing his girl friend, Rosie.
It was quite an adventure; we took it in turns to sleep in the
back, while three of us were in the cab. We drove through
the night, caught the early morning ferry, and with the
sunrise behind us, and the rose coloured glow on the snowy
mountains ahead, we sailed to Our Island. As soon as we
arrived at Gorton Jockie, tired and dirty, the first thing I did
was to strip off and plunge into the sea, much to the
amazement and delight of the others.   In the romantic
surroundings of a cold damp cottage by the shore, Chris
and Rosie became engaged, much to our joy. In later years
they were to return many times with their four wonderful
children, Jacob, Samuel, Miriam and Sebastian.

We went to Arran every year, and often went twice.
Slowly we made the house and garden our own. Once, we
had a mini sabbatical of five weeks on the island, which was
wonderful. Welcoming different families on the pier and
then waving goodbye to them a week later made us feel that
we lived on the Island. Peter and Isabel MacArthur always
remember one evening when they drank a bottle of whisky
with us, by candlelight, in the old kitchen with its ancient

wooden floor, and warmed by a fire in the small open Victorian grate – an evening dreams are made of.

On a Sunday morning I sometimes rowed across the Bay to join the two families in church. The tall tower of the kirk stood proud against the background of the hills, and as I moved over the calm waters of the sea, I could hear the clear notes of the carillion bells playing the tunes of the hymns we were going to sing; I could hear the words in my mind. What better way could there be of preparing for worship? For many years our Minister was Douglas Fulton, whom we knew well; his manner of preaching, praying and reading was straight and unadorned, full of perceptive human wisdom and dry wit. On the first Sabbath of our holiday I would often weep as the tensions of my own church responsibilities fell away from me; then I could hear the beauty of the Gospel afresh, shown in the stories of shepherds in the hills and of reformed villains from the Gorbals. In the Lord's Prayer, we learnt to say 'debts' instead of 'sins', and only one 'for ever' at the end – very Scots and plain and straight! We sat to pray, and I remembered the old taunt about the Episcopalians

> *Piskie, Piskie,*
> *Amen;*
> *On your knees,*
> *Then up again!"*

Years earlier, in Brodick, we had heard the Minister pray "And we also ask Thy blessing, O Lorrrd, on the puir people of England, which, as Thou knowest, O Lorrrd, lies a hundred miles to the south of us;" – just in case the Lord had forgotten where these poor, benighted people lived.

It was good having our own home, but also good being only a hundred yards from Broich, where my mother would always have a really good meal waiting for us when we arrived. Often we had drinks with them in the logie overlooking the sea and Holy Isle, bringing our guests with us, or meeting theirs. Whenever we left at the end of our holiday, my father and mother would see us off, waving a large bright towel until they were just tiny figures on the pier. Some years later, when my father was eighty, we all went for a walk above Lochranza; the track went up a gentle hill overlooking the loch, and then dropped down to the sea. When we reached the top of this small hill Father said it was enough for him, and he would make his way back to the car. We walked on, and after about a hundred yards turned, and looking back, we could see him outlined against the sky, looking out to sea; when we next turned and looked back, he had gone. We have always treasured the memory of that moment – the dear, gentle old man, standing peacefully and content, on his own, and then, a minute later, just the bare hill and sky.

Before we bought Gorton Jockie my father and mother nobly had both children while we had a week on our own, sailing on the Broads. They believed that it was important for a young couple to have time away together. We were very lucky. After Mary had suffered one long spell in hospital, we dipped into our capital and had a holiday in Morocco, - Tanzier, Marrakesh, Agadir – exotic, and our first experience of a bazaar.

One Boxing Day we were staying with Mary's parents and I answered their telephone, as they were out. A man asked if her father could lead another pilgrimage to the Holy Land, in a few weeks time. I knew he was already committed, and rashly offered myself; with some misgivings, they accepted – time was short. So, with enormous excitement, we prepared for our first flight to the land of Christ's birth, life and death. I couldn't believe it. I had to lead a party of forty, with both spiritual, pastoral and administrative duties. I took it very seriously, and halfway through I was exhausted and spent a day in bed – much to the relief of the harassed pilgrims! We had arrived at Jerusalem at night; the first sound we heard in the morning was a cock crowing over the city. The apostle Peter had denied that he knew Jesus – "the cock crew, Jesus looked at Peter, and Peter wept bitterly". The cock crow was followed by the call to prayer from the mosques all over the city – very Eastern and very evocative.

Over the years I led my own parties, from each of my three different parishes, arranging my own itinerary. Whenever possible, we walked through the fields or hills, or up the mountain stronghold of Masada, where the Jews held out against the Romans. When the soldiers finally scaled the height, they found the mountain top strewn with bodies. In defiance, and preferring death to slavery, every man had put his wife and children to the sword, before offering himself to the sword of his neighbour.

After the Romans had sacked Jerusalem, the Jews were scattered all over the Mediterranean; but with such stories of heroic resistance, they kept their national identity down the centuries, even to the present day of Holocaust and the founding of Israel. Our first guide was Hagai, an Isreaeli, and he fired us with the account of the 1967 war and the recovery of the Wailing Wall of the Temple. It was only on later trips that we saw the Palestinian refugee camps and heard the other tragic side of the story. I usually took our pilgrims to Yad Vachem, the Holocaust Museum; they came out, very silent; it was powerfully understated, with black and white photos of piles of teeth, shoes and spectacles. On my third visit we went round the new memorial to the million children who had been killed by the Nazis. We walked in darkness, the only light being that of electric candles; with the help of mirrors there were a million flickering little flames. The only sound was a recorded voice giving the names and ages of the children, "Jacob, aged nine……., his sister, Rebekah, aged six…….Mordecai, aged four……..Sarah, aged eight……..and on and on and on………….When we emerged, nobody spoke.

We went to the Church of the Nativity in Bethlehem; the only entrance was through a low door in the stone wall, probably built to keep out invaders on horseback, but our Arab Christian guide pointed out that even a king would have to stoop when going to the birthplace of the Prince of Peace. With awe and devotion we climbed down the narrow winding stone stairs of the small chapel made from the rock cave under the church, venerated from the earliest times as being the very spot where the Christ was born. We had a palpable sense of holiness, and some of our pilgrims knelt to kiss the many pointed silver star fixed to the stone floor, marking the place where millions of pilgrims have believed that God entered His world. We sang 'O come all ye faithful………. and it really was, 'O come', from all corners of the world, to this smooth stone floor, hallowed and worn by the feet of worshippers down the centuries. We had hardly started to sing when we heard the unwelcome clump of boots on the stairs and heard the sound of German voices. We flinched. One of our number visibly stiffened. He had suffered at German hands as a prisoner of war. As soon as these unwelcome newcomers were all in the cave, they joined us in the carol, singing, in German. Silence. Our former P.O.W., tears staining his old wrinkled face, stepped forward, slowly took the hand of the nearest German, and holding it firmly, looked into his eyes. No words came, and none were needed.

Historically, this may not have been the place of Jesus' birth, but for this pilgrim it was where Christ the Redeemer had brought peace and reconciliation to an embittered heart.

There is a good modern chapel on the hillside above the Sea of Galilee. It is called the Church of the Beatitudes, but why, oh why do we define and limit Jesus' spontaneous words by neatly labelling them with Latin definition?! I imagine Jesus sitting with his friends and closest followers; as he looks at them, with his deep compassion and keen insight, he encourages them with words, personal to each one of them. The word 'blessed' has lost some of its original Hebrew earthy power; it has become religious; so, speaking with a Scots accent, I would paraphrase his words. To a gentle, reconciling person he would say, "It'll be all right for you who make peace, for you'll be called the sons and daughters of God," and seeing a tearful widow, he would say, "It'll be all right for you who mourn – you'll be comforted." Pilgrims still talk of their memories of the immediacy of that moment on the hillside overlooking the Sea of Galilee. Once, when we returned to the Chapel itself, we saw a number of rifles stacked outside the door and heard African singing coming from within. Soon we were surrounded by black faces – in fact, from Fiji – men dressed in the pale blue of the United Nations. One of them had recently been killed while serving on a peacekeeping mission.

Each evening in our hotel we gathered in a circle to share our experiences, thoughts and feelings of the day. This could be very moving. Often the party would include somebody who would be complaining, attention seeking and difficult. After a few days she might break down, weep and tell us of some terrible thing which had happened to her lately. She would be amazed at the love and understanding which would then surround her; and she would be relaxed for the rest of the pilgrimage. For many pilgrims the whole journey could be very immediate and personal; for those who had only worshipped in a church, it was a new experience to pray and sing on a street corner, in a garden or a boat. We usually ended with a peaceful, healing celebration of Holy Communion in the gentle garden of the resurrection. It may not have been the actual place – it overlooked the Arab bus station, where the shabby old buses stood in stark contrast to our gleaming modern coaches; this earthed it in the life of the modern poor; but the garden did include a stark rock face reminiscent of a skull – Golgotha – and also a first century tomb. For us, anyhow, it brought the peace and victory of the Risen Christ.

In all, I took eight pilgrimages to Israel. They involved a lot of work and organisation beforehand; once we had met at the airport I was tour leader, spiritual guide and pastor. It was demanding, but inspiring, and friends always helped me with the different tasks.

In those days the tension between Arab and Jew was not so great, but even so, we were very aware of the difficulties and injustices. Our groups were mostly middle aged and elderly, and usually only included a few men. Even so, we had a lot of fun, especially when eating, drinking and dancing; but I did dream of leading a pilgrimage of young men, sleeping rough and walking from town to town, but sadly I never turned the dream into reality.

Back in Sandwich the bond between the pilgrims remained strong, and during Holy Week, faces in the congregation lit up at the mention of the places in the Holy Land which we had visited.

On both Easter Sunday and Christmas Day the church was packed, the golfing weekenders attending in force. Each Mayor asked me to be his or her Chaplain and I said prayers at the meetings of the Town Council. The Cinque Ports ceremonies were approached with mock seriousness; the Essex port of Brightlingsea was one of our Limbs, and each year its Councillors came to Sandwich and solemnly paid their dues of five shillings and seven pence into an ancient horn. I went with Bill Chesterfield when he was Mayor when the Queen Mother visited Dover Castle as the Lord Warden of the Cinque Ports. We were then driven to the Town Hall for formal luncheon, and the crowds cheered us just because we were in the Royal cavalcade. It was fun waving back. On another occasion I joined the MP, the Mayor, Town Councillors and others to bless the new and much needed Sandwich By-pass. After my solemn blessing the traffic started to flow, but before we had moved, a lorry had overturned. No wonder that people looked worried when I said I would pray for them! I felt that one of my sad duties was to prop up the Mayor in the weeks after his or her term of office had come to an end. They suddenly had to adjust from being the Queen's representative in the town to being an ordinary citizen once again.

Remembrance Sunday was always a moving occasion. The band of Manwood's School marched through the streets – boys not much younger than those who had been killed. With the Mayor and Councillors we processed from the ancient Guildhall to the town square. I knew most of the people who stood there, and knew of the tragedies that lay behind their drawn faces. We then went to the church for the service and ageing Richard Denison-Pender spoke the immortal words, "They shall grow not old, as we that are left grow old................" I have never heard them spoken with greater dignity and feeling.

One of our congregation was Jim Swanton, the famous cricket commentator, whose deep and dignified voice had been known throughout the world – or at least the cricketing world – for generations. Each summer the choir of St. Martin's came to sing Evensong, and Jim and Ann gave them all tea in their lovely garden beforehand. Ben, the crucifer and keen cricketer, held out his hand after we had left, saying that he was not going to wash it, as he had just shaken hands with Jim Swanton! Jim had been in a Japanese P.O.W. camp and had been upheld by his Anglo Catholic faith. Because of his grave manner, he was known amongst some of his friends as the Archbishop of Canterbury! I asked him to be my Churchwarden; he was genuinely touched and humbled – apparently it meant more to him than many of his sporting honours. He was most supportive, but I was also somewhat apprehensive when I opened one of his letters or heard his voice on the telephone. He had high standards and with a mixture of decent respect for his Rector and firmness as in a headmaster, would comment on any church slovenliness or heresy. We had many meals with them, and I was impressed by the way in which, after a weekday lunch, he would return to his study and typewriter. He was disciplined. He also had a phenomenal memory, not only for cricket scores from years ago, but also for the appropriate anecdote or quotation, usually linked to the well known name of a friend of his. Amongst many others, John Major held him in great respect. His kind and lovely wife,

Ann, died shortly before him, and dear Jim heaved himself up to the lectern and read a Biblical passage about heaven; he made it sound more real than the earth. Although he was already weakened by cancer, Robert Runcie, former Archbishop, gave a magnificent tribute at Jim's funeral – they clearly knew each other very well.

One of the doctors in the town was Dick Richards, a merry and free thinking practitioner, who ran sex therapy sessions as well as conservative medicine. Like many other friends they rented Gorton Jockie for a holiday. They enjoyed themselves, but he pointed out that the springs of our brass Victorian bed squeaked when he and his lively wife, Pixie, put the therapy into practice. As I say, he was a swashbuckling character, and somehow got mixed up in a crime in the United States, for which he was imprisoned for a few years. I think we tried to keep in touch with him and also support Pixie in Sandwich, but with hindsight we should have done more. We saw him again, in Dorset, where he turned up with a cartridge belt around his waist and a gun in his hand – he had a share in a local shoot.

Sandwich is a small town and we often met each other wearing different hats, so to speak. At one party our doctor asked his friend, the Town Clerk and Solicitor,

"How can I stop my patients coming up to me at a party and telling me their symptoms?" "Next morning send them a bill for professional advice."

The following day the doctor received a bill for £5 from the Solicitor, "for professional advice given at a party"!

Of course most of my time in Sandwich was taken up with the ordinary round of parish life, Sunday services, christenings, weddings and funerals, church meetings, and regular visiting in the cottages and council estate of the town, looking after the mixed congregation, trying to care for those in trouble, go to the schools, appear at town functions, and generally show the flag. I also became Chairman of the Sandwich Youth Club, up on the estate. One of our keen Church youth workers started a social evening for the Church youngsters. I discovered it was on the same night as the town Youth Club, and all hell broke out. Some of the Youth Club members threatened to break up the church social; even my most loyal friends and supporters on the Youth Club committee felt I had betrayed them and said I should resign as Chairman straight away. I persuaded them to let me stay until the next A.G.M. a few months away. I felt hurt and misunderstood – I had not been aware of the clash of dates, and, anyhow, I thought there was ample room in the town for both groups. For some weeks I went about the town, dejected, and feeling that everybody was looking at me critically. I was not popular with all the Church people either – some did not like my new ideas.

Over the years fewer of the robed town councillors came to the civic services; they did not like my preaching left-wing sermons at them!

Happier times were the visits from St. Martin's and our return excursion to London, when we filled a coach with people and sacks of toys for the St. Martin's Christmas tree and magic carol service. We continued the visits to High Beeches and gave hospitality to single parent groups. Under the guidance of the Kent Industrial Chaplain, I regularly visited the three large factories to the north of the town, Pfizers, the pharmaceutical form, Petbow's engineering and Haffendens rubber works; it was a different and interesting world. I don't know that my visits achieved much, but they did seem to be appreciated by my parishioners who worked there – it helped me understand an important part of their lives. Once, a stranger, in blue overalls, came up to me and belligerently asked me, "Is it true that you make your parishioners pay for your holidays?" I was dumfounded, and only later did the penny drop. Often at a Church raffle I would joke, "The profits, of course, to the Rector's holiday fund!". Somebody must have taken me seriously.

We often went to the beach at Sandwich Bay. We either drove, or walked by the river, over the fields and across the Golf Course. I loved the sand dunes and wide open skies of the East coast. When in London we had gone to the Boat Show, and for £99 I had bought a Mini-sail; on the way home we had launched it in the fountain of Trafalgar Square. It's first proper outing, later in January, was in Newhaven Harbour, and I was careering about, trying to get the hang of things, when the rudder fell off. I nearly capsized, and when I looked up I saw one of the cross channel ferries approaching. In fact, the rudder was in the water, still tied on by a piece of twine, and I managed to get back to the beach. After a time we swapped the Mini-sail for a Skipper, a plastic 12' dinghy on a trailer, and had many a happy Sunday afternoon, sailing from the beach or up the river.

Many of our neighbours played a very high standard of golf, at St. George's, so I was too daunted to pick up a club again myself – I hadn't played in Sheffield or London. One day we were walking on the golf course at Blackwaterfoot on Arran and I was inspired to start again. I wasn't good enough for St. George's, and anyhow, you had to be invited to join; I knew which members of my congregation belonged to the Club, because they often wore the tie. The story goes that many years ago an Australian millionaire put in to join, but was blackballed, and so built his own championship course further along the dunes instead, Princes. I easily joined, was given lessons by the pro and, as Rector, a much reduced subscription. I played a lot, became as good as I ever shall be, and loved it. On my day off, a weekday, the course was not crowded, the sun shone, the sea sparkled, larks sang, and often I drove a 250 yard drive. I also played St. George's many times, at the kind invitation of friends; Tony Johnson often asked me and helped me slow down my swing. Some members played a two ball foursome, moving very fast; trying to hack my way out of a bunker, it was daunting to see four golfers and four caddies bearing down on me.

While I was at Sandwich the Open was held at St. George's, and occasionally I would watch a top professional play a difficult hole in four, when only a few weeks earlier, by sheer fluke, a long putt of mine had dropped into the hole for three. The pure, noble white and red flag of St. George fluttered against the perfect green of the grass and the sea danced with white waves. It is such moments of sheer joy that make us indifferent golfers persevere with a game that can be so infuriating.

When I first came to Sandwich as Rector, I gathered that my predecessor but one, was a popular man, but was fond of alcohol. My predecessor was a disciplined man, perhaps appointed to redress the balance?! With my arrival the pendulum began to swing back. I could visit all the houses within the walls on foot, so there was no fear of drink driving. The people living in the lovely old houses were very hospitable, and knowing my love for Scotland, poured me enormous whiskies – all their fault of course! After a few pastoral visits I might wobble home, very happy. One Boxing Day there was a good noonday drinks party near the

Rectory. Our wise and kindly retired priest, Charles Craft, pointed out to me that I only just managed to navigate the wide open door. I arrived home, not only very merry, but very late for lunch. In exasperation, Mary poured all the gravy over my head and onto the jacket she had given me for Christmas. I was duly repentant, but only for a while.

Once the children were at school, like many young mothers, Mary felt that she needed a new dimension to her life. After much encouragement from me and her brother Chris, she went to Kent University for a degree in Art and Movement studies. She worked very hard, hugely enjoyed it and did very well. Later she did a P.G.S.E. and taught at Betteshanger, an Adult Education Centre and Honiton House School, as well as selling her paintings in her own exhibition. She was also a great help to me in the parish, listening wisely to my worries, and picking up important news of parishioners when we were at any gathering. Her gentle manner helped people open up about their troubles; this was more important than running church organisations.

I knew one family who lived on the estate – their children went to the playgroup. She left her husband, and I went to see her in a caravan she was renting, to try and reconcile them – very noble of me, I thought. A few days later I met her husband in the street and he wisely advised me not to go again, as she was telling everybody about my visit, putting a very different construction on it! Looking back, I realised the significance of her giving my hand a special squeeze when we were dancing in a circle in the Church Hall.

In the last few years at Sandwich we received much real support and inspiration from the weekly study group.

Amongst those regularly attending were Alister and Beryl Hoda. They had a baby son, Alexander, and I baptised both him and his father in the Sunday parish Eucharist. Wearing my full vestments, I gave Alister a bear hug – a new addition to the liturgy for the congregation at St. Clement's. There were also many, many other people of whom I was very fond and who did so much for the Church. I inherited our tiny, thin, elderly part-time verger, Jessie Harris; she was full of spirit, and rattled her bunch of keys if the sermon was too long. If anything had gone wrong, she would say, in a cheerful voice, "You can't win, Rector, you can't win". If we had just finished a wonderful service in a packed Church, she would rattle her keys and cheerfully say,

"You can't win, Rector, you can't win!"

Very true.

I used a visual aid at a Family Service, to illustrate Jesus' saying "Hide not your light under a bushel". I held a torch in one hand, and covered it with a bucket with the other – very clear and memorable, but I could not understand why the congregation were grinning; the bucket was made of yellow plastic, and the light shone through it!

Throughout my time I received much help from Peggy Rossiter, our wise, humble, gentle Churchwarden and Jim her husband, ascetic, sensitive, creative. One morning the telephone rang after breakfast; in great distress they told me of sad family news which had just arrived in the post. I was touched and humbled, and only wished that other troubled people could have asked for my help in the same way.

A letter arrived from the Bishop of Dover, Dick Third, asking me to meet the Churchwardens of St. Peter-in-Thanet, Broadstairs, with a view of being their Vicar. It is a parish of about sixteen thousand, and one of the most thriving in the diocese, with two curates, a retired priest and lay readers, a brand new hall with an efficient parish office, verger and secretary. To be offered this post was a boost to my ego, but it was also rather daunting, and anyhow, if we had to leave Sandwich, we wanted to go west. When another Vicar in Thanet heard of the offer, he said, in a discouraging voice, "Oh, they're trying to get you to take it on now, are they?!" Before I had even met anybody, I got the impression that there were the problems of success; but both wardens were humble men and I gathered that they needed somebody with a gentle approach, so when I accepted, it was with spiritual arrogance – the greatest danger of all – a real "holier than thou!" attitude. When I told the Sandwich P.C.C. that we were leaving, Dave Collins said, "Oh yes, we knew already". I was startled as we had not said anything to anybody. His fellow undertaker had seen our old brown VW camper van parked outside St. Peter's Vicarage.

Our final big occasion before leaving Sandwich was a televised Songs of Praise for the BBC. It was based on our wonderful Harvest Supper in the magnificent medieval space of St. Mary's Church. Some of the hymns were chosen by a girl shepherd, a fisherman and a coal miner, and of course, all the town churches were involved. We sat, with our Wardens and wives, at the high table where the altar would have been. I had a short speech of welcome prepared, but during a wait before filming began, the producer asked me to tell the viewers what it was all about, so, off the cuff, I described the meaning of a Harvest Festival. When I had finished, Jim Swanton turned to me, and said, "That was brilliant broadcasting" – high praise indeed; but also full marks to the producer who had created the occasion for me to speak naturally. It was broadcast the following Sunday. What a way to end our nine years at Sandwich!

There had been times of great anxiety and sadness, but also times of much caring support, wonderful services, interesting people, and many, many happy family occasions, in our garden, on the beach or on walks in the countryside, not to mention all the parties! The most encouraging farewell was from Gordon Chapman; he had not always approved of my modern ideas, but said,

"I don't suppose that the people of Sandwich have ever been so loved by their Rector". You can see why I thought I was such a wonderful chap; and I can see the devil rubbing his hands in anticipatory glee.

Chapter XVII

ST. PETER-IN-THANET, BROADSTAIRS -
promotion? - great moments - my father - pride and fall

The old town and harbour of Broadstairs are full of character, with Georgian houses, cliffs and beaches where we spent many happy hours. The huge parish of St. Peter's encircled the town parish and had a complete variety of houses, many of them beautiful, in lovely surroundings. It also had a golf course. St. Peter's is a magnificent medieval church; Victorian additions reflected the nineteenth century respectability of its congregation; I would have liked to re-order some of the church but it was much loved and well cared for. Many of the staff, leading lay people and members of the congregation were deeply committed, caring Christian people.

I was instituted by the Bishop of Dover; I felt a mixture of pride and inadequacy – a considerable, daunting task lay ahead of me. Just before the service the Bishop had met my mother, and in his address he referred to her when he said, "I can see, now, from where Hugh gets those twinkling eyes, known to millions" – laughter, but only from those who had seen Songs of Praise the week before! At the bun-fight afterwards, there were poignant moments when I was greeted by people from Sandwich, bidding me farewell and good luck, their eyes and whole bodies expressing profound emotion, which I returned, without effort. The next instant their place would be taken by a friendly member of St. Peter's, welcoming me; but perhaps we had never met before and inevitably the feeling in me was less powerful and it required a colossal effort of will to switch immediately. This was a vignette of clergy life – taking both a funeral and a wedding on the same day.

After we had moved into St. Peter's Vicarage, but before my institution, we had a short holiday – vital to begin the process of breaking from Sandwich, where we had received so much deep love and support over nine years, a kind of bereavement, which we needed to work through before being totally committed to St. Peter's. In fact, this took more than a year; it was made more difficult because we were only about ten miles away, and during Sandwich's interregnum I was called back several times, especially for the funerals of people whom I had known well.

Behind all this, of course, lies the old dilemma for any priest of achieving the right balance between detachment and involvement. On the one hand, the priest should find his refreshment coming from his own prayers with God, the guidance of his confessor or spiritual director, the friendship of other clergy, and if married, the love and support of his family. This detachment means that he is available to all, rich or poor, intelligent or slow; it means that he is trustworthy and can make unpopular decisions when necessary, because he does not need to be popular with everybody all the time. It also means that he is pointing people away from himself and towards God; it avoids the personality cult. However, I found this approach difficult, because I do so like to be loved! I also react against the wrong sort of detachment, which can appear distant, cold and superior.

On the other hand, there is another approach, more relaxed and more human, when a priest is truly involved with his people, allowing his feelings to be stirred, so that he can "rejoice with them that rejoice and weep with them that weep". This approach allows for a natural growth of warmth and mutual friendship, with the priest admitting that he is vulnerable, needing and sometimes asking for help from his parishioners, which usually they are only too willing to give – as in the hymn:

> *Brother, sister, let me serve you,*
> *Let me be as Christ to you;*
> *Pray that I may have the grace to*
> *Let you be my servant too.*
>
> *I will hold the Christlight for you*
> *In the night-time of your fear;*
> *I will hold my hand out to you,*
> *Speak the peace you long to hear.*
>
> *I will weep when you are weeping;*
> *When you laugh I'll laugh with you.*
> *I will share your joy and sorrow*
> *Till we've seen this journey through.*

This is the way that I followed, both by inclination and with conscious thought. Of course, it can lead to favouritism, an inner clique around the Vicar, leaving others feeling left out; and also it can lead to a loss of godly detachment when needed.

St. Peter's Vicarage was a modern five-bedroom house, larger than usual, because of the importance of the parish? In the garage was a gleaming bright red Sunbeam Talbot, almost new; it was for our sole use, both parish and personal – it was quite a factor in making our decision! Once, driving to the golf course, I stopped suddenly, and a car bumped into me from behind; there was no great damage, but the car lost its value, and was no longer perfect – prophetic, in a way.

I inherited two curates. Before ordination Michael Burgess had been on the stage; he was a committed priest, had run the parish in the interregnum and helped me settle in before moving on a few months after my arrival. The other Michael had been a teacher; he was also totally committed and competent; this was his second curacy, and he was to be in charge of St. Andrew's, our daughter church. It must have been difficult for him; he had been appointed by my predecessor, John de Saumarez, a great and good man who had led the parish for many years. Michael had only arrived a few weeks before me; he had to make his mark and at the same time adjust to a different kind of Vicar.

I initiated a weekly staff meeting which included the readers and Sally, our wonderful verger – she loved St. Peter's and served it well. An issue arose about a parish function, Michael wanted a change, on spiritual principles; I was very doubtful and consulted the churchwardens who were quite sure everybody wanted to stick to the established pattern. At our next staff meeting I told Michael that we had decided not to change. Michael was critical, and continued to press his case. I warned him that I was getting angry; but he went on; I finally exploded, swore and told him to shut up. Stunned, shocked silence. I was not strong, confident and wise, but unsure of myself and still finding my way; I could not cope with such a strong challenge to my authority. Word went quickly round the parish that I had sworn at Michael. Many months later he told me that he had never been spoken to like that before; but he gave the impression that it had made him think. But it didn't do me much good.

Early on in my time at St. Peter's Michael Burgess told me of a sad death in the parish. My immediate reaction was to go and see the family; but in his next breath told me that he knew them and would be taking the funeral. I held my tongue and realised that I now had to share my ministry with other priests and theologically educated lay people, very different from my role in Sandwich. In my daily way of working, I was behind St. Peter's, where the implications of lay-led ministry had been thought through and acted upon for years.

I inherited a baptismal policy which required the parents to attend a course before their child was baptised, and a promise of full church commitment afterwards. I was doubtful, but sincerely tried to operate this policy, which was new to me. I found that it left people feeling hurt, inadequate and rejected by the Church. Whatever the theological reasons, they felt that their child was not good enough to be baptised – the opposite of the gospel which says that God loves us as we are, and we do not have to earn his favour. I tried this policy, and slowly abandoned it, returning to a way of open baptism, gladly welcoming anybody who wished to bring their child to be christened. All too often I have had to absorb the hurt caused by priests who have adhered to a "strict baptismal policy". Sadly, I undermined some of the activities at St. Peter's by bringing in my own ideas which made it difficult for the lay leaders.

However, there was a very good response to my introduction of Quest, a well designed programme for Church teenagers. We had about six groups, each with two adult lay leaders and we all had great times; and there were large numbers for Confirmation. Almost by chance, one of my first visits was to Wyndham and Joy Hughes-D'Aeth; they welcomed me like an old friend; I immediately felt at home as I sat in their comfortable, faded armchairs and drank their whisky. They were also new arrivals in the parish and were deeply committed to church and the care of people. Joy lived up to her name with a lovely smile; she was wise and deep. Two of their six children, the youngest daughters, came to my group of Quest and I was told that my open and questioning approach to faith saved them from too violent a teenage rebellion. One of their elder brothers was Jonathan, whom I met several times. Needless to say, there were many other totally dedicated members of St. Peter's, including Olive and Margaret who took good care of us

I was not good at making decisions; I often took them spontaneously and failed to consult leaders who would be affected indirectly by my latest enthusiasm. Sally, our verger, asked if she could use some of our large garden to grow vegetables. I readily agreed, but over the weeks I just couldn't decide how many rows of carrots I wanted to grow, and so how much space she would have! Naturally, she gave up! One Palm Sunday I was getting ready to go over to the Church at 9.30 for the 10.15 service; a breathless churchwarden came to find me; I had forgotten that the clocks had just gone forward. The choir and congregation seemed amused – or most of them did.

There was a very good prep school in Broadstairs, Wellesley House, where I preached quite often. I knew the

Headmaster who was a good friend of Jim Swanton, and he agreed with me that I did not seem at home at St. Peter's, and did not preach as well as I had at Sandwich. We agreed that I may have suffered from over-promotion, as often happens. There was also a Social Security house for old men, where I did feel at home! I also visited a home for very mentally handicapped youngsters. I went to their joyful Christmas party, took very simple services and blessed each boy and girl as they lay, helpless and uncomprehending, in bed. I felt that this confirmed their spiritual worth, and was encouraging for the staff. One day, on returning to the Vicarage, I was greeted by our retriever, Barnie; he gave me a great welcome and in the course of the day, was able to express every emotion just as well as the most handicapped of the children. I no longer believe that we have souls but animals do not – we are far too similar, and are all of spiritual worth.

At Sandwich we had bought James an adorable Labrador puppy, whom we named Harry. When we were at St. Peter's, James, aged about fourteen, had a friend to stay, and the two of them took Harry for a walk. They came home desperately worried, as Harry had slipped his collar and disappeared. Later he was found dead by the electric railway line. The boys were up half the night making a coffin; the undertaker was very good in fetching him and burying him in our garden. It was Holy Week, and at a service in Canterbury Cathedral I told the Archbishop, Robert Runcie, of our family distress; he took it seriously.

I arranged a one-day Conference for sixth-formers from different schools in the town. The most memorable speaker was a young Jewish rabbi, a swashbuckling character, with flowing black locks and long black boots, very attractive to the students. He gave a plausible and compelling account of Jesus of Nazareth, the greatest of Jewish prophets; as a Jew he seemed to understand Jesus better than we did – and there was no need to attempt to define his divinity.

I was automatically a governor of St. George's Secondary School, but fortunately not Chairman, as my predecessor had been. The meetings seemed rather aimless and discouraging. There was also a Church Primary School near St. Peter's, and I was the ex-officio Chairman of Governors; I think I was able to give good support to the Head Teacher and also helped to get new lavatories for the children. There had been much procrastination by the authorities, so we called in our M.P., Jonathan Aitken, and I got to know him. He was at the height of his career then, but later he was in prison because he had lied about his expenses. While there he became a more deeply committed Christian, and has written about his experience. I met him again at St. George's Golf Club and he told me that Jim Swanton had come to visit him in prison. Jim was nearly ninety, and I was ashamed that I had not made a similar effort.

Edward Heath had been a choirboy at St. Peter's and I was told that he still attended occasionally. The only time I met him was when I took the funeral service at Barham for one of his family. Even with his family around him he seemed to be a lonely figure. Mary played the cello at one of the concerts he conducted, and had a hand written letter of thanks. Years later, he gave a lecture to the Salisbury clergy on religion and politics. He spoke like a statesman, especially in his long term vision for Britain's place in Europe.

One spring I was in bed for nearly a fortnight with 'flu – the real thing. I got better just in time to lead our parish trip to the Holy Land. We arrived at our hotel in Jerusalem;

after dinner I got the pilgrims settled and was telling them about the next day's visits, when a porter came to tell me that my sister was on the telephone. She told me that my father had died, suddenly and peacefully. I heard the full details when we got home, but it was a terrible shock, as he was quite fit and well when we left. I immediately told the travel company; but kept the news from the pilgrims until a replacement leader was ready to be flown out; mercifully, Mary was with me, and I could share my shock with her; she also was devoted to my father. I told the pilgrims on the Mount of the Ascension; they were deeply disappointed that we were leaving them, but also were very loving and helpful. Even in our short time in Israel I had been able to share some of my special insights about the life of Christ; the whole experience drew everybody close together.

A return flight was arranged, and we went straight to Sussex to be with my mother, Colin and Alison. I heard how my father had been sitting one evening by the fire in the library, and had suffered a short blackout, but he quickly recovered. He thought he was quite well, but my mother insisted on keeping him in bed next morning, and sent for the Doctor; he examined my father, and pronounced him well. My father asked him "Is it all right for us to fly to Jamaica on Thursday?" "Yes, certainly". "Good", said my father, "because Amy does need a rest," – and died. It was a massive clot on the brain. He was 82. A few months earlier he had had a fall in the woods, and was in hospital for a few days. I was able to be with him and saw him looking frail. Mercifully, the last time I had seen him was at a gentle day we had spent at Lloyd Square, and he stood at the door, waving us off, with a lovely smile on his dear face.

Shortly after we arrived back at High Beeches I ran down the paddock in front of the house, full of regret that I had not seen more of him in the past months and shouted "Sorry, Father, sorry". Then it was as if I saw his face, to my right, looking much younger, and saying, "It's alright, it's alright!" I was immediately reassured, and never had any regrets later. I've always felt him near me and even closer than when he was alive.

I use the phrase, "as if" I saw him. Later I realised that those words are often used in the Bible to describe somebody's unique mystical experience – "as if it were the appearance of the likeness of a lion". It wasn't imagination, and yet nobody else could have seen my father's smiling face in the air. It was an unforgettable unique experience, somewhere between those two descriptions; and it did bring about a lasting change in me. In religious writing, all too often pious people use definite language to describe something which cannot be put into words; they even talk about the absolute mystery of God as if they knew what they were talking about! This makes it very difficult for the literally minded, used to technological definitions and not familiar with the language of myth, poetry, mysticism, and personal experience.

The shock for my mother was appalling – they had been so, so close, He had a lovely funeral at their church in Coleman's Hatch, and Eva, his cousin and sister-in-law, gave an inspiring, amusing and appreciative address; she ended with abrupt, controlled passion, saying, "It was a good way for him to go, but it was not good for me. I shall miss him dreadfully-every day". Then she stumped back to her pew. This made a deep impression on me – so much better than finishing with a pious platitude.

In the summer we buried his ashes in the Kilbride graveyard above Lamlash, overlooking the hills and the sea. His stone gives his full name, Edmund Theodore Maddox, and the words "A lovely life". Later in that week on Arran, we went on our walk above Lochranzar, and in our mind's eye we saw him standing on that gentle hill top – and then he had gone. The worst time was when our steamer slowly pulled out from Brodick pier, and my mother stood alone waving a towel, not two figures, but one, becoming tinier and tinier as the ferry steamed to the mainland.

It was about five years before her grief began to lift, but in all that time, and up to the age of ninety-eight, she had a stream of guests, of all ages, at Broich.

Back to St. Peter's. After about two years there, Michael was about to leave, to be the Vicar of his first parish. The Bishop sent me Simon Franklin to be a possible successor. We got on well from the very beginning; he has a delicious sense of humour, a warm, open, engaging manner and a faith in God that was integrated with life. Thank God, he and his delightful young wife Ann agreed to come; he got on well with Mary, James and Anna and seemed to be thoroughly at home with us. It was a great relief and I really looked forward to working with him. About this time some of the lay leaders alerted the Bishop that I might be heading for a breakdown because of strain. I was sure I was not, but I certainly was finding life difficult. I had made some bad decisions, was muddled and disorganised, had hurt some key figures and had to withdraw from others to whom we had become too close. Shortly before, the leaders had taken the Quest teenagers away for a Church weekend. One of the fifteen year old girls came back with a love bite on her neck; her parents were angry that I had allowed it to happen, and were angry that I was not worried. They spread alarm among other parents.

The Bishop came to see us, in a kindly and caring way; he suggested that we should immediately have a fortnight's leave. We went to our old Sandwich friends, John and Judy Henderson, who had a small farm on the edge of Dartmoor, and then we had a week on our own in Dorset, staying in a cottage in Carey on the edge of Wareham. On the way back we stopped at Abbotsbury, and as we looked up at the chapel on the hill, Mary said, "That's up there, just for its own sake; perhaps that is something you need to remember – doing things and leading worship for its own sake, not looking sideways for other people's reactions" – a useful reminder for all clergy. We had no idea whether we would ever come to Abbotsbury again.

Shortly after our return to St. Peter's the Bishop came to see us again. In the interval he gathered that parishioners' worries about me had grown, and very gently, he advised me to resign. It never occurred to me to refuse and fight: I know that he cared for us as well as for the parish. I have always found that if I have been open with the Church authorities they have been understanding, kind and supportive; it saddens me to hear of battles between bishops and clergy. A week or two later he sent me the resignation papers to sign, if I was still willing. That was a very painful moment; there is no signing of papers when a Vicar moves to another parish or retires, so I took my pen in hand with a heavy heart and a sense of failure.

The Bishop asked me to go and see him in Canterbury several times; sometimes he just listened for an hour while I poured out my story and my feelings. He wisely asked me to write down and show him a list of things which had gone well. There were nearly fifty items, which was encouraging. I think the Bishop felt partly responsible for my difficulties, as he had asked me to take on the parish; he said that I could go on Sabbatical leave, on full pay, until I found another post, and that he would give me a good reference. He had heard that the Theological College of the Scottish Episcopal Church in Edinburgh were looking for an honorary chaplain for the summer time, and we gladly followed up his suggestion.

He chose a very wise way of announcing our departure to the congregation. He decided to come to the daughter church, St. Andrew's, to licence Simon Franklin as their curate and tell them then. I was in the vestry with all the Wardens and choir before the service. Some of them knew what was going to happen and some of them guessed that something was in the air. For me it was a time of terrible tension which I shall never forget. In his address the Bishop said that I had been under great stress, and he was giving me Sabbatical leave ....but at the end of it I would not be coming back. Many of the congregation were shocked and dismayed as they were profoundly grateful for the help I had given them.

We could have left straight away, but I wanted to see Simon settled, I also wanted to celebrate another Christmas, and, to be honest, I wanted the Vicar's board in the Church to give my name and the dates 1981-1984, instead of 1981-1983 which would have been too much of a giveaway to posterity. We paid the price of having a few extra weeks of gut-wrenching tension, but it was worth while, even if only for one poignant memory. The annual Christingle service was a wonderful event, with over five hundred present, mostly families. Simon gave the children's talk, with jokes, visual aids and an easy manner, with throw away jokes at his own expense. We were both wearing our golden copes, and as he came down the pulpit steps, I smiled, and said to the congregation, "He's a fool, isn't he?!" Simon came to me, put his hands round my neck, and pretended to throttle me. The congregation loved it, and afterwards one perceptive person said, "It's a real shame that you are leaving now, because you two really get on, don't you?"

One day he was at the Vicarage and saw me preparing to go visiting; as I was putting on my battered old green cap he said, "Yes, that's what it's all about! Some people love you for being so laid-back, but others don't think you are 'a proper Vicar'" Yes, we could have worked together and overcome some of the difficulties, but it was too late. I had also prepared for my last PCC very carefully, everything was thought out and organised. I chaired it firmly, and one of the wardens, loyal to the end, said, "What a pity that you couldn't take all the meetings like that – it went well."

I was determined not to slink away and on the evening of Epiphany, 6th January, I celebrated a Choral Eucharist with a full church; although some of those most worried or hurt by me wisely were away. In my sermon I used the three gifts of the Kings to highlight the faults in Church life, hinting all too obviously at St. Peter's – no hint of an apology for the hurts and disappointments I had caused, - spiritual arrogance to the end. They gave us a handsome cheque at the farewell party afterwards; I did, at least, thank them for all their love and support, followed by goodbyes, often tearful, from everybody as they left. It was difficult for Mary, as she had settled at St. Peter's, had made friends and led a full life with her music and painting – she had had a successful exhibition; but it was also a relief for her.

All our furniture went in store, and we set off with the car heavily laden for all we needed on Sabbatical. We even packed a sack of coal; the car began to limp, and we turned off to stay the night with our dear friends, the Hodas, outside Sandwich. We drove away from the Vicarage with much sadness, a sense of failure, but also profound relief that all the tension was over. I felt that God, through his Bishop, had rescued us from ourselves.

Chapter XVIII

SABBATICAL - freedom - Hampshire - new work? -
Edinburgh

Robert and Lorraine Tollemache were very good to us,
letting us live in their little old cottage in the village of
Steep, near Sheet in Hampshire. James was at Cranbrook, a
mixed, boarding grammar school in Kent; it had much of
the quality and facilities of a public school, but we only had
to pay the boarding fees, and there was a good social mix –
ideal. After we had left Sandwich Anna continued happily
at Northbourne, and before long went as a weekly boarder,
with the help of a Church charity. Sadly, they no longer
thought this funding was necessary, so Anna started at a
convent school in Broadstairs, and boarded there when we
left. This was very difficult for her, as she did not know
where we would be living; but we knew that we had to be
free to be away a lot, looking for a new job.

Apart from this anxiety, which grew as the weeks went
by, it was a great relief to be free of all Church
responsibility, doing everything together, shopping, walking

in the lovely countryside and thinking what to do next. I saw an advertisement in the Church Times for a post as the caretaker of a hall, with accommodation. I was tempted! One day I was walking down a village street and saw a notice for a Christian Aid coffee morning. I felt an immediate tightening of my stomach, the tension caused by the thought of having to persuade people to do and give more than they really wanted. I thought, "Let the buggers starve!" I was weary of doing good.

Mercifully I had decided to go on a silent Ignation retreat; each day I had an hour with my guide; he would already have given me a short passage of Scripture to read.

I was given a passage from the fifth chapter of St. Luke: When Jesus had finished speaking to the crowds, he said to Simon (Peter) "Launch out into the deep, and let down your nets for a catch", and Simon answered, "Master, we toiled all night and took nothing!" I exploded, shouting out loud and swearing angrily at God, "All my life I've been working for you, and look where it has got me, no home, no job, nothing!" It wasn't all His fault, of course, but I carried on shouting until my anger had abated, and I felt somewhat calmer. I picked up the Bible again – I had hurled it across the room – and read Peter's next words, "But at your word I will let down the nets". Something like this then went through my mind, "I've tried to do your work, and it has gone wrong – but if you want, then I will start working for your church again, but not in a thriving, demanding parish, but in some gentle way". I now felt much closer to God and said my daily Office with sincerity once more.

We looked at a market town in Cumbria and were very taken with the magnificent country; we thought of a

Cambridge chaplaincy, a Church in Suffolk, one in Monmouth and applied for Painswick in Gloucestershire. It was a Crown living but there were already three people on the list.

It was a good time for Mary and me, as we travelled round the countryside together and then returned to the cottage. We tried to find out what God wanted for us next, or, in other words, what we would be good at and what we would enjoy. I realised that over the years I have a much wider experience of worship than many people who have only devoutly and loyally attended their own church all their lives. I have loved the corporate silence of Quaker Meetings, the free, uninhibited joyful Pentecostal worship in Africa, plain Church of Scotland services, the three hour liturgy of the Orthodox Church, monastic worship in Catholic and Anglican chapels, Cathedral Evensong, youth services with guitars and drums and worship on the hills, at sea and on the seashore.

Latterly, I have been caught up in worship in mosque, synagogue and temple. Slowly I have come to see that it does not really matter what you believe or how you worship, so long as you lose yourself in the ultimate mystery of life and are inspired to give greater love to your neighbour.

In thinking of a new parish, we considered the needs of the people, and whether I could help them; we looked at the church and the house – that was very important! – the countryside, opportunities of music, and whether Anna could have a pony. We applied for Chapel-on-the-Frith, a fine stone built town on the edge of Stockport, near Manchester and running into the Derbyshire moors. In January we went to look; we liked the Vicar and his vision for the Church, the stone Vicarage and warmth of people; it included a large housing estate, 8,000 in all. We had also looked at a vacant parish in Dorset; we did not follow it up, but it sowed the seed of how wonderful it would be to live near the sea in my father's old county. Then, at John Kirkham's instigation, the Archdeacon of Dorset rang me about the Red Post Parish, five small villages in south Dorset. Earlier on I had not seriously considered country work with congregations of fifteen instead of one hundred and fifty; but I met a college chaplain who told me of his previous work in a similar parish. "The good thing about working in the country", he said, "was the possibility of knowing everybody living in the parish; in a town you only know the congregation". This rang a bell with me, a very human approach, God's love for everybody, and not only for the devout; it reminded me of a nineteenth century hymn:

> *"There's a wideness in God's mercy,*
> *like the wideness of the sea;*
> *there's a kindness in his justice,*
> *which is more than liberty.*
> *There is no place where earth's sorrows*
> *are none felt than up in heaven;*
> *there is no place where earth's failings*
> *have such kindly judgement given.*
>
> *But we make his love too narrow*
> *by false limits of our own.*
> *and we magnify his strictness*
> *with a zeal he will not own.*
> *For the love of God is greater*
> *than the scope of human mind,*
> *and the heart of the Eternal*
> *is most wonderfully kind."*

One day in early spring, Mary and I were walking in the country in Hampshire and saw a church standing alone in the middle of a field. We went up to it, and opening the door, immediately felt that it was loved and prayed in – fresh flowers on the altar. For me, in a strange way, it stood as a country version of Roland's vision – living amongst people, worshipping and being available.

In this way my mind was opened to the possibility of country work, which was very different from anything I had done before. I also remembered the comment of a wise old retired priest: "It is not the good which you can do for the country people; it is the good which they can do for you." This turned out to be very true; it seemed both to answer my need and be a corrective to my self-importance. So we agreed to drive down to Dorset and meet the Archdeacon outside Almer Church. He showed us the churches in the five lovely small villages with a total population of about eleven hundred. By chance we happened to meet Venetia Chattey in the road outside her house, and we were able to have a brief chat; she was the Patron of the living.

A few days later we drove north again, to Chapel, to meet formally with the whole PCC who would be interviewing several candidates to appoint their new Vicar. They were friendly and supportive; we liked the whole set up, but were daunted by the bleak weather, the dark houses and the lorries thundering up the road next to the Vicarage. Also we could not discover a school where we could imagine Anna being happy. The PCC told us that they would let us know their decision as soon as possible. We drove away on the busy, noisy roads, through some very grim areas and right down the motorway to Dartmoor; we wanted to get right away from it all and make our decision in the home of our dear wise friends, John and Judy Henderson.

Naturally, we were exhausted, but after dinner in their farm kitchen, the telephone rang, and it was for us. It was the kindly Warden of Chapel, a former President of the Law Society, who knew my father. With quiet joy in his voice he told me that the PCC wanted us and offered me the job. I had to be honest and tell him of our doubts and our worries about Anna. Poor kindly man, he sounded surprised, sad and disappointed, so I promised I would let him know as soon as possible. What on earth were we to do? There seemed to be no clear answer from the good Lord. Knowing my hatred of making decisions, I knew I must set a deadline and agreed with Mary that I would ring him at 9 o'clock next morning.

Whenever we were away I would ring our neighbours at the cottage, friends of the Tollemaches, and ask them to open and read any letters which had arrived. They usually just went into the porch where the mail would be lying on the mat; but this time Rob and Lorraine had been down for the weekend, and had put our letters on the kitchen table. For some reason which they couldn't explain, our neighbours went into the house that morning, where they found and read us a letter from Venetia Chattey, asking us to come and meet all ten Churchwardens of the united benefice. With just a few minutes to spare I rang her and asked if we would come later that morning, as our road home went right through the different parishes. I also told her that we had just received an offer from another parish. She was somewhat startled by the haste, as usually the procedure lingered on over several months, but she readily agreed.

Her family had owned the Bloxworth estate for four hundred years, and as Patron she could ask the Bishop to appoint her nominee. Walter Drax was the Patron of the villages of Morden and Almer. His family had lived at Charborough Park for a similar time, and he owned much of the land around and most of the houses. He had heard about us from Jim Swanton, one of my referees, as they had often met together in Barbados. The other two villages, Winterborne Kingston and Zelston were in the patronage of the Bishop of Salisbury; the patrons took it in turn to appoint. This time it was Mrs Chattey's sole responsibility to nominate, but out of courtesy she asked Walter Drax to join her in meeting us.

We sat in the lovely drawing room of her home, the former Rectory, where her forbears had lived for most of the nineteenth century. Walter Drax asked me what I would hope to do as Vicar? Weary of all the latest fashionable schemes for "mission", I just said, "I hope I would be able to help people love God and each other." That seemed to make sense. We briefly met all the other wardens in their homes, some in big houses and some in country cottages. We ended up in the hamlet of Almer where we immediately felt at home, first with a really lovely and genuinely Christian couple, Frank and Min Wallis, who lived in one of the estate cottages as Frank was a tractor driver, and then we ended with a cheerful welcome and a big gin at Almer Manor.

We went back to Bloxworth where we sat round the kitchen table, and reluctantly I had to ask Venetia if she were willing to make me a firm offer in writing there and then, as we were expecting a letter offering me Chapel when we got home. After briefly conferring, she wrote a short letter offering me the living of the Red Post Parishes.

We had asked about schools for Anna and were recommended Sandford Middle, a modern building set in very large grounds and the Purbeck to follow, at thirteen. We met staff in both schools and noticed the fossil set in stone at the entrance; it seemed to represent all that was good about this part of Dorset. It was only mid-February, but as we drove back over Wareham Forest the gorse was already in bloom. Then we drove home.

We now had firm offers in writing for two very different parishes. How on earth were we to decide? We considered every aspect, with my putting the advantages, and then swapped positions, with Mary being in favour, and me against. As the offers of the job and the house were made to me, we knew that I had to make the final decision; but we wanted that to be our joint decision, as far as possible. I am reminded of the story of a couple coming to a Vicar about their wedding; she was a large forceful woman, and he a mousy little man. When the Vicar asked them "Who makes the decisions in your life?" she said, "I make the minor decisions, and he makes the major ones." "And who will decide which are the important decisions?" said the Vicar, with a smile. "I DO", she promptly replied. Mary was not like that!

We agreed that I should walk up to the lovely little ancient church in the village, say my Daily Office of worship and make my decision by half past ten. Following my experience of Sandwich and Wimbledon, I wrote a number of letters accepting Chapel and another two accepting Red Post. I put them in their envelopes, stamped, ready for posting, and placed them in two larger brown envelopes, one marked 'Yes to the North', and one 'Yes to Dorset'. I would post one batch of letters and tear up the other. I knew that Mary loved the idea of quiet gentle

Dorset, but nobly was willing to go to Chapel if I believed that to be right. I laid the two letters on the altar, one a long typed letter, and the other a short one in Venetia's fine handwriting; the two large envelopes I laid down on the pew in front of me as I knelt at the back.

It was Lent; there was a large wooden cross, which said to me "Take up your cross and follow Me." Christ seemed to say "Do my work with a thriving congregation and many needy people on a large housing estate, and I will look after your family". A few minutes later Christ seemed to say, "Look after your family, lay aside your self importance, and I will look after you".

Having prayed and asked for guidance, it was twenty five past ten. I was fairly clear and calm about returning to the North ....then the Church door opened and two elderly ladies bustled in, with brooms and mops, and started cleaning.

Suddenly, my calm was shattered and anguished doubt swept over me; I was desperate; I would have been shouting out loud, if alone. My hands moved to tear up 'Yes to Dorset', then moved to tear up 'Yes to the North', and finally, hands trembling, ripped 'Yes to Dorset' in half. I stumbled up to the altar, scrunched up Venetia's letter and put it in my pocket, and carefully folded the other. I tottered to the door to post 'Yes to the North' in the pillar box outside the Church. To confirm that the decision was made I looked in the 'Yes to Dorset' envelope in order to see the torn up letters. I had torn the large envelope down the middle, and both letters of acceptance were safe and unharmed in one half of the big envelope. I posted them.

I walked calmly, joyfully and thankfully back to the cottage where Mary was waiting, dreading the worst. She was amazed and deeply relieved, equally joyful and grateful. A few days later we heard of hidden difficulties about the Derbyshire parish, but we also had a telephone call from the kindly Churchwarden there, offering to pay for a school for Anna if that would affect our decision. That disturbed me, and until we came to Dorset I was still occasionally wondering if I had made the right decision. Sometimes there is a difficult period between making a decision and being able to act upon it.

On that first evening, back in the cottage, we wrote to Anna saying that we had a home, she would be able to have a pony, and that we would fetch her as soon as possible. It was also very good having James with us for the spring holiday.

I have often thought about the strange way in which I made my decision to come to Dorset. To put it in anthropomorphic terms, it seemed as if I were making a costly offering to God, which he appreciated, but did not take up, knowing that the alternative was better for me, my family and everybody, in the long run. I was reminded of the profound, shocking, puzzling story of Abraham being prepared to sacrifice his son Isaac, through whom the nations of the earth would be blessed; it must have been an appalling decision to make, but eventually his trust in his God overcame his natural reluctance and he was ready to do the dreadful deed, as local custom required. He made his offering; God recognised it, but did not take it up. This story in Genesis chapter 27 (best in the King James Bible) helps me see that sometimes it is good to be prepared to surrender whatever we hold most dear. Is this a very human story, told in typical vivid Hebrew fashion, of a father giving up his protective, controlling love for his teenage son? Give up our children and they are given back to us?

Or was this way of deciding just my daft way of finding out what I really wanted?! I think and hope that what I really want is also what God wants, for God is deep within me, timeless, knowing the needs of all his children, deeper than either my conscience or my worldly drives? Perhaps God is nearer my subconscious than He is to my conscious mind?

After a relaxed, happy Easter holidays in the cottage, we took James back to Cranbrook, and taking Anna with us, put the car on the train for Edinburgh. At the end of January we had already been to meet John Armson, the Principal of the Theological College of the Episcopal Church. We were there for Burns night, a wild occasion with a student reading, with great passion, the Ode to a Haggis and plunging his skean dhu into the sheep's stomach as if it had been the heart of a Sassenach.

I loved our time in Edinburgh, the city of my forbears; the staff and students were friendly and interesting and there were many international visitors. We got to know the city, took up with cousins and old friends, explored the Pentlands, the Lammermuirs and the Trossachs as well as one memorable visit with my mother and Aunt Eva to St. Leonard's, their old school in St. Andrew's. More than once we went to Arran for the weekend – that felt very good and natural.

My duties were light, spending much of my time with the students and their families. Since leaving St. Peter's I had not taken any services. John Armson was very sensitive about my vulnerability, and gave me some weeks to settle in before I first led any worship. I was tense and anxious about doing so, but it was a relief afterwards to have taken the first step back into a priest's life. Those few weeks of the summer term went by all too quickly, and before long we were on our way to the lush South. I was very grateful for the chance of a Sabbatical of such joy and the opportunity to work as a priest in a new and gentle way.

Chapter XIX

DORSET – EARLY DAYS -a country parson - a great
estate - hunting

How can I possibly get the balance right in speaking of
the next twenty years? I have made so many loyal
friends, I've laughed at so many hilarious moments, and
been alongside so many dear people in times of anguish that
it is hard to know what to include. I want to leave out
anything that might be hurtful or even embarrassing as well
as fascinating things told to me in confidence. Oscar Wilde
said, "Which is worse - being talked about, or not being
talked about?" So, in many ways, this is a random
collection of memories, and most of the occasions and
names represent many others.

I was instituted as Vicar by John Kirkham, old friend
and fellow curate, now Bishop of Sherborne. Venetia
wisely chose Kingston as the church for the occasion, which
helped bind the five parishes together in one benefice. The
Vicarage is a happy house in a hamlet of only about twenty
houses, surrounded by woods and fields in gentle hills and

valleys. We made the dining room and drawing room into one, and the sun poured in all day; both house and garden were ideal for parties. We could not have been luckier with our immediate neighbours, Richard and Vivien Hares; they saw us through all our ups and downs, and over the years I was able to christen, marry and bury members of their family. Our neighbours on the other side gave us no trouble. Some of them had been asleep for centuries. In my first few months I hugely enjoyed wandering up a country lane to a cottage or farmhouse, built with a mixture of stone and the local soft brick, as well as meeting people in the three council estates, where many of the original village families lived. Again and again I was welcomed with genuine warmth, inherited with the goodwill felt towards my predecessors. I often heard of my predecessor-but-one, Will Sandey, a former naval chaplain, who would hop off his scooter to help the men in the fields. When the landlord of the Cock and Bottle was away, Will would serve behind the bar; he was popular with the men.

I loved to hear the Dorset accent spoken amongst the farming people with its soft gentle tones and endearing phrases such as "'ee said to Oi". It is not just an accent, but the outward expression of a whole way of looking at life, slow, wise, honest and trusting with a wry sense of humour that could see through the pretentiousness of town bred newcomers. A typical story was told of a suburban lady being shown round a country cottage which she thought of buying.

"Very nice", she said to the tenant, "but where's the toilet?"

"Oi'll shew 'ee" said the old man, as he led her up the garden path to the privy.

"Oh, but there's no lock on the door!" she cried.

"Don't 'ee wurry, ma'am, nobody around 'ere steals the shit".

Over the next months I tried to visit every home in the five villages, only about five hundred in all. I soon realised that these first visits were of unique importance, because often people would tell me their family history, including the tragedies they had struggled through; so I tried not to hurry those visits. After about a couple of years I had a good idea of who was likely to come to church and who probably never would; but I had enough time to go on visiting regularly, in any case. In a small benefice it was possible for me to represent God's love for everybody and not just the Church people. I only realised how much this had been appreciated after I had retired.

I went to see Cyril and Betty Legg who lived in Broadclose, as they were members of the large Legg family in Kingston; they had just made the big decision to give their young granddaughters a home with them. Years later Betty told me,

"I'll never forget how you went down to the bottom of the garden to welcome them – you always were the soul of our house."

I was very touched by that phrase which I had never heard before – trying to put into words part of the calling of a parish priest as he visits every home, revealing the soul of the home which is there already.

Dick and Deeny Yeatman ran the Cock and Bottle in Morden; he was a typical farmer-cum-host and Deeny a warm hearted, glamorous grandmother. Shortly after our arrival their youngest son, Craig, was killed on his motorbike. Most of the village and a crowd of youngsters were at his funeral and burial in Morden Churchyard. Some years later I took another tragic funeral in Winterborne Zelston. Neil Crofton had died in a canal accident. His mother, Heather, sang in the choir, and years later, his father, John, saw me struggling to paint a forest of wooden posts, the frame of our Stoborough sun room – he took them away in his van and painted them all himself – what kindness.

It was fascinating living and working near the heart of a great estate, where most of the land and many of the houses were owned by the Drax family who lived at Charborough Park, the great house set in the rolling parkland behind the long wall and great gates, along the road from Wimborne to Bere Regis. From the first we were made welcome there and received much kindness. Over the years I was involved with their family christenings, weddings and funerals which might be followed up by lunch in the lovely dining room overlooking the deer park.

I had glimpses of some of the best elements of the life of a traditional estate – the mutual care between landowner, tenants, staff and workers. Several times I travelled over to Southampton Hospital to see a family member of one of the tractor drivers, only to find that Pam Drax had been there before me. Albert Green looked after the culling of the deer and lived in a cottage deep in a wood, without telephone or television. He told me that Mr Drax had driven down to bring him to Charborough to watch a particular nature programme on television. Fred Hodge was the ever cheerful London born driver and odd job man at Charborough; after he had died from a long protracted lung cancer, I went to see his widow Hazel, and Mark, the tallest of the Drax sons, came in to comfort her. He tried to give her a hug, but he was too tall, so he knelt in front of her and was then the right height to enfold her in his arms!

I got to know the tractor drivers, and noticed that after I had stood with a group of them for a few minutes they easily accepted me and talked quite naturally among themselves, often using swear words to describe something. This confirmed my long held suspicion that swearing is not a moral or spiritual lapse, but just a custom that is accepted on some occasions and not on others. I also got to know the gamekeepers and their families and came to realise what a significant part is played in the country by shooting, both socially and in terms of employment. I remember ringing up a Vicar friend working in a city and he asked me if I had had a good congregation on Sunday?

"Oh yes," I replied, "we had a full church, because there had been a shoot on Saturday". "Good heavens, a murder?"

The guns might have been staying at Charborough for an old fashioned shooting weekend, or might be on a paid shoot. The beaters were a lovely mix, including real old countrymen and others who just loved being in the country. The tenant farmers would also have their own rough shooting.

We had the use of the glebe field next to the Vicarage and we were able to borrow a pony for Anna and later we bought her a horse. It gave me deep satisfaction to see and hear her trotting up the lane.

The hunting world was also much more of a social mix than many people realise; it includes the hunt staff, the stable girls and retired farm labourers who loved to follow the hunt wherever it was. There were also trades people who could afford a horse and hunted regularly. I borrowed a beauty of a fifteen hands half Arab and rode to hounds a few times. On the first occasion I was quite nervous, as I had not been out for thirty years, and coming up to a five barred gate I lost my stirrups, much to the alarm of the people behind me; but the training I had been given by that Army bombardier thirty years ago stood me in good stead, and gripping with my knees, I sailed safely over. On another occasion I borrowed a pony and as we moved off from the meet, the girth slipped, and I fell off before we had even reached the road. When I went into the pub that evening there was much merriment.

In one of my villages there was an old farm worker who was a passionate follower of the hunt. He told me of a Master who wanted his body thrown to the hounds after his death. It had been gently pointed out to him that this was against the law, so he reluctantly agreed that he would be cremated and his ashes scattered over the carcases which the hounds would eat. We could not arrange this for my parishioner, but a pair of hounds were present when I buried his ashes in his cottage garden, and the huntsman sounded "Gone Away".

On one occasion I was directed by the Field Master to watch for a fox in the corner of a field by the main road. As I sat on my horse several drivers hooted angrily at us as they drove past. It was strange being on the receiving end of a protest and made me feel guilty. I can understand why some people hate the idea of an intelligent animal being pursued by baying hounds, but we don't enjoy seeing the fox killed, as some anti's think – it is the unpredictable ride over country that is the excitement – the end is quick. It is all part of country life and I felt close to my people, to the land and to the past, when hunting.

Chapter XX

DORSET BELONGING - James - country characters

About a year after we arrived in Dorset, we had a very worried telephone call from James' housemaster at Cranbrook in Kent. James had been acting very strangely and had disappeared. We waited anxiously, and later his housemaster rang again, telling us that he had been found and taken by ambulance to the Psychiatric Hospital near Maidstone, suffering from a very severe mental breakdown, including an explosion of anger against us and all the pressures and expectations of sixth form life.

In a state of shock and heavy bewilderment we immediately rang the wardens in each church, telling them that we would be off first thing in the morning and did not know when we would be back. This was in the days before all the motorways were finished, and so it was after a long drive that we arrived at the huge, old-fashioned hospital. We could not find James' ward and finally made our way up an iron outside staircase to a locked door at the top; it was finally opened by a large, formidable black nurse. We went through the ward to the office and asked for James – we had walked past him and did not recognise him – he was so thin, pale and drawn with mental agony. We were told that he had schizophrenia, and the bottom fell out of our world. We had hoped that with time and rest from all pressures he would soon recover, but when the doctor explained the illness to us, we realised that it might affect him for life.

After an agonizing fortnight James was brought to the Forston Clinic, near Dorchester, under the care of Dr. Dick – we had been advised to find James a hospital in West Dorset, which provided some of the best mental health care in the country. We were on the border between the Health Authority districts, and I will always be profoundly grateful, that up to the present day, we have been able to see him in that lovely part of the world. I cannot tell his story – that is his privilege – but I need to write of my memories.

After we had returned to Dorset from Kent we were on the receiving end of so much kindness. Whenever I went visiting, in council house, cottage, farmhouse or manor, as soon as I had sat down, I was offered tea, and a question, in broad Dorset,

"How's your son, Vicar?"

or I was given a whisky and with a fruity but compassionate voice, my host would ask "Hugh, how's James?"

For the first quarter of an hour they looked after me, before I could begin to ask about their lives. That University Chaplain's prophecy had come true.

Brother, sister, let me serve you
Let me be as Christ to you;
Pray that I may have the grace to

267

Let you be my servant too.

The love and care which was given to me, Mary, James and Anna in those early years was, in a strange way, the foundation of the way in which I was alongside my people for the next eighteen years. It was also a new experience seeing James in the Clinic, encouraging on one visit, and heartbreaking the next; I was not there as a clerical visitor, in good mental health, coming and going as I pleased, but an honorary member of the ward, sharing in the robust humour and emotional caring and also exasperation of the members; and when we left, our hearts and minds were still on the ward.

I now knew that God had indeed guided me to tear up those letters saying Yes to the North and post those accepting Venetia's offer to come to gentle, loving Dorset. I couldn't have looked after James in a hospital in Manchester as well as eight thousand people in the parish. With a full heart I would say that prayer at the end of the Communion Service:

Father of all, we give you thanks and praise,
than when we were still far off
you met us in your Son and brought us home.

After some months James was living in a youth rehabilitation house, near Eastleigh, and was doing well, working in a café and even taking driving lessons. He was home for a few days and went to a Diocesan Youth weekend in Wimborne Minster, where he learned that haunting Taize song, "Oh, Lord, hear my prayer. When I call, answer me." We felt calm and grateful. He returned to Eastleigh, and with the prospect of having to leave and go to a Richmond House in Cambridge, he had another major breakdown and was back in hospital.

I went into Morden Church and knelt at the back, as I often did. I usually felt that it was a holy place, full of the mystery of God's love. Now it was cold and empty. I shouted out,

"Why? Why?"

There was no answer. Only the echo of my desperate cry.

I always remembered this moment when, on Good Friday, I read out Jesus' final angry words on the cross, "My God, my God, why have you abandoned me?" On Calvalry, as at Morden, there was no answer.

James slowly recovered, but each summer for the next three years he had another breakdown and was back in hospital.

It was so difficult for us to get it right at this time – he had wonderful, genuine, professional care and modern medication, so it was necessary for James to find his own independence. His illness was basically a chemical imbalance in the brain – inherited from my father's side of the family, but we had been part of the problem as well, by sending him away to boarding school etc. However, we were given wonderful support by James' social workers and doctors. Compared to so many we were very lucky.

Over the next years James moved several times, back and forward from hospital to hostel, to a flat, to digs, to sheltered accommodation, a house shared with others and finally to a roomy, light flat of his own, not far from the harbour, owned by a Housing Association which gave him support.

In the flat below was a man who lived a troubled life; a former gang leader, he was gay and would pick a fight with anyone in a pub if he thought they were laughing at him. He could be friendly with James, but one night he came up and threatened James with a knife, unless he turned down his music.

One night James had gone to bed, but, mercifully, not to sleep. He smelt smoke, and hurrying downstairs, found it pouring out under the door of this man's flat, just beneath his own. Sam lived in the bottom flat and James persuaded him to call the Fire Brigade who came immediately. When they broke into the flat they found the man had been murdered and the flat set on fire. James and Sam spent much of the night with the police, giving evidence of the background of the disaster. It was a traumatic experience, but James remained wonderfully calm and strong; many a weaker person would have panicked and remained disturbed for a long time.

James has been in his flat for more than ten years and runs his own life very steadily, with the aid of his Disability Allowance and his loving, demanding friendship with Linda in the flat below. Both medically and financially things are so much better than they were a hundred years ago. These days James is straightforward, witty, generous and affectionate. In his own way he has struggled and achieved more than those who have sailed into "successful" careers. I am proud of him, and very, very grateful; it has been a long uphill struggle for him.

A few months after our arrival in Dorset I was sent a form asking on which diocesan committee I would like to serve. I filled it in and returned it, thinking of some of the important things I had done in Canterbury. None of my offers were taken up. I was hurt. It brought home to me that I was unknown, and starting again, at the bottom of the ladder, so to speak. However, John Baker, our wise, learned, compassionate and holy Bishop of Salisbury asked me to lead the retreat, held in his house, for those to be ordained at the weekend, and to preach in the Cathedral at their ordination, - a humbling experience.

My sister Alison had been at Sherborne at the same time as the present Headmistress, and so I was asked to go and preach to the girls. A nearby Vicar chuckled when I told him and explained that it was often her custom to ask new clergy to come. As it was a privilege to be asked, I should not expect expenses, and, anyhow, I would only be asked once. I duly went to the school and talked to the four hundred girls – a larger and younger audience than my usual Sunday congregation. I then had dinner with the Headmistress and some very sophisticated young ladies. As I went to the car, the Headmistress accompanied me, pressed my expenses into my hand and asked,

"Are you very busy these days?"

"Not really, no, I just potter about."

"Would you be able to come and preach again?"

I think the chuckling Vicar had got it wrong – unless ....?!

Through a Gloucestershire connection I also knew the wife of the Headmaster of Sherborne (the boys school), and preached several times in the glory of the Abbey. I was also asked to speak with the staff at a voluntary meeting a few days before the school year began – an occasion for them to step back from planning the curriculum and think more freely. I was impressed by the number of staff who gave this occasion real priority. With James in mind, I reminded them of the dangers of putting on too much pressure to succeed. This led to a thoughtful and sensitive discussion about the needs of the boys. James' experience has given me an insight into many related difficulties thrown up by the stress on the individual in a highly competitive culture; a slower, gentler, more corporate and spiritual way of living is more healthy – at least, that is the way I justify my idleness!

On one occasion when I set out to preach in Sherborne Abbey my sermon was poorly prepared, and as I was in very good time, I pulled into a side road about two miles from the town, to rest. When I opened my eyes and looked at my watch, there was only a quarter of an hour before the service was due to begin. I raced through the town and met an anxious Headmaster at the door. That was my last visit.

I was also asked to preach at another first class boys school in the glorious setting of Milton Abbey. At that time the Headmaster's wife was the sister of a Corpus friend. I also went with the next Headmaster, Mr Hardy, whose mother had lived in Sandwich. My happiest times were with Jonathan Hughes-D'Aeth, whose wonderful parents had been so kind to me in Broadstairs; I had met him there several times, so we had a cheerful reunion. With his usual joyful exuberance he almost bounced up and down with enthusiasm as he told me of a staff meeting discussing a very difficult boy.

"People suggested several different ways of dealing with him, but nobody thought any of them would really work. After a sad silence, one of the masters said,

'Of course, what he really needs is just a lot of love.'" Then Jonathan said to me, "Nobody would have dared say that at my last school!"

I think that little story said much about both Jonathan and Milton Abbey. I also got to know and respect the school chaplain, Charles Mitchell-Innes; he had followed Andrew Salmon who had been at Milton Abbey for years – the best of the cricketing sort of chaplain, seeing services in the Abbey as part of normal life, tall, sporting, caring but unsentimental. Everybody had a natural confidence in him. Charles had been a master at Sherborne, but was only newly ordained and new to the role of chaplain. I was touched by the way he used my listening ear to talk through some of the puzzling issues of his work.

Because of my difficulties in both parish and family life, several clergy seemed glad to be able to share some of their difficulties with me. Several of the Wareham curates used to enjoy coming out to Morden, and so did the much loved Rector, Peter Hardman. He had come to talk thing over, especially the burden of his work load which included a major appeal for the Church roof.

"I have nothing to do with the buildings, or money," I said, "so I can spend my time with people."

He looked doubtful, but as he came out of the Vicarage he glanced up at Morden Church tower, covered in scaffolding. With a worried voice, he asked,

"Goodness, what's wrong?"

"I don't know" I replied, "the wardens are looking after it".

"Yes, you mean what you say", he chortled, and drove off on his scooter down the drive, wobbling with laughter.

Sometimes at Chapter meeting, a harassed looking clergyman would say,

"How on earth do you manage with FIVE parishes?"

"Oh, I don't know," I would reply, with just an element of truth, "I go sailing in the summer and hunting in the winter."

If Mary overheard, she would be cross with me and tell the others that I got to know and help my parishioners as members of my crew on the boat or fellow followers of the Hunt; besides, she would tell them, I knew the names of almost every man, woman and child in all five villages. But I enjoy shocking my fellow clergy and, hopefully, making them think. We don't have to earn God's love by rushing around frantically and organising everybody; instead, I felt that my calling was to point to the Kingdom of God by being amongst my people and listening to them – a sort of quiet presence (although sometimes loud in merriment); and in my personal worship I would "tell God" of the wonderful things my parishioners were doing, as well as of their sufferings. Of course, other clergy have a different, more active vocation.

In visiting, there was endless variety. I walked up the path of a small cottage, and found that the only person there was a very attractive young wife and mother, lying on a sun-chair in a bikini. I did not know where to look, but I think she enjoyed my embarrassment. On another occasion I called on a horsey woman living in a bigger house; on opening the door she said, "What the bloody hell do you want?"

Nervously I said, "I've come to see your mother."

She led me through to the drawing room, where her elderly mother graciously offered me a gin, which I gulped down. Some months later, I called again. The daughter opened the door.

"What do you want this bloody time?"

"A bloody gin, of course!"

She roared with laughter.

I tried to become more involved in the life of the farm workers, but there were fewer opportunities than in the old days, because of the use of modern machinery. Once I helped deliver a calf, pulling strongly on the rope attached to its forelegs. I was distressed when I listened to the bellowing of its mother a few days later when her calf had been taken from her. I was told that it was necessary, and that in a few weeks she would settle down.

Trying to be of use I offered to help a young farmer, Richard Gulliford, with the milking. I was successful with three cows, putting the cluster of four tubes on their teats, but the fourth lady was not so co-operative; she did not like my doing something so intimate, and after my third nervous attempt, she lifted her back leg and kicked me in the mouth. I was hurled backwards with blood pouring from my lip. Richard's wife, Sarah, patched me up, and instead of helping him build a small bridge as planned, I sat in the farmhouse kitchen, drinking tea. The next day they brought round a leg of lamb to make up for my shock and injury. It therefore cost them more in time and money than I was worth! I did not attempt to help with the milking again; but the story went round all their family, and bound us all closer together.

I tried to call regularly on every household, whether they ever came to church or not. If I had a special reason to visit a house I would also try to call on the neighbour each side. Each month I would try to deliver about twenty magazines, taking a different round each time. I might go in and linger if anybody was in; if it was obviously the wrong moment I could hand over the magazine and just ask,

"Everybody all right?"

In that way there was no need for them to ask me in. I might often hear of a neighbour or a family member in hospital; I would then try to see them wherever they were, Poole, Dorchester, Blandford, Wareham, Salisbury or any of the nursing homes. I was very impressed with the Weld Hospice in Dorchester, and Forest Holme in Poole where there was a calm and joyful atmosphere. These visits could take a lot of time, but were well worth it; it was not only the patient who was grateful, but also family, friends and neighbours. Before going onto the ward I would always try to empty myself of myself, and ask for God's love to flow through me instead. I usually would offer a prayer, thanking God for the skill and care of the hospital staff – nearly always people spoke very highly of them – while I held the patient's hand. I would ask for God's loving healing to flow through them, body and mind. We might say the Lord's Prayer together, other patients sometimes joining in, then a short blessing. Even if I were in a state of personal turmoil before going into the ward, many people said that I brought a great sense of calm with me. If this is true, it was because I prayed beforehand; so that it was God, not Hugh, who was bringing that sense of peace which can be so healing.

Early on in the parish I went to see Alan and Beryl Wellstead. Their son, Adrian, had been in the Royal Navy in the Falklands. At the time they were on a coach party from the village; they were talking and were not listening to the radio which was switched on. Everybody else heard the announcer say that Adrian's ship, H.M.S. Sheffield had been sunk. Nobody knew whether Alan and Beryl had heard, but after terrible anxiety, somebody told them. Adrian was not one of those who survived. Later on, Alan and Beryl went in the party of bereaved relatives flown out to the Falklands; they went out more than once and also joined in the meetings and memorial service in London. I think they did find help, comfort and friendship in the shared grief of other families. Adrian was married, and their small child was born after he had died, which was a comfort to Alan and Beryl. Their daughter-in-law married again and they all remained a close part of the family.

Within a few weeks of my arrival I heard about Michael Barnes, a married man of forty with two sons and a third child expected at any moment. In those days, Kingston had a good cricket team. Mike was batting, had a heart attack and died at the crease. The next day his daughter was born.

When I called I had to be sensitive to this extraordinary mixture of feelings, gratitude for the birth of the baby and devastation at her father's sudden death. The Church was packed for his funeral and a long line of silent mourners walked behind the coffin as we wound our way through the village to the cemetery – it reminded me of those black and white Greek films. I christened the baby, Elizabeth; years later I took the wedding of her older brother Richard. It was a privilege to become so closely involved with one of the real Kingston families right from the beginning. As the years went by I hugely enjoyed the company of Mike's mother, Barbie; as she recovered from her loss, her irrepressible humour constantly broke through. I have just taken her funeral and many memories made us all chuckle.

Chapter XXI

DORSET – SAILING - glorious days - terrifying
moments - voyage through Scotland

Two years after our arrival in Dorset I had a legacy and
bought a small sailing boat, a Cornish Shrimper. She
was nineteen feet long, was built in fibreglass, but had the
lines of a tough looking fishing boat, with wooden spars, a
high-peaked gaff, red sails, a lifting keel, an outboard
engine, a large cockpit and a small, low cabin which could
sleep two. We saw one in the Wareham river, and it was
love at first sight. We kept our eyes open for a second-hand
one, and in the meantime tried out several other boats – not
faithful to my first feelings of loyal rapture. Mary wisely
said that if we bought another boat, whenever we saw a
Shrimper sail by, we would regret our decision. A few
months earlier I had called on Andy and Jan King, at their
cottage in Winterborne Kingston, to arrange a baptism; but
it took some time to reach their door, because in the garden
I met Andy, working on his Dragon, a superb, graceful,
traditional racing boat.

I included them in a party at the Vicarage, and showed him an advertisement for a two year old Shrimper for sale in Anglesey.

"What do you think?"

"She looks good."

"Any chance of your coming to look at her for us?"

"Yes, of course; when?"

"How about tomorrow, our day off?"

There and then the four of us made arrangements for the children and agreed to set off at five o'clock in the morning. We drove through the magnificent hills of North Wales to Anglesey, where Andy inspected the boat and approved of her. We bought her on the spot and towed her home behind our big old Peugeot, after considerable difficulty with the trailer. Andy worked on her during the winter and I shall not forget launching her and sailing her down the river to Poole Harbour – our own little sea-going boat; we had been lucky to find a mooring at the East Dorset Sailing Club, at the bottom of Evening Hill.

We called her Catherine, after my godmother, Bobbie, as she had given me the money to buy her, and also after Mary's Aunty Kitty; it was one of the best decisions of my life.

She was both a very pretty boat and also perfect for our needs. She was small enough to spend the winter in the Vicarage drive, and large enough to sail out to sea. With her lifting keel we could creep all over Poole Harbour, although many times we stuck on the mud! We often took out another couple with us, sailing to Studland where we would anchor in sight of the fields above the cliffs, the golden corn in the harvest sunshine, dotted with the scarlet of many poppies – alas, no more. We would swim from the boat, share a picnic and a bottle of wine, and then doze in the long cockpit. Over the years we must have taken out hundreds of people, many of them parishioners, and often people who were troubled or lonely. On a summer's day I might be driving around one of my villages, see a group of bored teenagers and offer them a sail. They would race home, tell their parents and be back in a few minutes, for a glorious sail. Years later I was taking a funeral and three large cheerful young men reminded me of one such occasion when they had swum from the boat while I dozed in the cabin. I also took out dozens of small children on our parish day on the beach, perhaps eight at a time, with an experienced teenager to help, while other teenagers walked out to the boat, each with a child on their shoulders. Happy days. No Health and Safety restrictions – just common sense.

We would often spend a night on board, anchoring in the peace and beauty behind the islands. I took some of my nephews for a night on the boat, Jacob, Samuel and Sebastian, one at a time. We would cook and eat a simple meal in the cosy, candlelit cabin, and talk. It was a wonderful way of getting to know them well.

We joined the Shrimper Association and went to the dinners at the Royal Motor Yacht Club, as well as going on their week long rallies to the Solent. We enjoyed the dinners at the Yacht Club in Yarmouth, the pub at Bucklers Hard up the Beaulieu River, but my favourite nights were in the peace of Newtown Creek. One time, after a day's vigorous sailing, we ghosted up the Creek with only the whisper of an evening breeze, slipping silently along, past the big yachts where their owners sat sipping their gin. As we glided slowly past them, one quietly said, "Red sails in the sunset". I think we had made a perfect end to their day.

Once my crew was Fred Gulliford, a friend and experienced sailor; we left the Shrimper fleet in the Solent and sailed back on our own. I was in favour of hugging the shore, but Fred suggested we use the strong ebb tide to take us past the Needles, as there was only a light west wind against us. The wind rose to Force Five and with wind against tide the waves became short and steep, fully six foot high, while in our cockpit we were barely eighteen inches above the water. I was becoming alarmed and put in a reef, quite a perilous business in a small gaff-rigged boat in heavy seas. To keep the ability to steer, we started the outboard engine, to give us way; Fred suddenly called out that it had jammed in reverse; we could no longer steer properly and the boat was beginning to turn side on to the waves. I feared that we were in real danger of being swamped. Mercifully, Fred was able to unjam the gear leaver and we could move forward again just in time.

We had to tack past the line of buoys marking the channel; the furthest one seemed a very long way off, and we had to round it before we could turn to a safer angle and reach toward Christchurch Harbour near Hengistbury Head, which we could see in the far distance. As we turned we realised that we had been looking at the line of the Purbeck hills above Studland, and Hengistbury was close at hand. What immense relief as we sailed more comfortably to the Harbour entrance, where we anchored to wait for the tide to turn. After a time another Shrimper came by, heading for the entrance.

"Where can we spend the night?" I shouted to him.

"Follow me!" he called back, and led us right up the river, past the cows and horses browsing peacefully by the water's edge, past the glory of Christchurch Priory to the private quay at the bottom of his riverside garden. He invited us in for a shower and a drink before we cooked our hot meal in our little cabin.

Before we turned in we gratefully said the one hundred and seventh Psalm, from the Book of Common Prayer; verses 27 onwards:

"They that go down to the sea in ships: and occupy their business in great waters;

These men see the works of the Lord: and his wonders in the deep;

For at his word the stormy wind ariseth: which lifteth up the waves thereof.

They are carried up to the heaven, and down again to the deep: their soul melteth away because of the trouble.

They reel to and fro, and stagger like a drunken man: and are at their wits end.

So when they cry unto the Lord in their trouble: he delivereth them out of their distress.

For he maketh the storm to cease: so that the waves thereof are still.

Then are they glad, because they are at rest: and so he bringeth them unto the haven where they would be.

O that men would therefore praise the Lord for his goodness: and declare the wonders that he doeth for the children of men!

These wonderful words came from our hearts, - even if we did not believe that the Lord interfered with the weather, just for us!

I had been sailing Catherine for three or four years and was looking at a map of Scotland; I noticed that there was blue between Ayrshire in the South West and Cromarty in

282

the North East, because of the Crinan and Caledonian Canals.

It was a challenge, and I immediately thought that I would go for it; and why not make it a sponsored voyage for a charity? Two, immediately came to mind, the National Schizophrenia Fellowship for James and Michael, another parishioner, and Cystic Fibrosis, for two special families in the parish.

Like most families living in the country, we needed two cars and our two battered old vehicles depended for their life on the constant help of Ken Jenkins. We both had great respect for him; he had been brought up on a smallholding in Morden, and was the best of Dorset. After restoring a car to health he would join us for a cup of tea at the kitchen table. At the time his son Richard was about twelve and had C.F. We knew little about it, but were told it could be fatal. Because Richard was not allowed to play football or rugby, he played tennis, and I often gave him a game on the village court.

The other family also meant a lot to me; Reg Adams is a forester, a woodsman, and a champion axeman, with a powerful chest as hairy as a gorilla's and a heart of gold. He could fell a tree in seconds. He would sing "The Old Rugged Cross" at the funerals of estate workers with such feeling that many strong men wept. I would always arrive at the church early and would often find Reg kneeling by the organ stool, asking for help. He and Peggy had an equally powerful son, Terry: he and his wife Louise had three children, Amy, Holly, and Jamie. Both girls had C.F.

In case I did not finish the voyage I divided it into five legs, so that people could pay for any number completed. At a village fete one sun-tanned black haired young beauty offered to sponsor me and added, "and I will give you a kiss on each of your legs, for each leg sailed." As she was wearing a low cut blouse and no bra, the thought made me quite dizzy.

The sponsor forms were made available throughout the five villages and I posted them to many friends and relations. Many promised £25 and a few £100 for the full voyage. With growing excitement I began to realise that I might possibly raise a considerable sum. I also contacted Yacht Clubs, Harbour Masters and Canal Managers and they waived all fees, saving me hundreds of pounds.

I had planned the voyage while looking at a road map, but bought several charts of these dangerous waters, with swirling tides and many rocks. I knew nothing of navigation and attended a few classes with some friends; we met in Richard and Sara Harvey's ancient house in Morden. They were given by John Barkworth who was chairman of a charity, the London Sail Training Trust. Over the years he and his family became firm friends; he had a dry sense of humour but could be rather a typical peppery ex-cavalry colonel. In one of these navigation classes he set us the task of plotting a course from Poole Harbour to the Solent. I often got muddled with compass bearings, and ended up in Piddlehinton! In exasperation John burst out, "I give up! You'll just have to trust in God!" John was a good Catholic.

A few weeks before we were due to start, Ken checked the boat trailer and discovered that it needed considerable repair. Typically, he struggled late into the night to get it ready. A team of us worked on the boat, painting her traditional black, until she gleamed. She was in the Vicarage garden, with her newly varnished wooden mast pointing to the sky, against the background of the Church tower.

The night before we left we gave a party in the garden, attended by about fifty friends and parishioners. We danced eightsome reels in the drive and the Red Post Choir, all men, sang sea shanties, including,

"Our Vicar lies over the ocean,
Our Vicar lies over the sea,
Our Vicar lies over the ocean
Our Vicar's as sick as can be!
Bring back,
Bring back,
O bring back our Vicar to we, to we
O bring back our Vicar to we!

Andrew Babington, our Rural Dean, gave us a blessing. He was one of the old fashioned parsons, witty, caring, a grandson of an Irish Duke, with big eyes and an aristocratic nose; he was attractive to women, and at home with people outside the Church; for their sake he would bend the rules when necessary.

He had hugely enjoyed one occasion which he loved to describe. He and his family lived in the large old Rectory next to the Church in Blandford. The Church Commissioners wanted to sell it and two of their men came down from London to make a critical inspection. They wore formal dark suits, and carried those new, square, black briefcases, beloved of Yuppies, instead of the soft, leather cases, beloved of our generation. Having scoffed at the size of the house they went into the Rectory courtyard, saying,

"And what do you want all those sheds for?"

Opening the door of one of them, Andrew said,

"They are the stables for our hunters".

Baffled, the officials returned to London, and the Rectory was not sold until Andrew had left. There would have been a battle if they had tried.

After Andrew's blessing at our party, the sun began to set over the hill; we were given an emotional farewell by two Scottish friends playing on fiddle and guitar, "Wull ye no' come back again?" Up at five o'clock in the morning to take down the mast, load the provisions and strap her securely onto the trailer. Before leaving for Scotland I had to take the funeral of a special man, a retired policeman and member of our sailing club, who had done much to help us with our boat in the early days – strange timing, and another, very different, emotional occasion. I would not have neglected this duty for anything, but it meant that we did not leave the Vicarage until noon. Bruce and Joyce Randall towed us north in their Land Rover; they lived a few hundred yards away, he was Dorset born and bred and was the local builder; over the years they have become firm friends.

It had been a long day, and for Bruce a long wearisome drive, but I was determined that we make Gretna before nightfall. Poor Joyce still remembers her shock as I let out a terrific shout as we crossed the Border. My plan was to find a B & B for Bruce and Joyce, and to save money, I would sleep in the boat. We pulled into the car park of a pub, and Joyce was going to go and enquire about accommodation – Bruce was slumped at the wheel. She seemed nervous at going alone into a Scottish pub, so I gallantly offered to go with her. She went to the Barman and asked for accommodation.

"Och, no; we canna help ye. All the rooms are booked."

Then a pause and,

"but I can offer the two of ye the Bridal Suite, if you like?"

In horror, Joyce exclaimed,

"Oh no, this isn't my husband, it's my Vicar!".

Roars of mirth from all in the bar. Instead, we were recommended a kindly B & B, and Bruce insisted on paying for me to have a proper night's sleep. Our host was a young policeman, and had been on duty at the time of the Lockerbie crash.

Next morning, much refreshed, we had a pleasant drive to Troon harbour to launch the boat. We discovered that the inflatable dinghy had a leak, and also that the heavy anchor we had borrowed to hold her fast in strong tides weighed the bow dangerously low in the water. The Yacht Club patched the leak, and complete strangers on the neighbouring pontoon leant us a smaller anchor; the Harbourmaster allowed us to leave the trailer in the yard, free of charge. We had a trial sail that evening, and poor Bruce was highly alarmed as the floor tilted sharply under his feet and water came over the side. He was not reassured by my calm comment that she was just heeling; he had never been in a sailing boat before.

The next morning we were joined by my brother-in-law Chris, and his family; they crossed to Arran by steamer, while Chris and I sailed across the open sea towards the peaks of our beloved Island, to the sound of the pipes played on our tape recorder down below. A great moment.

A few weeks earlier John Baker, the saintly Bishop of Salisbury, gave James some money to buy something which would help with his recovery. He wisely bought a video camera, which he kindly leant me to film the voyage.

After two nights at Gorton Jockie, we started on the first leg, sailing along the East coast of the Island to Lochranza. With all the family on the beach, we were piped away to the tune of Wull ye no' come back again? – a very genuine question!. Chris left us at Ardrishaig in the evening, his place taken by Fred Gulliford, from Dorset. The trip up the Crinan Canal was memorably beautiful; the beech trees still carried their fresh green leaves, bluebells glowed at their foot and the gardens of the lockkeepers' immaculate white cottages were bright with colour. Fred and I spent the night in the loch near Crinan, and as the sun was setting over the distant hills, we climbed a brae and prayed for the people we were trying to help; we asked for God's protection in the difficult waters ahead where we would sail the next day.

Early in the morning we slipped through the Dorus Mor with the ebb tide for the most wonderful days' sailing of my life. The wind blew steadily and in unbroken May sunshine we creamed along Loch Linnhe, surrounded by the great hills of Argyll, and anchoring by remote uninhabited islands. The next day we anchored for lunch at a spot of great peace and beauty and were privileged to see Eider duck flying and alighting not far away. Then we heard the sound of an engine and saw a small bright red fishing boat racing from the opposite shore. Two shots rang out over the water, and the ducks, still on the water, were dead. I was deeply shocked by this sudden, loud violent interruption of life and peace. In the afternoon we had an exciting fast sail with wind and tide in our favour as we swept past the Island of Easdale with its jagged rocks to an anchorage amongst the smaller islands. We glided in by the evening light, dropped anchor, and cooked mackerel on the shore while the sun set most gloriously over the hills of Mull.

The following morning we sailed to Duart Castle, surrounded by sea and great hills. It had been the home of the MacLeans; Catherine, the daughter of the Chief, had married my ancestor Hugh Inglis in the eighteenth century. Mercifully, Fred was a better navigator than me, and the strong tide took us safely through the overfalls to Loch Creran, just north of Oban – another glorious sail. We anchored near Barcaldine Castle, a typically ancient, austere, battlemented place owned by Roddy Campbell of Barcaldine the Younger. I had baptised their daughters, when his wife, Jean had been the accountant at Charborough. At the end of the seventeenth century Roddy's forbears had owned many a hill and glen of the Highlands, and it was at Barcaldine that the MacDonald chief was detained for the night, so that he was late for his reluctant signing of the oath of allegiance to King William; the massacre of Glencoe was the result.

While he was in Dorset, Roddy worked for the Sea Life Centre in Weymouth, and a few weeks before we set off, I had a letter from the Centre at Barcaldine, asking if I would baptise a baby seal before it was released into the sea, and whether I would preach from the boat – they obviously knew the Gospel story. I got the delighted permission from the Bishop of Argyll and the Isles for me to bless the little creature, even if I couldn't baptise it! At my request, they made quite an occasion of the ceremony, asking the children from the local Primary School and visitors from the Centre to join us on the shore. We had a simple service, sang a hymn and said the Lord's Prayer. Standing in the boat, I told them the purpose of the voyage, of

289

schizophrenia and cystic fibrosis. Then we hoisted our red sails, weighed anchor, and with a gentle wind were piped away down the loch by a young man, in full Highland dress, standing above the bay.

At Barcaldine Fred left me and his place was taken by Mark Acton. I had met him in Bloxworth and he had already helped me a lot with the boat. He stayed with me for the rest of the voyage. Every few days I would ring home and I got a message to ring the new undertaker at Sandwich. This was in the days when mobile telephones were rare, and I would try ringing from ancient coin box telephones in remote lochside villages, and often my coins would run out. Slowly bizarre messages began to emerge about a funeral. The Fripps were a family in Sandwich we had known well nearly twenty years ago. Nickie had already died and we discovered that their son James had gone missing in the United States some time ago. Finally, I was able to speak to his father, John, and he arranged for me to fly down from Inverness, saying that he would meet me at Heathrow. It all sounded mystifying and tragic.

In the meantime we motored through the Caldeonian Canal and sailed the length of Loch Ness to Inverness, the home of my Inglis forbears. Throughout the voyage we had placed the boards saying Schizophrenia and Cystic Fibrosis each side of the boat, and had many moving conversations at the quayside. Here we met the members of the local C.F. branch; their Chairman, a former Head Teacher, saw us off on our final leg to Cromarty. As we stood on the quayside he offered us a prayer; we took off our hats and stood quietly while he, quite unselfconsciously, thanked his Lord for us, and asked for a safe passage out in the North Sea. As we sailed past the Soutars, the considerable hills guarding the entrance to

Cromarty Firth, we saw a dolphin leaping out of the sea to greet us.

We anchored off our old house, Clunes, and rang home – a profoundly moving and satisfying moment.

Later we motored round to the harbour, and at the pierhead saw the great figure of Reg Adams waving a welcome. He and Peggy had driven all the way up to tow our boat home. From the boat we saw a strange sight – the hammer and sickle flying above the royal coat of arms of the Royal Hotel. A Russian yacht club was paying a courtesy visit, and the Communist government had not yet fallen; only a short time later the flag would have been different.

I got a lift to the delightfully small airport at Inverness, and in an hour was in London. John met me, and as he drove me down to Sandwich he told me the full sad story. His son had been living an unconventional life in one of America's cities, and to earn some money had got a job as a taxi driver. He had taken a passenger way up into the mountains and was never heard of again. A year or two later a human jaw bone was found not far from a mountain road; after forensic tests it proved to be the only human remains of Jamie, the happy young teenager we had known in Sandwich. After a Catholic Mass in St. Clement's I was to bury its ashes in his mother's grave in the churchyard next to our old Rectory.

My amazingly varied and wonderful voyage brought out astonishing kindness from so many people, but it was tightly bracketed by two tragic funerals – it felt very strange.

I caught the train home to a lovely welcome by Mary and our retriever, Barnie. Slowly the sponsorship money came in, and reached £11,000. Don MacLeod kindly edited my video, and I accepted invitations to show it at the Royal

Motor Yacht Club Shrimper dinner and many church halls in the area. This brought the total up to £12,000.

It had all been one of the great experiences of my life.

After a few years of sailing in the Shrimper, we joined a flotilla of larger chartered boats, sailing in the Greek islands. We had a boat with a red-edged foresail which stood out against the blue sea and the white mountains of classical Greece. We either joined the others in a shoreside taverna or anchored in the remote bay of an uninhabited island; again and again I had to stop myself thinking, "This is what other people do!" We explored deserted villages, fields full of spring flowers, ruined monasteries and ancient sites. On our first flotilla holiday we often had to ask the others for help and advice; on our final day we joined in an organised race; we were able to hold a long tack, and much to our surprise, crossed the line first, to the delight of everybody, except to the crew of the boat which came in second!

Chapter XXII

DORSET – CHARACTERS & TRAGEDIES -
Friends and families in the parish - St. Margaret's Westminster

Once we were settled in Dorset, Mary continued teaching piano and cello to both adults and children. Before long she was in much demand to play in quartets and orchestras, and also sang in the Barn Choir under the guidance of Richard Hall; he would turn up on a powerful motorbike, covered in black leather and black helmet – a large, long bearded figure, looking like either a Rocker or an Old Testament prophet; he would then beguile you with a delightful smile and a warm enthusiasm. It is a good, small choir, hand-picked. Each summer they go to the empty chapel on the hill at Abbotsbury, have champagne and salmon sandwiches and sing, just for the joy of singing – a fulfilment of our Abbotsbury doctrine of years before, when we were returning to Kent, the doctrine of worshipping for its own sake – not looking sideways to see what effect it would have on other people.

I had a similar thought when visiting. I had sat in a cottage with a non-churchy family, chatting for about half an hour; they had no worries to share and I was not trying to get them to come to church. As I wandered down the pathway I was chortling with laughter at some joke we had shared, and as I closed the garden gate, I said to myself, "Yes, I've been a good parson today." As I drove away I wondered what made me think that? What was the theology behind it? I had enjoyed them, I was the man of God in that village, perhaps I had, indirectly, helped them to feel that God enjoyed them too? In contrast, I remember a Bible study where a lovely, devout woman liked the thought of "Jesus, friend of sinners."

"Yes, he enjoys you," I said.

"Oh, I know that he accepts me, but I can't think he enjoys me!"

"Oh, yes, he does, and so do we!".

We all gave her a hug, and I think she believed us. The Gospel, or Good News, is very simple: "God enjoys us so don't hurt Him."

I carried on with the custom of exchange visits with St. Martin-in-the-Fields. Once more we went to the Christmas Carol Service, taking up a coach full of parishioners and many bags of toys, collected in the churches and local schools. Rose and Joan are two wonderful ladies, true villagers of Winterborne Kingston, two good friends who led a team of workers providing excellent food at almost every function in the church and village. They always came on this visit to London and for them it was a day away from their responsibilities, a time of hospitality in St. Martin's Vicarage and candlelit magic and soaring singing by the red-robed choir of the Royal Parish Church, the start of their Christmas.

In the summer there was a return visit, with members of the St. Martin's Darby & Joan and International Clubs. They were given lunch, once in medieval Tomson Manor, once in Jacobean Anderson Manor and then in the library of Charborough Park, where Walter and Pam Drax renewed many links with their guests from Barbados. It was wonderful seeing so many black faces in our Dorset villages. In later years we gave them lunch in Kingston Village Hall where they were welcomed by the children from the village school; lunch was followed by hilarious entertainment and singing. In groups of three or four, our smartly dressed visitors were given tea in the ancient cottages and pretty gardens of several parishioners from the other villages.

When we had arrived in Dorset the organist at Almer and Morden was Frank Tatchell, a dear, gentle little old man, pure Dorset; he drove up from Sandford in an ancient Morris. I suggested that we pay him for playing, but he declined.

"Well, can't we pay for your travel, then?"

"Oh, I would have to ask my accountant about that".

Later, I realised he owned his own farm, a handsome farmhouse, six cottages and Tatchell's Tip!

Mick Gulliford, who played at Bloxworth formed the Red Post Male Choir. Mick had been brought up in Wales, as had his four sons and two daughters. His wife, Esme, was the sister of Vic Stone, one of the tenant farmers of Bloxworth. Vic was a wonderful character, and I had a great respect for him, a relaxed portly man with a cheerful manner and a keen mind. "Why did I spend the best years of my life as the lavatory attendant to a lot of cows?" he would say. His real talents were used when he became Chairman of the Governors of the Purbeck School and Chairman of the Purbeck District Council. His wife, Megan, was the daughter of a famous spiritual healer. She enjoyed telling me of a W.I. meeting in their farmhouse; as the good ladies walked down the drive they heard singing; it came from Vic, lying in the ditch; Vic liked his beer. They had two sons and two daughters, so when the Gullifords and the Stones were together it was a great family occasion, and they often included us.

Before I came to Dorset, I had read my predecessor's description of the parish of Bloxworth; he said that the congregation was small and the church's future was uncertain; he also said that there was a gulf between the Church and the Social Club – most of its members were people who had lived in the village all their lives. Vic was their Chairman, and so, at the end of an evening's visiting, I would often have a drink with him in the Club. One night I had already been given a pint or two, and then was offered a whisky by Herbie Hunt – the Hunts and the Gales had been in the village for centuries. Herbie is large and cheerful and had been the village special constable in Morden; so when I refused his kind offer, as I was driving, he said, in broad Dorset,

"Oh, go on Vicar, just put your wheel in the ditch and it will take you hoame!"

Of course I had to accept, and noticed that his comment was true. The Gullifords and other Church people were drinking in the Club, and before long the gulf was bridged. At the Club Harvest Supper, the Secretary stood up and said, "Now, the Reverend Hugh would like to see you all in Church for the Harvest Festival on Sunday". To my delight they all followed him in the next day. Very gratifying.

The Red Post Choir was remarkable. Most village Church choirs had a number of elderly ladies, two or three girls and two old men. Here we had a bunch of nearly a dozen men, most in their thirties or forties, no robes, some coming from the fields with straw in their hair, others from smart offices; three were the hulking sons of Mick Gulliford, Richard, Fred and Jim. They went round all the village churches, and were an enormous encouragement and support. They also did an entertainment for the Harvest Supper – Frank Tatchell did a wonderful, bemused, little farm labourer singing, "There's a hole in my bucket, dear Liza, dear Liza". Mick had a very senior post in the engineering side of television and often travelled great distances to be home in time for choir practice; he would have prepared everything meticulously – his commitment put me to shame.

Fred became a good friend through our sailing adventures. His brother Jim lived in Wareham; he had a cheerful, good-looking, friendly son, James who had been kicking a football about in a park; he collapsed and died instantly of heart failure. The shock and grief of the whole family were indescribable, and I was sorely stretched in trying to help them; all I could do was to be with them. Bloxworth Church was packed for his funeral and many of his friends, boys and girls from the Purbeck School, were there. One of their teachers thanked me for the service; I had said "Why can God possibly have allowed such a thing to happen?" …………….. After years of asking, I still have no answer……………………. All I can say is that I believe that James is alright, that God is with you and in each of you, helping you to look after each other." The teacher had especially thanked me for saying there is no answer.

In Kingston there was a traditional village school of about forty children, I knew most of them by name; in my early years it was entirely traditional, with the teacher sitting on a high stool and talking to the children; later, the building and the education were radically changed in a modern, imaginative fashion. Both were excellent in their different ways. To start with, I could wander in and out at will, but later the doors were locked and I had to ring the bell. At one stage the government was constantly criticising teachers. I was in the school corridor and heard a lesson going on, and the teacher was saying,

"Luke, what are you good at?"

"Writing".

"Yes, you wrote a lovely story. And Anne, what are you good at?"

"Adding up".

"Yes, you got all your sums right." And, Adam, what are you good at?"

In a downcast voice, "I'm not good at anything".

"Oh, yes you are! You're very good at being kind to people".

It was humbling to stand there and listen to such wisdom. Encourage, encourage, encourage. I wrote to the Minister of Education recounting this experience, suggesting that the teachers themselves needed such encouragement from the Government. I had no reply.

Early on in our time in Dorset a family moved into Morden Dairy Cottage, a few hundred yards from the

Vicarage. One day I saw an ambulance go past and stop outside the cottage; shortly afterwards, I went along to see if anything was seriously wrong. A tall man, Anton Simon, welcomed me and explained that his wife, Tess, had just been brought back from hospital after a bad bout of asthma. He took me upstairs to see her; after talking for a while it seemed right to tentatively offer a prayer; my offer was warmly accepted and, in the most natural way, Anton knelt on the old boards while I gave Tess a blessing. I immediately realised that they were an unusual family and over the years they have become firm friends. They are both Catholics, Anton having been at Downside with Antony Sutch, of Radio 4 fame, and many other friends who also turned up at their parties – and what parties! Anton has a very quick mind and quick wit, a great teller of risqué jokes and loyal and caring to his many friends; a strong personality, he would keep in touch for weeks with anybody bereaved, ringing them up every day to see if they were alright. His remarkable, open honesty gave him a great, perceptive knowledge of human nature. He was one of the few people who would cycle up the road on a Saturday morning, just to pop in, for no reason except to see us.

Tess is scrumptious, with a mixture of English, Irish, and Mediterranean blood, volatile, warm hearted, enormous fun, irrepressible, ever hospitable, a committed wife and a loving mother.

They already had a son, three year old Charlie, and a few months after their arrival in Morden she gave birth to a beautiful baby boy, Harry. One Saturday night, about ten, the telephone rang: it was Anton, "For God's sake, Hugh, come round. Harry is dead." I hurtled round; Anton was on his way to the hospital, but it was too late – a cot death –

unexplainable, no obvious cause. Mercifully, a friend was with them for the weekend, because Tess was wild with grief. I shall never forget it. Anton returned soon, and I stayed the whole night with them. As dawn broke, I walked wearily past the Vicarage and up Paradise Lane to the top of the hill – and complained bitterly to God; then I took the early Communion Service where I shared the news with horrified friends of theirs; for them, as well as for me, the whole service was about Harry, Tess, Anton and Charlie; and the crucifixion was sharp. Over the next few months and years they received much help from other parents bereaved through a cot death; and then helped others in their turn. Dom Antony Sutch, then Headmaster of Downside, part of the ancient Benedictine Community, joined me in taking Harry's service in Morden Church. A few years later Eugene was born and then Fleur, and both were christened at Morden.

Through all these family occasions we came to know Tess' parents very well, Mike and Meg Stopford. Mike was laid back, warm and humble, and Meg, like her daughter, was a riot. She had had her share of tragedy and could easily weep and then bubble with laughter. If any recently bereaved person turned up in Church I would make sure that they met Meg and I would then see them embracing a few seconds later. Mike's forbears were a mixture of Royal Navy and Maltese aristocracy, and they had a house in Malta which they offered us for a holiday; they even leant us their bright yellow 1960's Ford Cortina, an unheard of privilege. It had the gear lever on the steering wheel and although thirty years old, only had a few thousand miles on the clock. Before we went, we read the Kapillan of Malta by Nicholas Monserrat, a wonderful novel combining the rich history of the Island, the heroic history of the war years, the life of a priest and an enchanting love story.

Mike and Meg had a small swimming pool in their garden which was totally private so that we could swim with nothing on – always the best way, whether from my boat or a cold mountain stream. In the house we were looked after by two Maltese ladies; Malta is strongly Catholic and they were delighted to meet a priest with a lovely wife. Meg had arranged for us to have lunch or dinner with some of their family and friends – a great privilege to knock on the plain door set in a blank wall in a narrow street and be welcomed into a large hall and beautiful garden beyond.

Vera House had been Churchwarden of Winterborne Kingston for many years – a farmer's wife, she rode her high old bicycle to Church, getting everything ready and with a sweet smile welcoming everybody who came.

Tony Simpson was the other Churchwarden at Kingston and Jenny ran the Playgroup. They knew everybody in the village and always understood people in difficulty or trouble –Gospel values. I always felt at home with them. Many years ago Tony started the symptoms of Motor Neurone Disease, which was already affecting his hands and his feet. He told me that he had been given healing prayers and the laying on of hands some time ago. Almost uniquely, the disease did not spread until more than twenty years later. They retired to Devon and I took his funeral; I told the congregation how I had visited him in hospital shortly before he had died. He was asleep and Jenny was explaining how he had to have a rubber sheet under him. Tony opened an eye and said,

"Don't worry, Hugh, I've been using rubber all my life!"

John Webber was another Churchwarden in Kingston, a farmer, leading member of the NFU, a magistrate, much involved in many local and national charities, a strong man who did not waste words, with country ways and a country voice. Like many others I had a great respect for him and was moved by the steady look in his eye as he gave me Communion at the altar and then, when ill, from his chair at home. He was in a Plymouth hospital, dying of cancer; without telling him, I drove down to see him. As I appeared at the door of the ward, he just looked up and said, in broad Dorset,

"Well, booger me!"

I mentioned his surprised delight when I took his funeral; the congregation flowed over into the graveyard and the singing could be heard in the next village.

Simon and Susie Patterson, with their children Alexander, Barnie and Lottie, rented Almer Manor. They regularly came to church and sometimes Simon would bring one of the boys to the short, quiet 8 o'clock communion – a good habit. They now often have me to their home outside Wareham. They move in worlds very different to mine – business, journalism, psychology and politics, which gives me a helpful insight into modern life – they are warm and loyal friends.

One evening the telephone rang: it was Ann Jenkins, wife of Ken our mechanic friend, and mother of Richard, the boy with C.F., and his sister Clare. Ken had collapsed in the bathroom, had a massive heart attack – and died. He was in his early fifties. We were half prepared for Richard's early death, but not for this. We feared that in order to secure Richard's financial future, Ken had worked himself to his own death, often staying out late at night, working under a car in cold weather – always ready to help a client. Next morning I joined Ann and her brother who drove us up to Frimley Hospital in Surrey to tell Richard. Several times I had already gone to Frimley, to see Richard and take him out, when possible, but this was different. I am haunted, still, by the memory of Richard's shock and rage as he heard the news and fled from his room in blind anger.

The Church was packed for Ken's funeral, he was widely liked and respected in our part of Dorset. Richard was able to have some periods of reasonable health over the next few years and enjoyed the car which his father had bought him – it had the number plate beginning YOB, which amused him. However, it was not long before he was continuously in hospital; sadly, he had to be moved to a more specialised ward in a hospital the further side of Surrey, where he died. In Frimley both Richard and his family had been known and loved by all the nurses and doctors; they had responded to his courage and humour. I have often noticed how children who spend much time in hospital have an open, easy, direct way of talking with adults; Richard certainly did.

His funeral service was equally harrowing and draining, with a huge congregation, including lots of young people; it overflowed into the chancel and even the vestry. We laid him to rest beside his father in the churchyard overlooking the fields and woods of Morden. When it was finally over, I wearily dragged myself up to the top of the big field behind the Church, just to be alone. To my dismay, I saw a figure in the distance, approaching me up the hill. But it was Anton. He had seen me far away; looking through his binoculars he could tell by the droop of my shoulders that I was in trouble. He folded me in his arms and took me to the cottage for the malt whisky he kept especially for me; a true friend; a forceful personality, yes, but also sensitive and caring. Ann endured the next years, having lost both her husband and her son, and is now happily remarried. Clare is also living in Morden, and has done very well in the world of horses.

I was often asked for prayers of healing. I would usually lay my hands on the person who was suffering, holding their head, shoulder or hand; I would try to empty myself of my own thoughts and feelings, so that I could be a personal living channel for God's healing love to flow through me. I always asked for healing of both body and mind, leaving the final outcome in God's hands. I know that these prayers always brought some degree of peace to both the sufferer and also the anxious family. I am sure that a peaceful rather than a tense state of mind can help the process of bodily healing. Once, but only once, there was a remarkable result! Olive Blott was one of our lay readers in Broadstairs, a devout and prayerful woman. She was in hospital for an operation and I gave her the laying on of hands the night before. Later, she told me that when she woke in the morning, before the operation, she noticed that a large mole on her arm had disappeared. Up till then no medical attention had been successful. Who knows?

I was asked to help in this way when Stanley Chattey's sister and her husband were staying with them at Bloxworth. Stanley's sister, had a cancer, and after the service in Church I blessed her at the altar rail. She died some time later and I was asked to bury her ashes in the churchyard of Bingham's Melcome, the lovely ancient stone house in a hidden valley of deepest Dorset, near the village of Melcombe Bingham. Later, I met their daughter, Annie, and her fiancé Johnnie Cunningham-Jardine from Dumfriesshire, and at Michael's earnest request, I promised to take their wedding whenever it would be.

Very sadly, Michael fell ill and died before the great day was fixed, and I took his funeral at Holy Trinity, Brompton. A few weeks later Annie rang, asking if I could take her wedding at St. Margaret's, Westminster, the parish church of Parliament; it is a large ancient church, but overshadowed by its neighbour, Westminster Abbey. She gave me the time, half past two, and the date; to my dismay, when I looked in my diary, I saw that I had a wedding in Zelston that day at twelve o'clock. Annie was deeply disappointed.

She rang back later, saying,

"If we sent a helicopter for you, would you come?"

"Yes, of course – I could just do it".

On the day of the weddings the Dorset bride was held up. She was coming in a horse drawn carriage and it was held up on the main road. The minutes ticked tensely by, until it was nearly half past twelve by the time she entered the church. I calmed her down and took her wedding without hurry; I couldn't spoil the Dorset wedding for the sake of the London one; but I did cut down my address and left out everything that was not necessary. At the end of the service I walked slowly down the aisle and only when out of the church and out of sight did I hitch up my robes and run down the lane to the car where Mary was waiting to take us up the road to the helicopter, rotors whirling in readiness.

As we flew over southern England, again and again we saw the pattern of medieval England below us, a village, church, big house, Vicarage, farmhouse and cottages. The countryside was dotted with the blue of private swimming pools; they became rarer and disappeared as we approached the poorer parts of London. A grand car met us at Battersea and sped to St. Margaret's, in good time for the lovely and fashionable wedding and following reception at Green Park. At a party a few weeks later, I met a fellow wedding guest, Chips Selby Bennet, a large, loud, rumbustious man who immediately introduced me to a friend as "The Rotary Rev"!

Chapter XXIII

DORSET – YOUTH ALIVE - Fun Week - Huish - Bear Grylls

In successive years we ran a teenage group, Youth Alive. We put on youth services; one included some live drama, with one of the teenagers lighting up a cigarette in the middle of the service; one of the horrified adults bundled him out; my following comments were meant to prove something or other, about tolerance, understanding, acceptance. I don't think that it was one of our group who was responsible for another discovery – a condom on the carpet of the chancel floor; sacrilege, or a natural place for loving? I suppose that it might depend on the degree of commitment of the young lovers? Some of the congregation were horrified, while others, like me, heard the news with a wry smile. We took Youth Alive away for several weekends, combining much fun with some good work such as role-playing stories from the Gospels. On these occasions I got very little sleep at night and many a teenager still has a treasured photo of one of the many times I was found sleeping in a ditch the following day.

I couldn't have done this youth work without the help of some wonderful parents, Oliver and Liz Lucas, Wendy Carter, Don and Sarah MacLeod, Terry and Gail Wood, amongst others. Oliver became deeply involved in church life, both intellectually, spiritually and emotionally.

Don was the son of a Wee Free minister from Skye. By pure chance we discovered that he had owned and run Kingsmills Hotel in Inverness, the former home of my Inglis ancestors. It is now hugely enlarged and one of the smartest hotels in the Highlands. Don knew his Bible from cover to cover and had all the correct answers to everything; he used to refer to me as "Hugh without a clue," until he saw a copy of the separate Gospels in different columns, contrasting the different versions of the same story. It was a conversion moment for him, helping him to a wiser understanding of the Bible and a more tolerant understanding of people. Without any formal training or authorisation these helpers would often give the address at a Church service, usually well attended by the youngsters. The highlight of my week was often to receive Communion from one of them, standing at the altar, face to face. They knew me and my faults very well and it was both humbling and reassuring to receive the Body and Blood of Christ at their hands. They were members of the Support Group which met regularly at the Rectory, where we shared personal difficulties quite deeply, both giving and receiving understanding.

Oliver was the first leader of our Children's Fun Week, and Terry Wood the second. I did not have the energy to run it myself, and so delegated, even though this meant that the children did not get to know me so well. We planned it months ahead; about a hundred children came, from all five parishes. We took them swimming in several private pools in the parish, up in the park at Charborough, Huish, North Farm, amongst others. We took them walking, camping, raft making, taught them arts and crafts and gave them a day on the beach at Studland. We ended with a riotous disco in Morden Village Hall. Teenagers, too old to join, returned as responsible young helpers. Originally, in my mind, the week was to include some spiritual input, and on the Sunday I commissioned the helpers at the altar. After every visit to a private home, the children would raise their arms and voices in a great shout of "THANK YOU!" Sadly, the teaching was never included, the commissioning was not really wanted, and even the "thank you's" became more muted and finally disappeared. The Week was very carefully organised, so that we could live with the knowledge that we never knew how many parents would be free to turn up each day. With all the increasing burden of Health and Safety regulations, the Week became more and more difficult to run, and finally died. Typical. Who missed out? Both the children, the parents and the helpers.

Tony and Jo Davies lived at Huish and played an important part in our family's life – they gave interesting dinner parties, hosted the Church fete and invited us to their swimming pool. They did a lot for the Dyslexia Society both locally and nationally and when they bought Green Island in Poole Harbour, they shared it with the Green Island Holiday Trust, which they started. On six separate weeks they gave six disabled people a wonderful holiday; they had the help of different volunteers each time. As you can imagine, those weeks were much appreciated; also by giving hospitality at Huish in the winter, Jo created a strong sense of a Green Island community.

The island itself is a gem; it is a joy to walk round near the shore, and have glimpses of the sparkling sea through the trees. At low tide the mudflats teem with a wide variety of feeding sea birds. Jo and Mary shared a fiftieth birthday party, held in the glade in the middle of the island; all the guests were ferried over in one of the Harbour pleasure boats – a magical evening. Jo and her new husband, David Pope, very kindly gave my sixtieth birthday party at Huish; old friends came from some distance, we swam in their pool, ate and drank and to the skirl of the pipes danced an eightsome reel; my mother, aged a mere ninety-three, danced a pretty pas de bas with the best of them. I also treasure the memory of Patrick Mayhew, a large man, doing the washing up, while my tiny mother dried up beside him.

I have been involved with four generations of the family of Bear Grylls, adventurer, television personality and now Chief Scout. His grandfather was a distinguished Brigadier and devout churchwarden of Winterborne Zelston. Stupidly, I tried to introduce a few minor modern changes to the service, which caused him much distress. I went to see him in his cosy study in Zelston House and sipped sherry on his comfortable old sofa by the log fire. I said,

"Ted, I'm sorry if I have upset you with the idea of some changes. Even though they are very small, they seem to really distress you. May I try to put into words why strict adherence to the Book of Common Prayer means so much to you?"

"Yes, of course".

"Well, we live in disturbing times, crime is rising, public and private honesty is disappearing, divorce is growing and society seems to be falling apart. You are an upright man and have lived your life by the old standards of decency. You see the monarchy, St. George and the Prayer Book as forming a rampart against the tide of immoral modernity;

move one brick and the wall will crumble. Is that, perhaps, why the Prayer Book is so important to you; because if that is so, I quite understand?"

The dear old man looked somewhat surprised and gratified.

"Yes, yes, Hugh, I think you put that very well."

We grew in respect and friendship for each other and worked well together. I think this can be a good way of creating confidence and communication between people of different views.

In contrast, for any vicar, it is easy to be dogmatic and ecclesiastical... a little girl's pet mouse died. She carefully made a tiny coffin and filled it with flowers; she thought of a prayer and chose a hymn. With great solemnity, the family gathered around the little grave, heads bowed.

Suddenly her daddy said, "It's just moved; it's alive! What shall I do?"

"Kill it!" cried the little girl.

This is a timely warmly to any vicar who has exactly the same feeling about a parishioner who spoils his carefully prepared service! The ceremony must go on, even at the cost of a life!

I had several meals with the brigadier in the dining room of that lovely house. Later he was in hospital; I was sitting in my car in the lay-by of a country road outside the parish, having taken an assembly in one of the neighbouring village schools. A car pulled up and Tony Simpson, churchwarden of Kingston, came to me,

"We've been searching for you. The Brigadier is dying and wants you with him."

I went straight to Blandford Hospital so that I could give him the blessing before he died. In preparing for his funeral I learnt of the important, skilled work he had done after the War, rescuing top German scientists from the clutches of the Russians.

The Brigadier's son was Sir Michael Grylls, Tory MP for North West Surrey. He and his wife Sally, daughter Lara and son Bear, moved into Zelston House. Michael was always well dressed but relaxed, warm and welcoming in manner, fun, enthusiastic, not judgemental, colourful, devout and a great support to me, both personally and in the parish – a truly remarkable man.

Sally is unique. She has an unmistakable classy voice and is genuinely at home with everybody. She also is full of enthusiasm and new ideas; a keen organiser, a strong personality, eccentric, a one-off, with a firm faith in a personal, caring God to whom she is committed. Utterly loyal both to me and my successor. Early one morning she heard of a tragic death and drove straight round to the family's cottage, still in her dressing gown and slippers. They have never forgotten the comfort she gave them. She crashed her BMW and bought an old yellow VW Camper van instead. It broke down in Piccadilly, but she was able to steer it onto the double yellow lines. It was late in the evening, there was nothing she could do, so she bedded down for the night. The police knocked on the window and asked,

"Name?"

"Lady Grylls".

"Yeah, come on, stop fooling, who are you?"

Sally used to love telling this story against herself.

On another occasion Sally was driving home from London in the yellow camper van; she stopped to help a man standing on the roadside, thumbing a lift. Making casual conversation she asked where he had just come from.

"I'm on my way home; they've just let me out of prison."

"Well, I'm glad you're free now. What were you in for?"

"Murder"

Totally unabashed and unafraid, Sally asked him for a cup of tea at Zelston House before he went on his way. She has a heart of gold and great compassion for anybody in difficulty.

Michael and Sally gave innumerable lunch, dinner and drinks parties, but my most regular visits were to their big old kitchen where we sat around their table for a meal and Bible study – a good group of people from different backgrounds. I took the wedding of their daughter, Lara – she longed for it to be in Zelston Church, but it was too small; so they just added a marquee on the side! Many of the Cabinet were there as guests. I was also included when Michael's former constituents gave him a flag pole as a thank you present on his retirement from Parliament after 29 years. He asked me to come to the "erection" party.

Through their family occasions I got to know their son Bear while he was still at school. Why the name Bear? – his real name is Edward ....Ted ....Teddy ....Teddy bear ....Bear. Once he was asked to read the lesson at Zelston Church; he was barefoot and jumped over the pews to reach the lectern. Bear came to 'Youth Alive' and our teenagers were impressed by his sincerity and irrepressible freedom and humour. I was in Zelston House when he was in hospital in Kenya with a broken back. His parachute had not opened properly when he had jumped out of a plane. I spoke to him on the telephone and gave him a healing prayer and blessing as he lay in his hospital bed thousands of miles away – the first time that a prayer of mine had been instantly heard far away, horizontally as well as vertically. If I wanted a picture image of my prayers for our family in Australia, I would usually imagine my prayers going to God, as to a satellite and then down to earth again – my prayers would be purified by God's love for them. All picture language, of course.

I shared with Bear's parents their anxiety whilst he was making his successful attempt to climb Everest, a lifelong ambition. When he returned safely he was surprised to learn that he had become the youngest Britain to ascend and safely return from the summit. He has written a very readable book about it, "Facing Up". It includes the time when he fell down a deep crevasse – having only just fixed on his harness which held him dangling far below. A few years later he made the most Northerly crossing of the Atlantic undertaken in an open 'Rib' boat. There were moments of terror even greater than anything on Everest. He writes of this expedition in 'Facing the Ocean', a mature book.

A few years earlier, he had brought Shara, his new fiancée, for a sail with me, one Sunday evening after Evensong. The tide was ebbing fast and the boat would soon be on the sand, so we waded out as quickly as possible; I tore off my trousers and Bear and Shara were highly amused to see me paddling through the water in my old fashioned and rather stained white Y fronts, dark shirt and dog collar! As we sailed along I discovered that I had met her mother in our teenage years in Woldingham; in fact, my father had acted for her grandfather, Dick Stafford. I was touched to be asked to take Bear and Shara's wedding at Tandridge, not far from Woldingham. With the wedding invitations they had sent a request for pieces of advice about marriage; in my address I read out some of the wise words; these two were the most popular:

Together, live each day like your last,

And each night like your first!

To Bear: Hug and squeeze her daily, and if the daily doesn't like it,

try the au pair!

After the gales of laughter had subsided, the congregation were ready for my own thoughts on God and on loving.

The beginning and end of the day were typically unconventional: the ushers wore morning suit tailcoats and pyjama trousers tucked into long socks, which gave them an absurdly Regency appearance. At the end of the reception the bride and groom flew off in a helicopter.

One morning I had a call from somebody in Zelston saying that Michael had had a massive heart attack and had died instantly. He was only 67 and his sudden death left a big hole in our lives. I helped with his inspiring funeral in Wimborne Minster; the service sheet included many sayings and poems. This was the one most typical of Michael:

From quiet homes and first beginnings
Out to the undiscovered ends,
There's nothing worth the wear of winning
But laughter and the love of friends.

Some years later I christened Bear and Shara's second son, Marmaduke, using water that had been frozen snow from the top of Mount Everest. Since then, Scouts throughout the world have voted Bear as Chief Scout – a great honour, but also a brilliant choice as Bear has all the courage, flair and enthusiasm to captivate the young. I recommend his autobiography *Mud Sweat and Tears* (ISBN 978-190502-648-7); it reveals his tenderness and self-doubt. It is a good read,

I have written at length about this remarkable colourful family because they have played a large part in my life in Dorset... but there are many others in the parishes who shared lakes of wine and distilleries of whisky with me, wept and laughed with me and gave me continued support; but I would need another volume to describe you all.

Chapter XXIV

DORSET – VARIETY - a difficulty - Eton - counselling

O ne of the dilemmas for a parish priest was the question of church marriage after a divorce. Broken families can be the cause of so many difficulties, and the Church should give full support to couples trying to keep their marriage vows, staying together "till death do us part". How can the Church take those vows seriously if it ignores the breaking of the vows by divorce and allows remarriage? On the other hand, marriages do break up for a variety of reasons, and it can be a wonderful thing if a man or woman finds a good new partner, has a fresh start in life and so want to be married in the eyes of God, in church.

In practice there seems to be no way of reconciling these two opposing principles. When I was first ordained remarriage in church was not allowed, and a divorced person could not receive Holy Communion without special permission. Recognising the spiritual needs of a couple seeking remarriage, the Church grudgingly allowed a service of blessing following a civil marriage, but it had to be in a side chapel, no music, no bells, no special flowers. Slowly these restrictions were ignored and then dropped. This was especially helpful for a bride who had not been married before. I have now devised an order of service for a Blessing which includes the traditional vows, but puts them in the past tense, "I have taken this woman to my wedded wife, to have an to hold from this day forward, for better, for worse, for richer, for poorer…..etc."

When I was Vicar I used the official Prayers for a Service after a Civil Marriage; I always offered the same service to everybody, and never remarriage in church. In those days, these were the guidelines of the Church of England and of our Bishop, and I think it was the right approach, illogical compromise though it is. It is vital that the same rule applies to everybody or else refusal is felt to be a personal rejection, but sometimes it went tragically wrong and one bride's family stopped coming to church, wrote to the Bishop and the Archbishop and over a period of years were unable to accept any of my explanation. I suspect that they thought I was an heartless ecclesiastic, and their friends in the parish seemed to think the same. It was all very sad. Mercifully they started to come to church again some time after my retirement.

Today, as a retired priest, I follow the custom in this parish, and am willing to remarry in church if appropriate.

At one stage I went to a wedding anniversary service for Tess and Anton. It was held in the Church in the grounds of Lulworth Castle, the first Catholic Church to be built in England since the Reformation; King George III had given his permission, provided it did not look like a church.

Unfortunately I could not go to the evening dinner party which followed so a few weeks later they asked me to Dairy Cottage to see a video of the hilarious evening. As usual Anton gave me a good whisky, topped up with water in a tumbler. I drank it and he asked his younger son, Eugene, to get me another. Eugene was about eight at the time and did not know the difference between whisky and wine, so poured an enormous dram into my glass. I was so involved with the video that I just did not notice, and finished the lot. As I left, Anton was telling me some racy Dublin jokes in a broad Irish accent. As I stumbled out into the pouring rain I carried on the repartee in the same loud Irish brogue. Suddenly I switched to roughest Glasgow and found myself consumed with blind anger which I hurled at the Almighty, violent oaths shouted into the black night and crashing rain. I don't know what the anger was about – probably a gut reaction to the frustrations of life. Shouting and swearing, I fell into the ditch; immediately my angry shouts turned into gales of laughter and by the time I reached home I was soaked to the skin and very content, set free from all my anger. Some weeks later I told Bruce and Joyce Randall of this crazy walk home. He said, "Oh yes, we heard that shouting and swearing – so it was you, was it?!" Their house was two hundred yards away, their windows were shut against the rain, so they couldn't possibly have heard me – it was a total leg pull.

George and Christine had moved into Morden and before long they organised a good, old-fashioned village concert. We devised a skit of our own, swapping roles. Mary dressed up as me, the Vicar, beard, dog collar and all; I had a skirt, some magnificent purple bloomers and a blonde wig. I had a fag dangling out of my mouth and scraped away at a cello between my legs. There was much laughter as we acted out each other's prejudices, using each other's language.

Mary (as Vicar)   "Sorry, love, they hate the times you've given them; you must arrange the Flower Rota all over again."

Me (as Mary)   "Oh shit!!"

Total collapse of the whole audience.

At the invitation of the School Chaplain, Charles Mitchell-Innes, I had often preached at Milton Abbey. He moved to Eton as the Conduct, the Senior Chaplain, and he asked me to preach there. I stayed overnight with them; and my heart went out to them, as in their first term there, they had heard that their son Andrew, a temporary prep-school master, had been running with the boys, had collapsed with heart failure and died – just like James Gulliford a few years earlier. I went to his memorial service in the College Chapel – a beautiful, inspiring, very Christian service.

I had been given the choice of an informal time with all the younger boys, including Prince William, or a sermon for the older boys in the Chapel. I chose the latter. At the start of the service I was led to the seat at the West end overlooking the boys and facing the altar. The Provost stood aside to let me in and I sat between him and the Headmaster; I had to pinch myself that it was real. I talked about James's breakdown, of the dangers of too much pressure to succeed and of the way my parishioners looked after me, of the dignity of vulnerability. The following year Charles asked me to help with the day of preparation just before the boys were to be confirmed. I had prepared a question and answer session for the morning and another one for the afternoon. During the lunch break I told

Charles that I was exhausted and that my thought processes were going awry. He had noticed this happening in the morning session, when I had asked the same question several times. He took over for the afternoon session. I slept deeply, and was all right for the bus journey from the retreat centre back to Eton. I had a profound conversation with an intelligent, deeply spiritual boy sitting beside me. I helped with the chalice at the Confirmation Communion next morning.

I became involved in the counselling world, learning through the Clinical Theology course; the group was led by Peter Graham, a priest, a hefty former Spitfire pilot, and widely experienced in counselling and group work. We practiced counselling about each other's real personal issues, we discovered our own hidden emotions through acting in role plays, and fantasy journeys. It was fascinating and very helpful, a sort of post Freudian exercise in the context of God's unconditional love for us. We aimed at discovering as much as possible about ourselves, so that we could listen to others with greater compassion and understanding. Great emphasis was laid on damaging experiences in the first years of life and how a person could be liberated from them by talking or acting out the experience, so that hidden damage could be exposed and its power diminished. We explored many personality types, and found we had something of each difficulty in ourselves – whether it was attention seeking, paranoia, depression, or whatever it might be,

It was a two year course, meeting for three hours once a fortnight during term time. It was highly organised, with a tight discipline. We did a third year and then I trained as an Assistant Tutor and led one group as a Tutor myself. People came to me for help, and I spent a proportion of my time seeing people in organised counselling sessions. Some asked for my help, while others were recommended to come; I also offered help to people I met, either in the parish or elsewhere. Some I saw over a regular period of time. I tried to help the men who had not been recommended for training for the Church' ministry; they had a strong sense of rejection. Some of the first women priests also came to see me, asking for help with the opposition they met. I was sad to hear how badly they were treated by some men who were always courteous under different circumstances.

I now find it very hard to get into the skin of those who still reject the priesthood of women. I remember reading a letter in the Times by a Jewish rabbi; he said that just because the Scriptures describe God as Father, does not mean that God is male. God is beyond gender, even if we describe Him as male because of the limitations of our language and imagination. In Genesis it says, "So God created man in his own image …. male and female he created them". Christians believe that God revealed himself in Jesus of Nazareth, caring, challenging, suffering, but Jesus could not be hermaphrodite, he had to be either a man or woman, and in the culture of the time it was natural for Jesus to be a man. I see no possible theological objections to women priests, only ecclesiastical ones, Apostolic Succession etc. Where church discipline conflicts with humanity; we can guess what Jesus' reaction would be. What do the opponents of women priests or bishops think the Gospel is all about?!

In listening to a number of men over the years, I was saddened to hear how many had been badly damaged by being sent away to boarding school at the age of seven. Several devout women came for help with their depression.

Sometimes depression is largely chemical, and can be treated with medication; sometimes it can also be caused by suppressed anger; the effort of denying the anger and keeping it in can make the sufferer very weary. I tried to help people understand that there was no need to be ashamed of their strong feelings, but rather that they should listen to them and not be ashamed to ask for help. There was one exercise I often used with some success.

"What does a baby need to survive?"

"Love, food, drink, water, air, sleep, nappy changing".

I would ask her to imagine herself as a baby again, and tell me where in her body she would feel pain if she lacked any of these necessities.

"If I lack food, I feel pain in my tummy, if I lack drink, I feel pain in my throat, if I am dirty, I feel pain in my bottom, etc."

"If you feel pain, what do you do?"

"I cry".

"Even if this irritates your parent?"

"Yes."

"If you don't cry, what happens?"

"I remain hungry, thirsty, dirty etc."

"What happens then?"

After a moments thought, and with horrified realisation, she would say,

"I die."

There might then follow a long silence, while the present implications of this sunk in; I would then help her repeat:

"I have basic needs. If my needs are not met, I feel pain and I cry.

If I do not cry, my needs are not heard,

My needs are not met ....

And I die."

I was humbled to discover how often this helped a woman, feeling guilty about complaining, to understand that she needed to demand help.

We were taught that, morally speaking, there are no such things as "good feelings or bad feelings, but just feelings". Every emotion that goes through a man is an inevitable, hormonal, response to what happens to him, or does not happen to him. He feels hungry because he lacks food, he feels sad because of loss, sexual arousal because of unpremeditated attraction, hatred and anger because of a threat of attack or neglect, etc. All these feelings are necessary for survival – in our basic animal nature attack may be the only form of defence. All too often I would hear a person say,

"I know I ought not to feel angry with my mother/father, because they did so much for me... but I do."

I tried to help him see that there is no meaning in the phrase "I ought not to feel ...."; it is, literally, non-sense, because I cannot help how I feel; I am only responsible for what I do with my feelings, how I act upon them; if I steal food, seduce a woman or hit my attacker, that is where morality enters, not at the point of having negative feelings.

Instead, we should listen to our feelings, see what causes them and deal with the need, whether it would be to move to the fridge if I feel hungry, or stand up to a bully if I feel angry.

It is also possible to have mixed, opposite feelings at the same time, and then it is wise to avoid the temptation to make a neat, celebral packet of explanation but instead, to acknowledge each emotion separately.   Another useful exercise was simple, but remarkably effective:

"How do you feel?"

"Depressed".

"How do you feel?"

"Confused."

"How do you feel?"

"Angry".

"How do you feel?"

"Calmer".

"How do you feel?"

"All right".

I was often astonished at how quickly somebody might deal with an emotion simply by acknowledging and naming it.

Often this helped in sorting out a woman's conflicting emotions with regard to her father or God, her father in heaven: grateful for some things, and angry about others, because of what had happened to her – and feeling guilty for feeling angry.   Some religious people found it very difficult to acknowledge that they were angry with life, with

God. "I ought to love God, and I do." I might help them talk to God in a chair opposite them.

"Do you feel He is listening to you?"

"Not really, no."

"Then imagine Him sitting there, with His back to you, and tell Him what you think of Him not listening to you."

Hopefully, some honest talking to God might follow, hurt and anger expressed – and then genuine love could follow and real praying could start again. Much depression may be caused by suppressed anger against people – and so against God. It is a lesson I am only learning slowly.

Every emotion can lead to a real, gutsy talking with God, and imagining His reply.

I believe that all feelings about life, about people, are feelings about God and can be dealt with best by straight talking with Him.

Years ago I was on an Ignatian retreat, and my guide was an Irish nun. I told her that I had lost the personal feeling that "Jesus had died for me". She guessed that I was seeing Christ as separate from myself, instead of seeing Him within me, as He had promised; St. Paul often took up this theme, Christ in me.

She suggested that I talk to Christ by looking in the mirror! This was easy enough, as I am bearded; but, of course, it is possible for anybody, man, woman or child. I was still feeling tense, so the Christ looked at me with a pained, anxious expression; and we looked at each other for quite a long time. Finally, the Christ recognised the mild absurdity of what we were doing and His lips twitched in a faint smile; then He grinned broadly and finally ended up roaring with laughter. The Christ within me had helped me laugh at myself. I am sure there are Freudian psychological equivalents saying the same thing. I suppose I tried to see something of the Christ in the men I visited in prison, either in Dorchester or behind the great, grey, grim walls of the Verne on the Isle of Portland. There, but for the face of God, go I.

Chapter XXV

DORSET – CONTRASTS - Dartmoor - Gorton
Jockie - Anna & Dominic - Corfe Castle

One day we went to stay with John and Judy Henderson on their lovely little farm at Holne, on the edge of Dartmoor. On the way we stopped, parked the car beside the road and walked up a hill. When at the top, we paused and looked back, only to see a car draw up beside our car, and then race off. Filled with anxiety we raced down the hill; sure enough, a window had been broken and my case stolen. We drove off in the direction the car had taken, and saw by the roadside, first a shirt, then later, underpants, trousers, one shoe and then the other, tossed out as the thieves drove away; but no case and worst of all, no sign of my diary, with all my appointments for that and the following year.

We went to report our loss at the Police Station in Ashburton; the burly police sergeant was most concerned for us, and said, with a broad Devon burr, "I'll pray that you find it." The next morning Judy helped us carefully search the ditches at both sides of the road. We went on for about a mile, even searching a thick bush beside the road. No luck. In despair I walked back to fetch the car. In my mind I could see that whenever I was out, somebody might be waiting for me at the Vicarage, and whenever I was at home I might be missing a meeting. I looked back and saw Mary and Judy waving wildly; as I drew closer I saw that Mary was holding my diary; it was unharmed and even my Bank cards were still there, tucked in the side flap. We had not seen it the previous evening because the diary was of a dark colour and the thieves had pushed it deep amongst the thorns of the bush. Judy had only discovered it because she had glimpsed something white in the middle of the bushes – one of my visiting cards had fallen out.

We went to the Ashburton Police Station and told the sergeant the good news and thanked him for his prayers. I certainly felt profound gratitude to God for the discovery, not thinking in terms of divine intervention or analysing its methods, but just expressing thankfulness personally.

Weary of arranging holiday lets for Gorton Jockie, we let it out on an annual basis; our first tenant was Craigie Aitchison, a son of the Lord Advocate and brother of the well known artist. With their common Edinburgh background he became an interesting neighbour to my mother. His life had not gone well for him, and sadly, he sometimes drank too heavily.

One afternoon I returned from parish visiting to find a distraught Mary standing at the door. She had just come off the telephone – a call from our next door neighbour in Lamlash; he had given her a running commentary:

"Gorton Jockie is on fire ....smoke and flames are pouring out of the window ....we have rung for the fire brigade ....they've just arrived ....and are breaking in ....they're dragging out Craigie ......they're laying him on the grass ......I think he's dead."

Yes, he had died, overcome by the fumes and smoke; he had left some clothes to dry close to a heater, and they had caught alight. Horrified, we got in touch with one of his relatives and arranged to take his funeral at the crematorium just outside Ayr, in a few days time.

Early next morning we drove up to Scotland. It was winter and there were no leaves on the trees; driving through Dumfriesshire we had views of hills and glens which we had never seen before; we had always travelled on those roads in summer. Our beloved Gorton Jockie was a sorry sight – much of the furniture and many pictures destroyed, the whole house covered in greasy black smoke; but it had not been burnt down, as we had feared. The walls, floors, doors, and most of the roof were undamaged. We rapidly made arrangements for the furniture to be stored in a shed up Glen Rosa belonging to the MacArthurs.

Poignantly, ironically, we took Craigies' cremation service, and drove home.

Later in the summer we stayed in the Byre for our usual summer holiday. We saw Gorton Jockie beautifully restored, but, very sadly, realised we had to sell it; it was bought by a genial sounding scientist for holidays and eventual retirement. We kept the Byre, and had several good holidays there.

Dominic is the son of our good friends and near neighbours, Rolf and Joy Shepherd. One day we were having drinks with Rolf and Joy; Dominic and Anna were there as well, having spent the night on the beach. We were all thrilled beyond measure when they told us they were getting married. Dominic is a painter, a strong character, both unconventional and traditional at the same time, imaginative, energetic, good looking and the ideal partner for Anna.

They did not want a large formal wedding, so it was just the immediate families in Morden Church – no hymns, no address, only a flute and a Shakespeare sonnet to accompany the lovely words of the Prayer Book marriage service which spoke all the more richly because there were no distractions, no gilding of the lily. Anna wore a sort of flimsy, pale purple dress which made me think of a Botticelli Venus. Her diadem was a ring of daisies from the Vicarage lawn and her bouquet some flowers from the hedgerow as I walked her to the Church. The service was followed by a meal at a long table in our drawing room; afterwards we saw them off from a quay on Poole Harbour, speeding away in a boat taking them to their honeymoon on Green Island.

They lived in a flat in Electric Mansions, directly above Brixton Market, a colourful, vibrant international scene. They nobly asked us all to dinner on Christmas Day, Rolf, Joy, James, Mary and me. I had just taken seven Christmas services, with only a few hours sleep in between; having driven all the way up to London I imagined that I would be too tired to be good company. When we had sat down I raised my glass in a toast,

"To the seven of us."

"We will soon be eight!" said Dominic. We were all thrilled and my joy immediately overcame my weariness.

Anna wanted to have the baby at home and the hospital agreed that it would be possible, provided the baby did not arrive on a Tuesday or a Thursday! Those were the weekdays when the market was in full swing and no ambulance would be able to get near, in case of difficulties. An adorable baby girl was born, looking so very like Anna at the same age, with two traditionally built West Indian nurses in attendance. The doorway at the bottom of Electric Mansions was often scattered with needles and stained with blood from a fight the night before. In spite of all this, the stall keepers and their rough looking customers were very protective of Anna and her baby in the pushchair. I christened her in the presence of a large gathering in Morden Church and gave her the names Nooka Sky Augusta McLaren Shepherd; Nooka was a princess in the Finnish children's book, Noggin the Nog, Sky – the colour of her eyes, Augusta, the month of her birth and McLaren after my mother. At the age of twelve she is a lovely girl, bright, alert and a voracious reader.

Dominic and Anna rent a cottage deep in a wood nearby. You reach it by a long track through the woods, avoiding the pheasants, the buzzards and the shy, gentle deer which stand staring, on the track and then leap away in graceful bounds. The track opens into a glade where you can see the house and the cottage. In winter, life in the cottage can be difficult, but in summer it is magic, especially when they give one of their happy lunch parties, either under the apple tree or in the front cottage garden ablaze with flowers. Four years later Caspar was born, and I named him at a joyful ceremony in the cottage garden. He is also very good looking, naturally (!), affectionate, imaginative and very much his own person. When he was about four he asked Anna about my mother.

"Mumma, Grannie Amy's very old, isn't she?"

"Yes, she's 101."

"Is she going to die?"

"Yes, one day." Long pause ....

"When the time comes, are you going to shoot her?"

My mother loved the story and told it to one of her nephews; she was delighted that he used it in his speech at some grand dinners.

I am very lucky to have my family so close; James in Weymouth, and Anna in Morden.

I was always interested in the idea of restoring an old house, but sadly all too many old cottages in Dorset had been modernised, often with very little sympathy or respect for the past. I started looking for an old house for our retirement, although it was seven years off. Once I started looking I could think of nothing else; so after seriously considering several possibilities we bought two cottages being sold as one, in East Street, Corfe Castle. The whole project involved major work and expense – far more than we expected, as usual! Terry Wood was our very imaginative architect, and Bruce Randall our loyal, experienced cheerful builder. With the help of his sons and the rest of his team, he removed the whole roof and finally replaced it, carrying the huge Purbeck stone slabs down and then up ladders. They knocked down walls, removed the 1970's bathroom, turning it into a sunroom, built a new plain staircase out of scaffolding planks, added old style windows and created a four bedroom house of huge character – lovely old stone floors, old doors and fireplaces, exposed beams and a panelled sitting room. I spent far too much time there, hugely enjoying myself, removing rubble, stripping walls, prizing off inches of woodworm from vital beams and discovering rock hard wood underneath and then decorating throughout. Everything was done in the style of years gone by. I had noticed that one of the signs of the great age of the house was the way in which so little was straight. As the roof beams bent, the heavy roof sagged so that even the windows and door frames downstairs were slightly curved. When Bruce put in the new windows we tried to create the same effect, but when I commented that the wood still looked square and modern, he suggested that I could bash it with a heavy hammer, to create an uneven surface. I bashed, and he looked on with pained amusement. David Newton helped me lay out the whole large garden with its view down the valley. Many friends helped us with the work and joined us for a house warming party before the house was let out; everybody was amazed and enchanted by what we had created.

Chapter XXVI

SABBATICAL - Ghandi - Sheffield - Highland
Pilgrimage - Retreat

I had been in the parish for fourteen years and was
running out of vision for its future; I could not see
myself moving from our home and friends and starting all
over again, so I asked for Sabbatical leave and it was granted.
Instead of taking a sustained course of study, I finally
decided to fill the three months in a variety of ways. I
joined a small group going to India, following the steps of
Mahatma Gandhi. What a man! We were only there for ten
days, but he made a profound impression on me. On
arriving in Mumbai (Bombay) we were shown people
worshipping in a Hindu temple, and as we walked through
the streets we saw women washing their hair in buckets of
water, squatting on the pavement; poverty, but also a sense
of purpose and activity. We saw the room where Gandhi
was born, reminiscent of the chapel of the Nativity of Jesus,
but, in this case, historically accurate. We learnt of the
impression he had made on world leaders and saw dozens
of students weaving for an hour before lectures. We

travelled by train, the platforms, swarming with humanity; we saw men crawling like spiders, mutilated so that they could beg. I saw a woman and child asleep on a tiny traffic island and the lorries belching out fumes within a few feet of them. I was haunted by the memory of the face of a small boy who had dived through the traffic to stand on the wheel of our coach and knock on our closed window, his other hand open, begging for money; and mile upon mile of slums.

We stayed in Gandhi's ashram, sleeping on the rat infested floor, and praying in the compound at dawn. We saw the black telephone which the British Government had installed so that they could communicate with him – although he had no official position all, he had enormous influence. We walked in the actual footsteps which he had taken just before he was shot. Above all, I was impressed by his integrity, his unified vision of life – his asceticism, his self-discipline was at one with the demands of non-violent resistance, his spiritual nourishment was the source of his political commitment. In my view he was the most Christ like figure since Jesus, even greater than St. Francis. He inspired Nelson Mandella and Martin Luther King among many others.

Gandhi was, of course, a Hindu, with a great respect for St. John's gospel. As well as visiting Hindu temples we visited many mosques and the Sikh island temple of Amritsar. We had already been to the park which was the memorial to the British massacre of Indian men, women and children, under General Dyer. The temple is set in a vast compound and is surrounded by water. Thousands of Sikhs from all over the world were on pilgrimage there, wearing their traditional costume. All pilgrims were given a simple meal, which we ate sitting on the floor. The Sikh holy Scriptures are in a gold chest, rather like the Ark of the Covenant. By day it is in the centre of the temple, and I watched the evening ritual, as the beautiful gold cloths wrapping the Holy Book were ceremoniously removed, one by one; the tense expectation rises until there is a final gasp from the enthralled pilgrims. Throughout the day the whole area is flooded with hypnotic Indian music, played loudly over the loudspeakers, partly modern, partly traditional. The casket is carried, shoulder high, on two long gold poles, over the ornate causeway to its resting place for the night. The excited, hypnotised crowd of brown faces surrounded me as I joined them, the only white face amongst them. I easily imagined them suddenly turning against me in a torrent of anti-western hatred. Instead, they took my hand and placed it on the gold pole, so that, forever, I could remember that I had helped carry their sacred book home for the night.

With the help of this personal experience of so many different faiths I grew in respect for them all, and was able to let go of any idea that Christianity is the only way to God. For me, Christ is the supreme human face of God, but there are many others which are very similar. God is God and we all are His children – we do not have to be Christian to know Him and receive His love. "There is no royal road, by which men, in a bundle load, are carried to heaven."

Later in my Sabbatical I revisited Sheffield and stayed with Reg, my Communist friend, now owning his house and a member of a cycling group which took him all over the world, in the company of interesting people. I saw his ex-wife, Ann from Carbrook, now a successful academic. Nearly all the factories and houses in Attercliffe and Carbook having been pulled down, salmon swim in the river Don which now flows through a park – and there is a vast shopping area. In the middle of the gardens stands the restored Chapel of Jesus, which many years ago we could see from Carbrook Church House. I went in there with Arthur Liddel, churchwarden and friend, still loyal to the tiny, struggling congregation; we knelt in this simple, ancient, holy place, with its unique dedication; the tears flowed down his cheeks, and in his breaking Yorkshire voice, he said,

"Lord, why do so few people here love you? Why do we go struggling on, and you just don't seem to help us?"

It was forty years since I had first met Arthur, and he was still the same, a dogged, faithful, emotional lovely man, so easily affronted by anything wrong.

I walked with Reg round one of the lakes of the Peak District, drove through Chapel-en-le-Frith to an Ignatian retreat in a Catholic house near Liverpool. Once again I had the help of a wise Irish nun; she advised me to do nothing the first day, but rest, she leant me some good binoculars to enjoy the birds and dragonflies by the pond, she showed me a picture of Jesus, head back, roaring with laughter, and after a few days of steady thinking she sent me into Liverpool. One of my fantasy journeys took me to the original sexiness within God, male and female, the act of love creating new life, the greatest miracle of all, from the earliest beginnings, down to my forbears and parents to me and on to my own children – an exercise that was wholesome, earthy, loving, with a union of body and soul.

The final expedition of the Sabbatical was a pilgrimage led by the Catholic Chaplain of Edinburgh University. We started from the Chaplaincy in George Square, in the house where my great grandfather had lived. We went by train and bus to Loch Lomondside, where we started our long walk to Iona. We carried a life-size wooden cross as we journeyed through woods, over burns and along mountain tracks: it was spring, and we walked through sunshine, rain and snow. After an hour's walking we would stop, prop the cross against a rock or tree, and one of us would lead a meditation and prayer. For me the most memorable was the one in sight of Duart Castle, the home of my MacLean forbears. The worship was taken by a Gaelic speaker from the Western Isles. He told us of a Highland Catholic priest who had gone to Rome for his training and, rejecting the offer of city life, he returned to his own people; and translated the Gospels into the Gaelic. From this book our pilgrim friend read the story of the feeding of the Five Thousand. We were a wonderfully mixed group, students and oldies from seven different countries. As we walked I often listened to the others, their woes and perplexities, which eased me back into parish life. There was a sweet Hungarian girl in our party, and as we prepared to part, with fond farewells all round, she hugged me and said,

"Oh, I love you ......you remind me so much ......of my grandfather!!"

I hugely enjoyed telling this story back in the parish.

In planning the Sabbatical I had hoped to share some of it with Mary, but her teaching and musical commitments had made this difficult.

Even so, we were determined that we would end the Sabbatical together, before I was caught up in parish life. We had heard of one parish priest who, after his sabbatical, had taken to his bed for three days, huddled up in the foetal position, horrified at the prospect of return to all the demands and fake expectations of a Vicar's life. We spent two nights in Grantchester, and caught up with each other's news.

Chapter XXVII

DARK DAYS + PUZZLING - Adam - Kenya

Sadly in the autumn, Mary left the Vicarage and went to live in a rented cottage near Dorchester. I could see it coming – we had been drifting apart for some time, but it was devastating, none the less. We remain on affectionate terms and swap news when we meet on family occasions; but it was sad for both of us, because we had been through so much together; in her quiet, understanding, perceptive way, Mary had given me great support, both with the family and in the parish.

It was also a shame that there was no opportunity for the parish to express their gratitude for all she had done for them. Some years later she married again.

In the following weeks there was one evening planted vividly in my memory. I was absorbing another disappointment that morning; Mary was in the Vicarage, as she needed to return for the piano lessons she gave to local children; and we had a bizarre visit from a friend whose marriage had broken up; he had been devastated, but was suddenly buoyant, cheerful, ignoring our situation and asking me to take his second wedding!

The telephone rang – it was Scarlett Vanicci, a black haired, glamorous young mother who had come from London and brought vivid colour to one of our Dorset villages – she was great fun and threw herself into village and church life; two years later, when I took her wedding, she arrived, like a film star, in a white stretch limo. In contrast, on that evening, she rang to tell me about Viv Gale, who lived in Broad Close in Winterborne Kingston, worked in the pub, and I had married both of her daughters. She had taken up riding, and coming down one of the village lanes, her horse had stumbled; she fell to the ground and her horse trod on her heart, killing her instantly. I shot round to her home, and then called on her friend who had been riding with her and finally went to the pub, where she was much loved; they were all in a state of shock. Her funeral was just before Christmas and the Church was packed, with people from far and wide, captivated by her lovely smile, her infectious humour and her readiness to listen to peoples' troubles.

I also found it strange taking my first wedding that autumn – taking the bride and groom through their vows; but the members of the choir around me were understanding and most supportive; so was everybody else, Bishop John Kirkham, the patrons, the congregation and above all, my own family and Chris and Rosie Nye, Mary's brother and sister-in-law; for some time he rang up nearly every day.

In the New Year, at a conference for counsellors, I met a wise marriage guidance counsellor and went to see her for help in sorting out my tangled emotions. In the first session I told the counsellor my life story; when I returned the following week, she startled me by saying that she thought I needed psychotherapy. I gulped and agreed. She said that I needed a woman therapist and arranged for me to go to somebody in North Dorset. Twice a week I would drive along the lovely empty roads and talk and talk about my past life and loves – an old man can be just as besotted as a young man – and the usual perplexing confusion of emotions, rejection, anger, guilt, heady freedom and hunger for another woman. I also talked about the many tragedies and tensions in the parish during those months. The Bishop of Salisbury helped with the cost. It was all an immense help and meant that I did not burden my friends – too much! Vivien Hares said it was like living next door to a sex-starved teenager – they were wonderful, but it must have been very strange for my parishioners, living with all my hopes, excitements and disappointments, but they showed real human understanding of somebody in my situation.

At one stage I wrote off to a religious dating agency – yes, such things did exist, even twelve years ago! I filled in the form, which included some bizarre questions, and returned it with a rather flattering photo of myself. The woman who ran the Agency replied, saying that she was interested in me herself and enclosed her own details! I was tickled pink and very flattered, as she must have dozens of men to choose from. I rang her up – she sounded rather weird in some of her ideas – so nothing came of that.

In the summer Don MacLeod, one of my younger churchwardens, asked if I would have my beard shaved off to raise money for the Church. I loved my beard, but how could I refuse? Don said he had never found it so easy getting promises of sponsorship money. We chose the day of the Bloxworth fete; parishioners primed me with plenty of beer and took me to a red plush chair on the small round, raised green near the Church. They had arranged, free of charge, for Marc, the chic hairdresser from Poole to do the deed. A large crowd gathered round, laughing and cheering happily – until the moment when his sharp blade removed the final whiskers and they all went strangely silent; stunned, shocked by what they saw? I immediately leapt down and kissed all the women I knew. Everybody said I looked ten years younger, some said I looked more autocratic. The Church benefited by over £1,000.

It was August, and we were in the middle of Fun Week; after breakfast a man came to see me, saying "I'm a teacher at Corfe Hills School, and I believe that you look after Adam Carter – you know that he was captaining the school rugby team on their tour in Australia?"

"Yes, I know him well."

Looking at the expression on the teacher's face, my heart sank.

"I'm just on my way to see his mother, Wendy…….. to tell her that Adam has died – in the middle of a match – heart failure."

I couldn't believe it. Adam had been a member of our youth group for five years – he was bumptious, wicked, very endearing, and great fun. He was just beginning to settle down, taking (very seriously) his responsibility in the team, and he was much loved and respected by all. I dropped everything and went straight round to see his mother. We knew Wendy very well, as she was one of our youth leaders, came regularly to worship and Bible study, came to Taizé and Israel. She is warm, bubbly, with a great sense of humour, at home with all sorts of people, and especially understanding of teenagers – she loved them. She adored

Adam. She was stunned, but, somehow remained calm. I went with her to tell her daughter, Tash, a beautiful, fun girl who had also been in our youth group. I knew her very well. She was with her man, expecting their baby very soon. She, also, had been very, very close to her little brother, even though they had often squabbled. That visit was heart-rending, to put it mildly.

Next evening one of the Fun Week leaders came to the Vicarage, just to see how I was coping with the strain of the tragedy.

Some of Adam's school friends joined Wendy and Tash in helping me put together a service for him; Wimborne Minster was the only place large enough. We had to wait for the rugby and girls' teams to come back from Australia. I was asked to meet the returning coach and to talk with the anxious parents waiting in the School Hall. The boys and girls came out of the bus, exhausted and subdued, often flinging themselves into the arms of their waiting parents. Adam's funeral service was inspiring. Several of his friends spoke of him and said how much they owed him; he would have been a great leader in the Army, or whatever career he might have chosen. I had to give the main address, which I prepared very carefully, relying on written words instead of too much emotion, as I often did. Wendy led the procession of family and friends as Adam's coffin was carried out; proud and full of life, Wendy led the whole packed Minster in singing, "Swing low, sweet chariot, coming for to carry me home……."

Later on, his lovely sister, Tash, has remarried, and now has three sons; she has just recovered from serious leukaemia, nursing her new baby in the hospital ward. Typically, while she lay there, she was planning a new

345

charity which she called LEAF, raising money for the leukaemia ward at the hospital. It is still going on, some years later, and has raised a hundred thousand pounds.

Some time after Adam's death I asked Wendy to supper to meet Flappy Lane Fox. Flappy and Martin had moved into Jacobean Bloxworth House, Venetia Chattey's family home. I got to know them well very quickly, as Flappy's son, Harry, had been killed in a car crash. Flappy and Wendy lived very different lives; but they are both totally genuine and understood and helped each other from the moment of first meeting. I just fed them and listened till the early hours. Later on Flappy became heavily involved with the Child Bereavement Charity, twice organising a high profile Christmas concert at Holy Trinity, Brompton, raising many thousands of pounds. She has also written a powerfully honest introduction to an anthology, "A Heartbeat away – finding hope after grief and loss." ISBN 09521661-6X. I thoroughly recommend it.

It has a foreword by the Prince of Wales. Flappy showed me a handwritten letter which he had sent her on hearing of Harry's death; it came from the heart. I have always been a great supporter of his and have written several times when the media have been particularly spiteful. Royalty suffer in the same way as clergy do – people put us on a pedestal and then vilify us if we fall off in the same way that they do themselves! I am impressed with the way he moves so easily amongst people, laughing away with no hint of stuffy pomposity. Personally, I approve of his views on organic farming, climate change and architecture – I think Poundbury is very innovative; especially do I think that the Prince's Trust for young people is wonderful. I am sure that he would be gratified to hear that! It is good to see him so settled and happy with the Duchess of Rothesay, as she is called in Scotland. In a strange way, theirs is a Shakespearian love story, with the Princess of Wales caught up in the tragic consequence of the couple's enduring loyalty to each other.

I have received much kindly hospitality at Bloxworth and was able to return it several times by taking Flappy and Martin's granddaughters for happy expeditions in the Shrimper. Unbelievably, one of them, little Molly died of a brain cancer. Why? Why?

David and Judy Newton had been good friends of ours when they lived in Bloxworth; sadly they split up and David moved away. One night he rang saying that he wanted to move back, and did I know of anybody who could put him up? I said that I would have a think. Next day I realised I was living in a house with four bedrooms and two studies, so I rang him and offered him accommodation in the Vicarage. He was good company - except that he wanted to watch football on the television – and patiently listened to me at the end of a difficult day; I don't think he had previously appreciated the strains of a Vicar's life – people's tragedies and frustrating meetings. His daughter, Hannah, came to stay with us; I had known her for most of her life. At breakfast, in a worried voice, she said,

"Dad, I tell my friends that my father is living with a Vicar...?!"

David and I collapsed with laughter and reassured her that there were not two men more randy for women in all Dorset. She was clearly relieved and has just recently suggested that I title this book, "Two dirty old men." Young women did not speak to their elders like that in the old days!

As their Chaplain, I went with a group of Venture Scouts, boys and girls in their teens, going to Kenya. The expedition was organised by a compassionate adventurer. We were to spend a fortnight living in a Scout camp near the shanty town Kabera, on the edge of Nairobi where we were to build a medical centre. The Scout leader was Phil Ventham, assisted by my good doctor friend, Tim Harley – two of his daughters, Emma and Rebecca, were in the party and Jan King was the nurse. Tim gathered plenty of medicine and simple equipment and was able to examine all of the many boys in the camp. More than one had HIV. I was enormously impressed with the local Scout leaders, dedicated, generous with their own money, and exercising unquestioned African authority over the boys; whenever they were getting too rowdy, one stern word from the leader and there was immediate quiet. Several times I took an outside Communion service and was asked to say the final prayers at the evening barbecue on the last evening. I started by asking them just to listen to the sounds of the African night – unforgettable. I also remember the camp fires when we would all dance round the leaping flames, singing African songs; it was exciting and a little eerie.

We also all went to a Pentecostal service in a vast shed on the side of the shanty town. Some of our young people did not like the way it was led by a large American, with a diminutive Kenyan standing in front of him, interpreting; but I was caught up in the wild enthusiasm of the many hundreds of worshippers. At one stage we were all asked to shout out requests to God, either in desperation for ourselves or for others in trouble. I shouted with the best of them, but nobody else heard, (except for God?!) because of the deafening shouting all around. I found it liberating. My "friends" said that I would, wouldn't I?

After a fortnight of sleeping on the floor, makeshift loos and no hot water, I was glad that I was due to go home – I'm getting old. I also let my beard grow. The leaders said, "Ah, we've got our Hugh back again." The Scouts went on to climb Mount Kenya, and go to village feasts where they saw a goat being killed; the last week of the month was spent on the beach. The trip made a deep impression on some of the young people, and several, especially those who became nurses, returned again and again.

Chapter XXVIII

NEW LIFE - Vici - Colin

We had to sell our house in Corfe, as part of the separation agreement. It was a bitter moment when I went round it for the last time. Until then I had never seen it finished and empty of other people's furniture. We had never lived there, but had spent many hours in the house and garden; and had spent many hours dreaming of our future there. It must be even worse for those forced to leave a family home. Angrily I said to God, "You knew we were never going to live here. Why didn't you tell me?!" The only consolation was that the house was dark and noisy at times, and it had no parking. We had been misinformed before we had signed the contract to buy. We sold; and divided the spoil.

I looked at many houses in my new price range and was depressed at how small and dull they were – until I found a late Victorian cottage set back from the road and just ten minutes walk over the water meadows to the river at Wareham.

Vici had come to Dorset to keep house for the Draxes; I had met her at Church and at Charborough. She helped me decorate and it was not long before her loving ways had healed me of all my hurts and confusion. We were at a local dance in the village hall, and Norman Sheldrake, a sort of grandfather figure on the Estate and in the village, warmed my heart by saying,

"It's good to see you and Vici getting together."

Her father was a war hero, a doctor in both world wars, awarded the Military Cross in the First World War for rescuing the wounded from No Man's Land, and twice torpedoed in the North Atlantic when serving with the Merchant Navy.

We were married by the Registrar at a civil ceremony in the King's Room of Milton Abbey and our wedding was blessed at a Parish Eucharist in Morden Church in the presence of family, friends and parishioners, from near and far. Meg organised the food for a simple reception in the Village Hall. A few weeks later we went on a happy honeymoon in Minorca, joining a Rambling group interested in birds and wild flowers. We were taken on some wonderful cliff walks and visits to hidden valleys, rich in colour. We were just getting into the coach on our last day, when the hotel receptionist came rushing out, telephone in hand. It was Anton saying that Tess' mother, Meg, had died; he was asking if I would be back in time to arrange the funeral? At the service Terence Arden gave the address; he was very close to Meg and had known her well. He was brilliant; he made her live in our memories and he ended with a lively imitation of one of her favourite comments. The whole congregation burst into spontaneous applause. She was laid to rest next to her

Michael and other friends in the churchyard overlooking the fields and woods. Her death was a great loss to our whole circle.

My brother Colin now came to be important in our lives. He was diagnosed with lung cancer, and I made a special effort to have him in Dorset. Guy joined us both for a cracking sail, out beyond Old Harry Rocks; there we found big waves, so we turned and raced back, on a long reach in bright sunshine and a good wind. He said it was one of the best sails of his life. Many times I went to see him in Leeds, first in his home, then in a hospice, and finally in a nursing home. I went by train, collecting my mother in London, now in her mid-nineties, saw Colin and sometimes returned to Dorset in the same day. In the hospice he said to me,

"Hughie, you know I'm an atheist, so I am not scared of anything after death; and I'm a doctor, and know they can control the pain, so I'm not afraid of dying; but I would like a Church service, because I know it would help all of you."

His clear statement of belief put an end to our lifelong arguments over science and religion; and I knew his thoughtfulness was typical of his kindness. He died a few weeks later; I took his funeral in the Crematorium and a service afterwards in their Norman village Church of Adel. It was a bitter time for his family and for our mother.

I had been in the parish for nearly twenty years, I was sixty-six and although I loved the people, could help them in their difficulties and take their weddings, christenings and funerals, I knew that I was running out of steam, was not visiting new people, saw teenagers in the villages whom I did not know, congregations were dwindling and costs were rising. It was time to go. The parish needed a new man or woman, with energy and motivation, to bring new life.

My successor, Jeff Waring, has been most generous in inviting me to take part in the wedding or funeral of many a parishioner whom I have known well. Not every vicar is so big hearted. I am humbled and touched by his kind offer.

Chapter XXIX

BLESSED RETIREMENT - weddings abroad - Orkney - Terence & Brian - Australia - absent-minded - boat's farewell

We had sold Broich, my mother's house on Arran; she was frail, getting blind and could no longer give the amazing hospitality which she had loved; but selling was a wretched business. Our share of the money meant that we could add on to the cottage at Stoborough and make major changes. Bruce and family again did the work; we decorated but it was not finished before we moved in. It was not an easy time for either of us – re-marrying, retiring and removing, all in a few months. But we have survived and flourish.

In retirement my praying has become shorter and simpler. When I walk into Wareham early in the morning I would just say,

"Thank you, Father, that I am retired, and that I live in Dorset." Once I added, "and thank you for lifting from my shoulders the burden which you asked me to carry for you nearly fifty years ago." I nearly wept with relief. I was no longer responsible for twelve hundred people and the organisation of Church life. Instead, I enjoy preaching and leading worship in the fine medieval Church of Lady St. Mary and the Saxon Church of St. Martin in Wareham, as well as helping out in all the villages round about. I also take christenings, weddings and funerals for friends, relations and former parishioners. The fees paid for the expenses of the boat!

The other day I was taking a christening in Affpuddle Church. I got everything ready, heard footsteps on the gravel and went to the door to greet the family; but instead, framed in the medieval archway, I saw two lovely young women, their shapely figures clothed in bikinis.

"I've come to show my friend the Church" said one,

"We've been bathing in the Piddle" said the other.

It was a good thing that some minutes went by before the family arrived, so that I could calm down and regain my composure.

I often get calls from the local undertaker, Jonathan Stretch, of Albert Marsh; whenever he is arranging a funeral for a countryman or for somebody known in the hunting field; he says it has my name written on it. Mark, his deputy, met his wife when conducting a funeral; she fell for this kind, good looking young man in his morning coat – one of the perks of the job. The bearers are kindly, strong and, when appropriate, full of good humour, often at my expense; on the way back from a sad funeral this helps us get over our distress. Jonathan himself is not only highly efficient, but bubbles with good nature; he likes to pass on compliments he has heard about me. Jonathan's fifteen year old son has a friend, Robert MacLeod, grandson of the

Wee Free minister I mentioned earlier; Robert still lives in Bloxworth seven years after I had retired. He was at Jonathan's house and at the dinner table Jonathan asked him if he remembered me?

"Hugh? He's a bloody legend!"

One day I was ribbing Jonathan about some imaginary defect in his character; he agreed, "Yes, I hope I reach the gates of heaven before the devil hears I've died!"

I have just heard of a very old lady, a very strong personality and stubbornly independent. She was unconscious for nearly a week, but it seems she was unwilling to let go, and surfaced once more. She sat up and said,

"Am I going to be cremated today?"

Her exhausted daughter replied,

"No, but if you don't behave yourself, you will be!"

Flappy also rang saying that a close friend, wondered if she could twist my arm and persuade me to take her daughter's wedding in Switzerland. No twisting was needed. The bride's father and mother lived in Canada, he was Jewish and she an Anglican; the groom was Greek and lived in New York; the wedding was to be in the skiing resort of Klosters in Switzerland. The bride and groom changed their flight home so that we could meet in London. I went up by coach and then got a taxi to Claridges for tea with them both. We discussed the wedding service, trying to include all the religious traditions of both families; in choosing the hymns I had to remind them of the tunes by singing them heartily, much to the surprise of the surrounding tea-sipping dowagers. It was a very happy weekend in Klosters where they put me up in a good hotel and included me in the three different parties. I had never been skiing, so I enjoyed walking up beside the ski slopes in bright sunshine.

The next year Flappy rang again asking if I could help once more – by taking the wedding in Majorca of the daughter of another close friend of hers. I met them all at their house in Hampshire and later was flown out to stay in a five star hotel on the edge of Palma. I was taken to my room overlooking the sea and the porter showed me the panel of lights, one for the morning, one for the evening, one for reading and one for romance, etc.! I was confused by them all and later had to send for him again to help me turn them off. Not only did the restaurant provide first class meals but the hotel had its own beach and cove. A taxi took me up into the hills to the lovely farmhouse where we rehearsed the wedding in its great courtyard. The next day I joined in with a friendly golf competition amongst the wedding guests – many of them household names. On Sunday morning I went to a glorious Mass for Pentecost in Palma Cathedral, before taking the wedding in the afternoon. I was touched by everybody's gratitude; for me it was a memorable weekend.

In my retirement I miss my friendship with the farmers, the farm workers and village people, but I am now getting to know the local farming family, the Randalls, and enjoy the regular sight of the London coach in Stoborough, held up by a herd of cows slowly ambling across the road in front of it; I even enjoy the smell of cowpats around the pillar box.

I have sold the Byre at Gorton Jockie on Arran, daunted by the work needed on it and the complications of letting. It was a mistake; I allowed my regrets to spoil many a holiday. We still go back, renting a cottage, staying in a B&B or with friends, but we cannot offer hospitality to friends or free holidays to the needy and worst of all, we do not have that year round knowledge that wherever we are, we own a little house by the sea on our beloved island in Scotland.

However, this did mean we could more easily explore other parts of Scotland. Vici and I joined a group going to Orkney. We spent a night in a kindly B&B overlooking the river in Inverness.

Very early next morning I went for a long walk, intrigued by a road sign "Culloden 3". It was a grey day with the Moor on my right and low hills beyond; the official Centre with its car park and building was another mile on; beside the road was a fence with a notice saying "No Entrance" – so I hopped over the fence. I was immediately on the battlefield, a grey, dreich morning, silent, sombre and infinitely sad – and I was all alone. The lines of Bonnie Prince Charlie's army confronting the government forces, were clearly marked; small, dignified wooden notices bore the names of the different clans and the positions they had held, ready for the famous, terrifying Highland charge. I slowly moved along the lines, alone, on this grey morning, and read aloud the evocative, ancient names of the clans of the Highlands and Islands – McDonald of Keppoch, McDonald of Glengarry, Cameron of Lochiel, Stewart of Appin, and then my heart was moved as I read, MacLarens, MacLeans, Robertsons, all forbears; and I had not known that they had been at Culloden. The last fugitive from the battle had fled to hide in the policies of Kingsmills; they knew they would be sheltered by Hugh Inglis, my ancestor who had used his trading boat to bring arms for the Prince from France.

Our time on Orkney was arranged by Pilgrim Adventure, a Celtic spirituality walking group. We were taken to the seashore to see the ruins of a village five thousand years old, we walked to prehistoric standing stones and in this land of the far North, we worshipped in the Cathedral of St. Magnus, with its round Norman arches and soft pink stone. Wherever we went there was the sea and more islands. We went to Scarpa Flow; it was here that the ships of the German Navy were scuttled at the end of he First World War, and it was here, that at the beginning of the Second World War, a German submarine sank the Ark Royal with the loss of nearly nine hundred lives.

Back to Dorset: Terence and Brian had moved into the parish shortly after we arrived. For years Terence has been organist and choirmaster for all Red Post – a voluntary commitment surpassing most others. He is appreciated and much enjoyed. The two of them are first rate company; warm and witty. They are welcome guests at many a dinner party or Sunday lunch in Dorset. They are also unfailingly hospitable. Sometimes I would take Evensong in Morden or Almer Church. At six o'clock I might say, "Put your hymn book away; Terence has been out to lunch." People would always smile and prepare to say the lovely service – no bitterness, no hoity-toity criticism, because they love and understand him. This caring, human acceptance of one another's foibles is one of the joys of a small country parish.

When it became possible for a Civil Partnership to be legally registered, Terence and Brian naturally wanted their commitment to each other to be blessed in their own parish Church. Sadly this is not possible under present Church of England ruling, so after much discussion, we suggested a legal ceremony in the Registry Office, followed by prayers at our home in Stoborough. Out of openness, honesty and courtesy it was important to float this idea before Jeff, my successor. He agreed that this was a good solution, and on the morning after the ceremony he rang them up to wish them well. Vici and I went to the Registry Office in Blandford to join Terence and Brian and the other two witnesses, Richard and Carolyn le Fleming. We drew up behind their Discovery; the doors opened and out of each one appeared an arm holding a glass of bubbly, so we drank with them. The legal ceremony was conducted by a woman with a lovely blend of warmth, dignity and joy. At the end of the ceremony we told her we would go and finish our bottle. "You're not really meant to ......but why don't you bring it in here?" She enjoyed the well deserved glass of bubbly. Back at home, in our small sunroom overlooking the garden, I put on my priest's stole and conducted a short service – a reading, prayers for their loyalty and life long commitment to each other, ending with a formal blessing. Vici had prepared a first class lunch, we had already opened two bottles of good red wine (Terence does not approve of the cheap ones I often provide!), the le Flemings another pair and we started with two bottles of champagne, gifts from Charborough. We left the washing up till the following morning, and the other four tottered off in a taxi.

It was a good weekend – but why, oh why, can't the dear old Church of England match the degree of understanding now enforced in law? It would seem that there is a mixture of the male and female in every one of us – an aggressive man with no tenderness would be horrifying and a woman with no strength of character at all could infuriate and make her a victim. There is a balance of male and female characteristics in all of us, a degree of bisexuality in some, often more pronounced during the in-between years, between childhood and adult life, by which time most people are powerfully attracted to those of the other gender; most people, but not all – some have known from early childhood that they are homosexual. Whether this is genetic or the result of early relationships we don't really know; and that does not matter. People are what they are; a minority of the population are not 'abnormal' in the critical sense; they are just a minority who are different from the rest. By what he said and the way he lived, Jesus was guiding us not to condemn, but to love away the differences between each other. If you look for a comment of Jesus about homosexuality, you will find ....nothing, even though people were basically just the same then as they are now; the only thing that changes is that some cultures are more open than others. A friend of mine had a Church background and upbringing and he really made me think when he said,

"Why do so-called Christians lack compassion and condemn gay people, just because the opinions of one man two thousand years ago; - Paul of Tarsus?"

I have heard people say that the Bible is against homosexuality; whereas, in fact, there are only one or two references in Leviticus, along with other horrific sayings which we choose to reject. Then they mention the New Testament, where it is frequently condemned; but, as my friend said, these were all the writings of just one man, St. Paul; many people seem to give more weight to what he wrote than to what Jesus said and did. St. Paul was a spiritual and intellectual giant, with his bold, liberating doctrine of grace, the belief that we do not have to earn God's love; he was a mystic and a poet, but he was not right about everything. God can challenge, reassure and inspire us through the Scriptures, but he did not dictate them. Inevitably God's thoughts will be somewhat distorted when they are expressed through fallible human beings.

Fundamentalism is nearly always dogmatic, exclusive and oppressive whether it is the response to Das Kapital, the Bible, Mein Kampf or the Koran.

At one stage Brian was doing well and they bought Englander, a magnificent, fifty seven foot wooden motor yacht; and typically, they gave much hospitality on board, once giving a 21st birthday party, including some young cavalry officers who surprised their girl friends by appearing from below, wearing nothing but a sock over their willies. On another trip they took all the members of Youth Alive; and on another, a group of very mentally handicapped adults. I won't forget the surprised looks on the faces of holiday makers standing on Poole Quay watching this elegant great yacht gliding by, apparently manned by the members of a psychiatric ward – reminiscent of that magnificent scene in "One Flew over the Cuckoo's nest". One man had not spoken for days but as we sailed by the Quay he kept gleefully shouting "Boat, boat".

Terence joined me for a trip in the Shrimper to the Solent; we spent the night in Keyhaven and sailed back next morning. After breakfast I took the Porta Potti to the bow of the boat and sat there contentedly, enjoying the view; but we were anchored, so we swung head to wind and the smell wafted back to poor Terence, sitting in the cockpit. He claims that he has never forgotten the horror of it. As we sailed home I felt seasick, the one and only time on the Shrimper. The night before, we had eaten a rich game stew, washed down with a bottle of red wine; and Terence was on the helm. As soon as I took over the tiller I was alright.

When my mother reached the age of a hundred Terence and Brian gave a small party for her at Giles Cottage, and another one each year since. The family had already given her a party in her Club in Pall Mall. As we approached in the taxi we overtook a line of cyclists dressed in Edwardian costume and riding ancient bicycles; it couldn't have been more appropriate, but it was pure coincidence. Her birthday cake was piped in to a tune specially composed for her, "The Braes of Balquidder", the land of the McLarens. In the 1920s, women at Cambridge were not awarded a degree, but only a certificate of achievement. When some of my cousins realised this, they wrote to Girton; one of the Fellows came to the Club and presented my mother with her two degrees, a magnificent bouquet and a bottle of champagne from the College cellars.

Not long ago I took my car to the garage in the village. Steve, our friendly manager, rang to say it was ready; I walked down, exchanged the usual banter, came home, put the car keys in their place, and realised that I had left the car behind! I used to be very good at remembering names, but no longer. I often meet people in Wareham who greet me warmly, but I can't begin to remember who they are. By asking, "And how are all the family?" I sometimes get a clue and all comes back. Once I tried this with a woman I couldn't place, but with no result, so I finally said, "And how's your mother?" With a look of horror on her face, she said, "You buried her last month!" Ever since then I have admitted my ignorance: I was standing at the checkout of a big shop in Poole not wearing a dog-collar; a very good looking woman, smiling happily, greeted me,

"Hello, Hugh!"

With a hand on her arm, I said my usual

"Remind me?"

"You're marrying me in the morning!!"

Total astonishment on the faces of all around.

I told the Surgery nurse about my failing memory; she suggested that I book in for a memory test with the Doctor. I agreed to ring – but forgot!

Tess and Anton often ask me to join them for breakfast in Wareham. On the way back Anton lured me into the betting shop, saying,

"I'll choose a horse for you to put your money on, and then you can bless it, so that it wins!"

Standing there in the shop I merrily gave him some spiritual advice.

"No, Anton, we don't make our own choice and then tell God to make it happen, that would be magic, not prayer. No, we must ask Him to choose the horse for us." Anton readily agreed; as he looked at the names of the horses, divine guidance was immediately obvious; in my name he put a fiver, at 12-1, on Parson's Pleasure. It came in first.

Since marrying Vici I have twice visited Australia, to meet her family; she had left England with them in 1970. On the way to Adelaide I went to Perth to stay with my brother Colin's son, Ian; he is a doctor and had met Mary Ann, a medical student; he had brought her to join us on holiday in Arran, where he proposed to her on Goatfell, the highest mountain on the Island. He drove me from the airport past a soaring new bell tower on the city's seafront; it had just been built to house the original bells of St. Martin-in-the-Fields. Over the years they had become badly unbalanced, and were damaging the tower, so they were due to be melted down and recast. Horrified, an Australian business man offered to pay for the metal for a new set of bells for St. Martin's, if he could bring the old ones to Australia. The day after my arrival Ian took me to hear them being rung. I introduced myself to the Tower Captain who said,

"Hugh! Yes, of course, I remember you; you said prayers before we rang, back at St. Martin's."

One day at the end of the sailing season in 2007, I was pulling up the anchor: for the first time, I became so breathless that I had to lean against the mast. Earlier I had jumped into the water but could only swim as far as the bowsprit. My doctor friend, Tim Harley, quickly found that there was something wrong with my heart. I got better with the help of pills and various hospital 'procedures' – I get confused with all the similar sounding names. I asked the consultant about the wisdom of sailing; he immediately relaxed, became less official and more human – perhaps a sailing man himself? – but advised me to take care about anything that might put a strain on my heart, and also to make sure that I always had someone with me. With this warning ringing in my ears and the thought of all the work needed to be done on the boat, I thought about selling her. As you may have gathered from this book I find it hard making decisions and postpone them whenever possible! However, my sailing club membership had to be renewed in a few weeks, which gave me an immediate deadline. On renewal day I went to the Clubhouse with all the others, handed in my resignation and gave the Club a donation.

I had a few bad minutes standing in the clubhouse looking at the familiar, characterful old wooden jetty which had seen the start of so many happy days for so many people. A friend put an advert onto the Shrimper website; a British fisherman, living and working in France, came and inspected her, gave me a cheque for more than I had paid for her and came back with his wife a month later to collect her. We gave a farewell party at Anna's cottage in the wood, where the boat spent the winter. I asked about twenty of the people who had come out with me most often. I ribbed each one of them with mistakes they had made when with me on the water; someone raised her glass, "To Catherine!". We all drank to her future. She was then piped away down the lane by our "family piper"; "Wull ye no' come back again?" A lump in the throat and then more of the excellent wine which her new owners had kindly brought from France. So ended more than twenty years of amazing happiness, fun, laughter, drinking, sharing, swimming, exploring, moments of terror and of pure joy.

> *"They that go down to the sea in ships;*
> *and occupy their business in great waters;*
> *those men see the works of the Lord;*
> *and his wonders in the deep ....*
> *O that men would therefore praise the Lord for his goodness;*
> *And declare the wonders that he doeth for the children of men!*

A few months later I spent much of the money on buying a chairlift for Vici; sometimes she has great pain in her back; it was also necessary for my mother when she came to stay with us, aged 106. I kid my friends that I sold Catherine <u>in order</u> to get a chairlift; in me this would have been incomprehensible sacrificial generosity earning me an easy entrance through the Pearly Gates; but they know that was not true – it was just that the purchase of one followed in time from the sale of the other – my friends know me too well.

So the chair helps Vici; it helped my mother.........and one day it may help me in the months before I make my final journey upwards, not propelled by my own efforts at righteousness – thank goodness! – but drawn by the understanding, forgiving love of my Father God. What a relief!

Yes, when I was in my twenties part of me was very reluctant to become a clergyman, but looking back over my life I am grateful for all the opportunities ordination brought me, the vivid contrasts between different people and different situations. I am grateful for the God-given opportunities to help people and grateful for all the sensitive, caring, humorous support I have received, - both giving and receiving many hugs over the years.

> *Brother, sister, let me serve you*
> *Let me be as Christ to you;*
> *Pray that I may have the grace to*
> *Let you be my servant too.*

Please read the poems and lecture in the appendix – they are important.

Appendix

Hugh's 60 years, by Alan George

Of Hugh's sixty years I can only vouch for thirty eight,
But the record's always true and straight.
Hugh my fellow student installed in Christopher
    Marlowe's rooms,
00, the best of Corpus Old Court.
Hugh turns student poverty into a fine art,
Maintaining youthful opulence, silk kerchief in the faded
    well cut jacket.
If he ever ate beans, then never from the can.
He gave enchanting dinners, the silver lit by judicious
    candles,
And he a third year to my first, draining the best out of life's
    fine port
At such a tender age.
A life wildly touched by the Spirit,
But not averse to the occasional malt.
He must have worked, but it didn't show.
At Grantchester Hugh swims in the summer heat,
A frenetic pork pie hat bobbing above the Granta,

Whooping mad Highland Hugh,
Beneath the waterline, doubt a kilt.
Cutting back seas of rhododendra to reach the deserted
    chapel at Forest Row,
His voice breathes steam in the night,
A match spurts light onto the crumbling altar;
Hugh's vocation amongst the guttering candles is praying
    for the living and the dead,
Tapping not snuffing a long stream of praise in his life.
His parents, warm and gracious, so much of them in Hugh,
Are baffled by my new smart blue corduroys and orange
    chukka boots;
They say, as we take neighbourly tea with an ancient lady as
    fine as porcelain,
"This is Hugh's friend – he's an actor".
Sheffield back-to-backs scarring the hillside in sooty
    furrows.
Hugh is now curate in a manse satanic black with the
    foundries' smoke.
A vagrant scuttles to see him across the derelict land
A walking scarecrow, his head full of torment pelted by
    persecuting boys,
To find sanctuary in Hugh's kitchen.
Hugh heats food, the man eats desperately,
As much a sacrament as the wafer and wine.
A bath is taken, hair scoured and Hugh on the floor
Trimming the other's hard corroded toe nails.
St. Martin-in-the-Fields and Hugh, the exploiter, has me
    carrying teles and
Recorders into the crypt to play my programme about what
    now I remember not
To those whom I cannot recall; but I was pleased he asked.
Mary cuts exquisite glass and rolls a cig –
I drink from her kingfisher goblet still.

She draws out the joy and music in Hugh's life.
The Rectory in Sandwich resounds to Mary's pictures
And I can see dark cello tones seeping under the door.
Hugh, sixty times you have been born to this high day.
All our gifts of love please spend
Priest, son, husband, father, sailor, counsellor and friend.

A selection of poems by James McLaren Maddox

The Sweetie

> And he held out his boyish hand,
> Stretched out to me; an offering,
> A round red button in his tiny palm.
> They'd punched a hole right through his hand.
> He said – "I only wanted to give you a sweetie".

our father

> "Well!", he preached today,
> "the Lord is forgiven" I said today,
> "Oh good!" he said today,
> "does this mean I can have some
> peace and quiet for a while, and watch the telly, and have
> a cup of tea, which I DON'T have to bless yet again?"
> "You know, you can go right off people",
> said God, "especially the ones with bald, sweaty heads,
> who have been blessed at least twenty times today, flipping
> greedy, and the new-borns who scream into your ear hole

371

when you're trying to bless them, peeing into the font,
and all down my habit!".
And no you can't Hail Mary today,
she's having a day off!
You could have given her a week off, at least, God,
somewhere for an annual holiday, somewhere exotic,
France maybe; I'm tired of trekking up to Jerusalem and
back!
"Brush well under your skin, and keep
your nails clean!"
"Thank God for normal people, said God."

Christmas

My old man carefully puts the
firewood in the gentle hearth,
Soon the warm flames crackle,
and the room is filled with
love, and good cheer.
Gentle is the winter's holy day,
And we rise into the hazy morning, with
excitement. The lights on the Christmas tree
are so very apt, and the glow of the
fire mingles with the memories of Christmas
past, with such good and genuine affection
that we can't see the twinkling lights
through our happy tears; some expressed,
some held and enjoyed within, and in this
snowy celebration, a red robin breast
sings a merry anthem.
After breakfast, dad, still drained from taking
the midnight mass, gathers his priestly attire
for the glory of Christmas morning.
"Where's my granny gone?"

I hear myself saying some years from now.
"Gone to join the heavenly babe"
I hear myself reply.
Down the lane, the cattle are lowing, as
my sister and I watch the calf, newly born,
in the five o'clock shadow, with still and peacefulness.
His breathy, childlike steamy nostrils, warm our hands,
mingled with the quiet, yet chilly winter fog.
Exciting and beautiful.
"I LOVE YOU LORD!"
I hear all of creation shout and sing.
"us too!" my sister added.
We sneaked back indoors, to see mum making a Christmas
breakfast – chocolate, satsumas, and cornflakes.
"why does God allow people to go hungry?"
I ask my dad.
"the only honest answer is, I don't know"
he replied.
"and I don't think I ever will".
"Happy Christmas everyone!"
"Happy Christmas"
we all reply!

Rest

As loved ones come and go,
their beauty within
is warm and gentle.
Their heavenly peace still shines
upon us
never far,
never gone.

A Hole in my Hand

There's a hole in my hand to let in the rain.
There's a hole in my side to let out the pain.
My head and my feet, are where pain and love meet;
in my heart, though it hurts, there's a home for you, my
precious lamb.
Come and rest with me, oh Lord,
draw close and feel me near.
With you in me I have no harm,
for those I love, no fear.
At your feet there are my feet,
yours are broken, mine are neat.
At your hands my hands would fight,
yours are open, mine clenched tight.

Purbeck Open Lectures

Questions of Life and Death

RADICALCHRISTIANITY

What can we throw out and still believe?

A talk by Hugh Maddox

R adical: the root. What is fundamental? What is it truly all about? Not some old priest lecturing away, even if he does have beer in his hand!

No, it is people living it out, men and women captivated by the Christ, by his compassion, his freedom, his challenge, his crazy generosity, his love – "If someone takes your coat, give him your shirt as well" – his refusal to condemn, his willingness to give all.

There are the 20th century heroes of the faith: Mother Teresa; Desmond Tutu; the Community of Taizé in France, where the Brothers have given up success, celebrity, sex, and where they listen and worship so deeply that many thousands of young people flock to them because they are counter-cultural; or, more locally, here in Dorset, the Pilsdon Community, men and women who welcome people with all sorts of difficulties; and I can think of lots of ordinary people who seem to understand troubled teenagers.

Radical Christianity is people who, together, live it out.

I have just come back from a week on a boat in Turkey. Not having much exercise, I became constipated, but after some days, when sitting on the loo, I was finally successful – in a big way! – and immediately said, "Oh thank you, Father, thank you!" I then laughed aloud at my absurdity.

There we have the agenda for this lecture: believing in my heart and questioning in my mind.

Maybe Richard Dawkins is right and there is no God, there is no purpose, there is no meaning, all growth is random, chance, ruthless. I find this possibility very disturbing, but I have to live with it, facing the grim reality that he may be right.

I am sometimes asked, "How can you believe in a God, a figure in heaven?" I usually reply, "I do not believe in A God, a separate Being whom I can imagine."

We must start from a different place. Whatever is at the beginning, whatever is at the end, whatever holds all things together – that we inadequately call G.O.D.

The question is not "Is there a God?" but "What is the nature of reality?"; or, put another way, "What is the nature of God?"

In the 1950's J. B. Phillips wrote a book called *Your God is too small.*

St. John reminded us that God is love and he who abides in love abides in God.

So I throw out the belief in A God, a separate being, like us, but believe that God is life, everything that is, everything that happens to me is God. Every emotion is a reaction to God: joy in family togetherness; hurt in marriage breakdown; anxiety in illness; dread at death.

We may say of a man: he loves life, living it to the full; he trusts life –both people and groups; he is bitter about life because of repeated hurts and blows.

This is what we mean when we say

> He loves God
> He trusts God
> He hates God

For God is life.

So how do we relate to the ultimate mystery, to God? By working together with others: cooking or repairing a bicycle with a child; in music, when we are taken out of ourselves; in making love, vibrantly, deeply, calmly, aware of the beloved and joyfully, profoundly alive in myself, two becoming one, and creating life in doing so.

We can relate to the ultimate mystery in silence, at peace with another, at one with nature, in the mountains, at sea, or eye to eye with a gentle deer in the wood. The mystic is at one with the universe. God is both within life and beyond; paradoxically, after the universe ceases to exist – God is.

But unique to humans is the gift of language in relating to each other and to God, our greatest gift and our greatest need. How everyman, every woman, needs to hear from the other the words "I love you".

In the play Fiddler on the Roof, Tevye, a hardworking, loving father of five romantically minded daughters, asks his wife, Golde, "Do you love me?" At first she dismisses his question as stupid, but then answers: "After 25 years married? After bearing you five daughters? Yes, I suppose I love you."

God, by definition, is beyond description. But I need words to express my thoughts and feelings so I speak AS IF to a father, a loving and caring father. It is so important to remember those words AS IF when trying to communicate with a puzzled friend.

Some of you may be getting restless and saying, "When is the old fool going to tell us what else he throws out as well as the belief that God is a man in the sky?"

I throw out the idea that God is male. How can the ultimate, the indefinable, be limited to one gender? Voltaire said: "God made man in his own image, and man returned the compliment!" I love the myth that the male God made love to the female God and so created the universe. We can call God "Mother" and venerate Our Lady, as the Catholics and Orthodox do. That is good psychological sense.

Often, in times of hurt, anger or despair, we can rage against the idea of the sovereignty of God, that he intervenes with the laws of nature and human affairs. There is no explanation for the horrors of the trenches in the First World War or the Holocaust in the Second. I once attended a lecture given to some students by Michael Ramsey, the learned, wise, holy former Archbishop of Canterbury. They asked him "How can God let such things happen?" After pacing up and down, great eyebrows twitching, with heavy distress in his voice, said, "I don't know, I don't know". After a profound silence, he talked of possible ways of living with suffering and redeeming it.

Instead, I believe in the weakness of God, his suffering, redeeming love. God does not intervene, but He can influence us if we are willing to listen and offer ourselves as part of the solution, whether climate change or a personal problem. We may call God "Father" but we do not mean that he is a powerful father of a helpless, dependent child. Instead, I see him as a father, without money, power or possessions, listening and talking with an adult son who is free to make his own decisions.

Some say that we are like children, terrified of the dark, unable to face the grim reality of human life, wickedness and chaos, and so we invent a powerful father figure to protect us. Perhaps a mature Christian faces the reality that the world and its future are out of control and so finds meaning in the crucified Christ instead.

We can sit light to the belief in miracles if we mean intervention by a supernatural power in a mechanical way. But we can remain hopeful, expectant of an improvement in health, the body's amazing ability to heal itself. A confident, hopeful attitude of mind can change everything. We should place no limit on the power of the mind. Speaking of a friend's recovery, we may say, "It's a miracle" – meaning that it is wonderful, beyond our previous experience.

We need not believe, literally, in the nature miracles recorded in the Bible, immensely inspiring though the stories are.

You will soon have the chance to get back at me in question time!

You may remember a hilarious mocking of similar views in the mouth of Bernard in *Yes, Prime Minister*, in the episode "A Bishop's Gambit".

But, before the question time, one more important issue. I believe that we can sit light to the belief that God dictated every word of the Bible and with it the idea that we can prove everything by quoting the Bible. I am always wary of people who say "The Bible says….." as if it were one clear directory of behaviour. Fundamentalism can lead to fanaticism, whether the Koran, Das Kapital, the Bible or Mein Kampf.

The Bible is an anthology, 66 books of infinite variety, written, rewritten, edited, translated by many people over a long period of time. It recounts historical facts, such as invasions, battles, kings, and, usually, interpreted facts seen through Hebrew eyes. They thought of God as their saviour who brought them out of slavery in Egypt through the Red Sea and the wilderness and gave them the Promised Lane of Canaan. This was their interpretation of their own experience. The UN would condemn it as invasion and unwarranted aggression.

The books of the Bible also contain superb poetry and spiritual writing of great beauty and insight, with recurring themes of right behaviour to our neighbour, trust in life, care of the poor and the foreigner, and the need for repentance and forgiveness. They tell of a developing idea of God, from the vindictive, vengeful, tribal God through to St. John's loving mysticism.

Above all, it is contradictory, paradoxical. In other words, it reflects human life and the widely different experiences of its many writers. It soars to great heights and also expresses terrible thoughts, recording hideous crimes. All its heroes have clay feet.

But we must be wary of quoting one of the Biblical writers to prove a point. This finally came home to me when a friend, the son of a vicar and grandson of a bishop, said to me, "Why do so many Christians condemn practising, committed homosexuals just because of what one man, Paul of Tarsus, wrote 2,000 years ago?"

In spite of all this, I do believe that God speaks to us, through the Bible, in the sense that a passage of scripture comes alive for us personally, whether comforting or challenging, a different message for each person, each community, each day, a living, changing relationship.

I do not believe the Bible is a textbook. I do believe it is like a love letter, speaking to our hearts. The language of religion, the scriptures, ritual, prayer, is the language of poetry, not accurate descriptions in prose.

Belief is not a matter of the mind, to be analysed and argued about. It is an attitude to life, to people, which leads to loving action.

(Interval)

I do not think that we have to believe in the virgin birth of Jesus. It is not mentioned in the Gospels of Mark and John or in any of the writings of Paul. It is an impossible idea to modern ears and is often mocked. Isaiah had prophesied that "a virgin shall conceive and bear a son and his name shall be called Emmanuel, God with us" – a wonderful promise. But I believe the Hebrew word "virgin" can equally be translated as "young woman".

The early church believed that Jesus was the Son of God, so they wrote of his birth to prove it, perhaps distorting the facts to fit the theory – always a dubious thing to do. "Virgin birth" neatly describes how Jesus could be both human and divine, Mary as mother and the Spirit as Father. It is more of a Greek ,metaphysical idea than an earthy Hebrew one and denigrates the dignity and miracle of human sexuality, doing much damage down to the present day.

Instead, I see the wonderful Christmas stories as inspired poetry, both the risky birth and eternal significance of Jesus, and as I read them and sing about them I am profoundly moved, especially when they are told in the incomparable English of the King James Bible.

I question the belief that Jesus is the only begotten Son of God, coming down from heaven, and my modern friends find it incomprehensible. To prove the theory, some New Testament writers tried to show that Jesus was like God, without sin; but Mark, perhaps the earliest Gospel ,records Jesus as saying, "Why do you call me good? None is good, except God alone".

George MacLeod, the great visionary leader of the Iona Community, a mystic involved in politics, a holder of the Military Cross and a pacifist, used to say: "It is not that Jesus is like God, but God is like Jesus." This is not a theological theory but truly, personally, an act of faith, of trust, to live as if life is compassionate, challenging, forgiving, with redemptive, suffering love.

Christians sometimes tell agnostics that they must "have faith", rather as if it were a thing – but faith is "not believing 12 impossible things before breakfast" but trusting life.

I give an example of how trust is needed when trust has already been broken. Parents ask the young teenage daughter of friends to babysit. When they return they find their toddler unconscious at the bottom of the stairs. The girl had not heard his cries because she was watching telly. On seeing the toddler she is distraught and bursts into tears. Do the parents trust her and ask her to babysit again? She might fail again; or she might be all the more careful – because trust would heal her. Trusting is always a risky business, especially when you have been hurt.

So to believe that God is like Jesus is to trust people, to trust life, whatever the cost. It is not a dry theory but a living, personal response to life.

At Christmas we sing: "He came down to earth from heaven, Who is God and Lord of all". Impossible to describe but inspiring to believe.

It led Father Borelli to leave the security of his presbytery in order to help the scugnizzi, the street kids of Naples, becoming one of them in order to help them.

oooOooo

Jesus was fully human and so the Incarnation is nothing weird, but is "the enfleshment" of God, not only in one man but in all of us. Jesus is special because he is especially close to his father in heaven, but he is special to remind us that we are all special. I am wary of any theology which separates Jesus from the rest of humanity. God is in us all, and in all creation.

oooOooo

In order to believe Christ lives, and that we can pray to Him, I do not think we have to believe in the bodily resurrection of Jesus. Although my spirit soars on Easter morning, my mind is with my questioning friends. Because the disciples could not face the fact of Jesus' death and the end of all their hopes, did they descend to wishful thinking? How can modern man accept the strange Biblical stories of the resurrection appearances – outside our own experience?

But we do have two facts:

1. Jesus was killed.

2. The Church grew, believing he lives.

The disciples had a life-changing experience of the Risen Christ, expressed in bodily form I can believe this because of my seeing my father's face and hearing his voice after he had died (p.242). Many people have had similar experiences.

But nowhere is it recorded that Jesus walked down the streets of Jerusalem to prove he was alive. It is only recorded that he appeared to those who loved him. In other words, belief in the resurrection is a personal response to life.

David Jenkins, Bishop of Durham, famously said: "My faith would not be shaken if they found the bones of Jesus of Nazareth on the Mount of Olives; the Resurrection is more than a conjuring trick with bones."

Belief in the Resurrection is not a theory of what happened to other men 2,000 years ago but the belief that God can bring new life to me now. Believing in the Resurrection is a way of living: expecting a marriage that seems to be dead to find new life, or a project that seems to have failed, to find fulfilment; it means having hope in eternity.

In my heart I believe that Jesus died for me and for us all. That is the main source of my gratitude to Him in my spiritual and liturgical life. But I find this hard to explain to modern man, especially the strange, metaphysical idea that Jesus made this sacrifice to appease the wrath of God. If misinterpreted, it can have three disadvantages:

It is incomprehensible to the modern scientific mind.

It gives the impression of an angry, demanding God, a threatening, dark figure in our lives.

If only those who accept Christ in this way can be saved, it excludes most people from union with God.

Yet, strangely – and it is hard to put this into words – somehow, without the crucifixion at the heart of our faith, talk of God's love for us can become sentimental. Perhaps this is because, in our hearts, we have each painfully discovered that, if we love, we become vulnerable and will be hurt. Those we love most can hurt us most.

If Jesus on the cross shows us what God is like, then there is suffering, self-sacrificial love at the heart of God.

In Helen Waddell's book on Peter Abelard, the mediaeval theologian, his student points to the rings of the grain in a tree trunk running the length of the tree, but they can only be seen where the trunk has been cut through. So, the crucifixion is where we see the agony of God, in all people and all creation; we are shown God's suffering, redeeming love for everybody, whether we respond or not. St. Paul wrote: "God was in Christ, reconciling the world to Himself".

There is another, less metaphysical and more human understanding of Jesus' death: the new promise, sealed in his blood. In other words, he would not go back on his belief in his God-given role to heal, provoke, and by his life and his words, make real God's love for us all.

It is a supreme example of similar sacrifices made by many men and women down the centuries:

> Sir Thomas More, going to the scaffold rather than deny his Catholic faith;
> Dietrich Bonhoeffer, hanged because of his opposition to Hitler.
> The seven Melanesian Brothers murdered on their journey of reconciliation.

Their sacrificial deaths were the final culmination of their beliefs and their lives.

Supremely, Jesus' promise of the Kingdom of God is sealed in his blood. His willingness to die proved what he had said and done in his life.

ooo0ooo

I sit light to the traditional doctrine of the Trinity, that God is one and God is three, although I love the belief that at the heart of creation is a community of love, the ever-renewing relationship of Father, Son and Holy Spirit.

> I see God as One.
> Jesus shows us what God is like.
> We are inspired by his memory, his spirit.

I wonder if the Church can define any doctrine about Christ. He was a spontaneous, paradoxical, will o' the wisp teacher. To box him in is like trying to" catch a rainbow in your hand".

So I am puzzled by the belief

> That God is a separate Being and male;
> That God intervenes;

386

That anything can be proved from the Bible;
That Jesus had a bodily resurrection;
That Jesus made a sacrifice to appease the wrath of God;
That you have to be a Christian to be close to God;

And I question attempts to define the Trinity.

What matters to God is the way we respond to life and to Him and the way we treat each other. Everything else is of secondary importance.

I must be honest about my intellectual questioning, but I believe with my heart. I listen and talk with God as if to a father; I love him and try to obey him; and I lead public worship with all my soul. In my old age I have learned to live comfortably with the apparently contradictory and paradoxical ways of the heart and the mind.

If I define a doctrine, I make an enemy
If I live a doctrine, I make a friend